THE WORLD
OF THE CHILDREN

By

STUART MIALL

Volume Three

THE CAXTON PUBLISHING COMPANY LIMITED

Morley Hall, St. George Street, Hanover Square, London, W.1

First Published . . . September 1948

Reprinted . . . March 1949

Reprinted . . . June 1949

Reprinted . . . July 1949

Reprinted . . . March 1950

Reprinted . . . November 1950

Reprinted . . March 1951

Reprinted . . . August 1951

Printed in the Netherlands by
Mouton & Co. of The Hague
C. 3. D.

CONTENTS

Volume 3

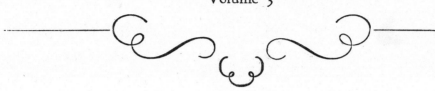

SECTION 8

THE YOUNG SCIENTIST

CHAPTER   PAGE

Junior Science (Introduction) . . . 1

(a) MECHANICS

1 A Spin in the Car 6
2 Acceleration 13
3 The Well 17
4 Playing Ball 24
5 A Ride in the Rain 28
6 The See-saw 40
7 The Lever 43

(b) SOUND

1 An Introduction to Sound . . . 46
2 The Clothes-line 51
3 Waves that Speak 64
4 How to Measure the Pitch or Frequency of a
    Note 80
5 An Instructive Toy of Cardboard . . . 83
6 Sounds from Afar 89

CONTENTS

(c) LIGHT

CHAPTER   PAGE

1 Evening at a Country Cottage . . . 100
2 New Lamps for Old 108
3 Peter in Trouble 117
4 The Eclipse of the Sun 126
5 Pin-hole Camera 133
6 The Mirror 147
7 Some Optical Illusions 156
8 A Real Camera 166
9 How a Lens Works 179
10 Colour 193

(d) HEAT

1 Fire 205
2 The Expansion of Air by Heat . . . 221
3 Temperature and Thermometers . . 226
4 What a Thermometer Tells Us . . . 233
5 The Expansion of Solids . . . 250
6 How Does Heat Journey from Place to Place? . 257
7 Ice, Water and Steam 266
8 What is Heat? 282

(e) AIR AND WATER

1 The Air We Breathe 286
2 Syphons and Pumps 302
3 Is Water a Solid? 310
4 Pressure and Vacuum Gauges . . . 316
5 What Makes Things Float? . . . 321

CONTENTS

(f) MAGNETISM AND ELECTRICITY

CHAPTER	PAGE
1 Magnetism	330
2 Electro-Magnetism	345
3 Electrical Measurements	365
4 Alternating Current	376
5 Beware !! Electricity can be Dangerous !!!	382
6 Static Electricity	387
7 Radio	399
8 Atomic Energy : Will it Save or Destroy Mankind ?	415

THE WORLD
OF THE CHILDREN

Volume 3

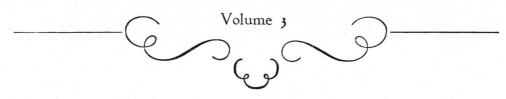

JUNIOR SCIENCE—INTRODUCTION

SCIENCE is more than a collection of studies such as heat, light, sound, mechanics, electricity, and so on—it is an attitude to life. The scientist is a person who likes to be sure of himself before he speaks, and whose speaking goes as far as is justified by the facts but no farther. The facts are either determined by careful experiment or are deduced from the results of such experiment. A training in science inculcates the love of truth—of exact truth—and it breeds humility. "I think" and "I believe" will not do in talking of things scientific. There is no room for self-assertion and bombast. A thing capable of proof IS and a thing capable of disproof IS NOT; the court of arbitration is the test laboratory. Compared with other men, scientists talk with "still, small" voices, because they are unaccustomed to argument. They do not have to shout or bully to make their propositions seem true—they ARE true, and if anyone is determined to be sceptical, the scientists can quickly stage a demonstration to dispel all doubt. A dreadfully convincing confirmation was given at Hiroshima of seemingly far-fetched scientific views about atomic energy.

The reason why science has had to wait so long before finding favour as a study in our schools is not far to seek. It cannot be taught by the same convenient classroom method that suffices for Latin, arithmetic, ancient history, and so on. In science one learns through a process of discovery; one does practical experiments, and one learns from these rather than from any human teacher.

Without there being facilities for making experiments, the teaching of science must be a fiasco, because the science teacher who asks children to accept without question the results of other people's experiments is being like the teacher of all the other subjects (mathematics excepted) in asking them to perform an act of faith. This may be necessary in some subjects, but in science nothing should be taken on trust. A truth is not a truth unless it will stand the test of experiment.

Children, then, do not learn science in their schools at an early age, solely for the reason that it is difficult and costly to teach. Indeed, it is impossible to teach when classes run to thirty, forty and fifty children.

The fact that children are not taught science in their schools does not mean to say that it is too difficult for the children themselves. The difficulties are all on the teaching side and not on the learning side. Children can have their science at the small private school, or in the home or, indeed, wherever there is somebody able and willing to make or provide facilities for simple practical experiments. And when we consider what science can do for the child character by its insistence on honesty, preciseness, clear thinking and exactness in statement, we shall probably feel that the training which omits science is, after all, a woefully incomplete training.

In some quarters instruction in Latin and Greek are supposed to be the hall-mark of culture; some day, in the not very distant future, it may be thought equally important to ensure that children get a grounding in science. Lacking this grounding, many children are growing up to-day with the idea that truth is how THEY want things to be, not how things really are. To make a good story many journalists have trifled with truth; to ensure for Germany the highest and most honourable place among nations, the Nazi teachers of history and biology trifled with the truth; politicians, lawyers, men of business and priests have, at various times, all manufactured special brands of "truth" to suit their particular purposes; scientists alone are concerned to represent things as they really are, and that is why every child should receive a grounding in science.

Science has to do with things that are unalterable by Man—things that are of God or of Nature (whichever term is preferred). In this respect science—including mathematics—differs from every other study. The problems encountered in science are steps that must be climbed on the way upwards and forwards to that heaven which awaits the discoverer of ultimate truth. The problems encountered in Latin and other man-created studies have more to do with human fallibility than with cosmical law and order.

It is not my purpose, however, to become involved in matters controversial. My concern is to meet the undeniable needs of children. While grown-up people argue as to which are the noblest studies to put before the child, he himself has in all places and at all times called out for science. From infancy the child is an experimentalist, and the true lover of children can do no less than afford him every assistance in his quest for first-hand knowledge.

The place given to science in this book is a big place, because every child knows that science is vitally interesting and vitally important. In this introductory article parents are asked to believe that all children need more science than they are at present getting in the primary schools; they are asked to make opportunities for letting their children perform simple experiments and even to assist in constructing the necessary apparatus. The father of Mary and Peter is, in this respect, an ideal parent.

The penalties that follow upon an ignorance of science are often very heavy, and girls are the chief sufferers, because theirs is only too often the deeper ignorance. I have seen people narrowly escape death by failing to take into consideration the most elementary mechanical principles when boarding or leaving moving vehicles; I have known people who have lost their lives or their homes as the result of some simple error that a slight knowledge of electricity would have prevented them from committing. Yes, it almost amounts to criminal negligence in these days not to teach science to children from the very earliest possible age.

How difficult is science?

It is not really difficult at all, but the old idea was to refuse to undertake any formal teaching of science to pupils who were not possessed of considerable mathematical knowledge. It was as though one had to know everything in mathematics up to, and including, the solving of quadratic equations before one could profit from instruction in science and in the scientific method. This was incorrect and may now be admitted as a pedagogic excuse for postponing to the secondary stage of education a subject that was, and still is, hard to teach at the primary stage, owing to the vastly greater number of pupils involved.

Children are now getting a little elementary science teaching in primary schools conducted by the more " go-ahead " local authorities, and the value of such teaching is beginning to be recognised by the Board of Education. There remains, however, great scope for further advancement. A teacher who is at one and the same time versed in the physical sciences and gifted with an understanding of young people should be able to go a long way into his favourite subjects with pupils not yet eleven years old.

If proof be wanted that very little mathematics suffices for the serious young science student, the following pages will afford it. In writing these pages I have given the child credit for knowing only how to add, subtract, multiply and divide. Of algebra he need, at this stage, know nothing, and of geometry no more than the use of ruler and compass. Yet the ground I have covered is extensive, embracing the better part of what must be mastered by matriculation students.

Teachers of elementary science have in the past been hampered by the want of suitable texts that could be placed in the hands of young children. Science has for so long been confounded with a lot of complicated algebra by teachers bent on making it a classroom subject fit for exposition with chalk and blackboard, that text-book writers have perforce favoured the mathematical approach. The subject of the average science text-book, even now, is not so much science as mathematics with a scientific flavour. Even in books for secondary-stage pupils, there is still reflected the old pedagogic anxiety to keep science a classroom subject as far as possible. Limited laboratory facilities have hampered science teaching for so long that the habit of spinning out the theoretical side of science at the expense of the experimental side has become deeply rooted, and it is not yet wholly eradicated. There still exist teachers of the old school who are more concerned to teach children about the lens formulæ and the law of minimum deviation for prisms than to let the children obtain first-hand experience with lenses and prisms themselves. Such teachers may be horrified at discovering the scope of the present work, avowing that I have written matter more suitable for students of fifteen, sixteen and more years old than for children of under eleven. Fortunately, the new idea is that children can learn faster by actually doing things for themselves than by sitting and watching their teacher from a bench or desk.

In concluding this introduction, I have to admit that parts of my science chapters will make hard reading for the child unless he has previously done some experimenting. Particularly does this apply to the articles on sound. The boy or girl attempting to read these chapters must carry out the more important of the experiments described therein, and I do most earnestly recommend parents to see that their child makes, or has made for him, the wave-imitating discs described on page 83.

CHAPTER ONE

A SPIN IN THE CAR

MARY and Peter were going North in their father's car. They had been travelling since daybreak, and now, at 11 o'clock in the morning, they were already weary of the long and tedious journey. The Great North Road seemed to be all the same—mile after mile of it.

"Get your great legs out of the way," Mary said sharply to Peter; "you don't give me any room."

"Get out yourself," retorted Peter. "I want to stretch."

Father realised that the children would soon be quarrelling in real earnest unless he gave them something to think about. "Come over in front beside me, Peter," he said, "and you can watch the speedometer."

Peter scrambled over into the empty front seat beside his

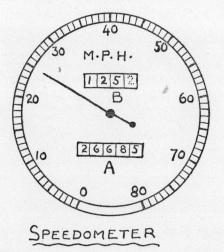

SPEEDOMETER

The pointer shows how fast the car is going by pointing to a number round the edge of the dial. It points to 30 when the car is travelling at a speed of 30 miles an hour; to 40 when it is travelling at 40 miles an hour, and so on.

The figures at A show you how many miles the car has done since it was first put on the road. (26,685)

The figures at B show you how many miles the car has run since the start of your journey. (125 miles and 2 tenths of a mile)

6

father. "The needle is pointing to forty-five," he said. "What does that mean, Daddy?"

"It means that if we kept going like this for a whole hour—not any faster and not any slower—we should travel exactly forty-five miles," his father replied.

Having said this, Father trod harder on the accelerator and the car immediately began to go much faster.

"Oh!" cried Peter. "Now it says fifty, now fifty-five, now sixty, now sixty-five, now seventy. I say, Dad, aren't we going at a rate? It's stuck at seventy-five now—I don't think it'll go any faster, do you?"

Mary jumped up and down in the back seat with excitement. "Keep it up, Daddy," she cried. "We shall be in Scotland in no time if we keep on going like this."

But Father saw a cross-road ahead, and so he eased the accelerator, and the speedometer needle dropped to 30. Then he saw a big round disc on a post at the side of the road, and in the middle of the disc was the number 30, very large. He pointed it out to the children "You see that?" he said. "That means that we are coming into a built-up area, with houses and shops and side turnings, so that it is not safe to go at more than thirty miles an hour. Sorry, Mary, but I can't oblige you. If I did seventy-five miles an hour here I should be risking our necks, and other people's too. Besides, I should be breaking the law, and I might be stopped by a policeman."

"Oh, Daddy!" protested Mary. "How long have we got to go along at this crawl?"

"Till we see another round disc with a black line streaked across it," her father answered. "Ill tell you what we'll do though, to make the time pass. Here's my watch, Mary; you and Peter can see if my speedometer is working properly. If we are *really* going at thirty miles an hour that means thirty miles in sixty minutes, or one mile every two minutes. There are mile-posts along this road, and Peter can look out for them. When we pass one he can shout out to you to notice the time. Then, when we pass the next one, he can shout out again, and you can read the time again to see if it is exactly two minutes

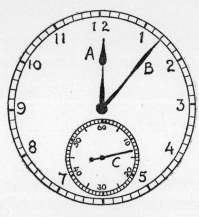

Hour Hand A goes round once in 12 hours.
Minute Hand B goes round once in 1 hour.
(Each small division round the big circle is occupied by hand B for 1 minute—there are 60 of them because there are 60 minutes in an hour)
Seconds Hand C goes round once in 1 minute.
(Each small division round the small circle is occupied by hand C for 1 second—there are 60 of them because there are 60 seconds in a minute)
Most pocket watches tick four times in each second, as you can find out by counting while you watch the seconds hand.

WATCH

later. You had better use the seconds hand, as you will then be able to judge the time more accurately. I will keep the car doing a steady thirty."

"Here comes a mile-post," cried Peter. "Get ready, Mary."

The mile-post flashed past, and Peter shouted out "Right!" at the same instant.

Mary started counting the seconds half out loud, half to herself; "Five—ten—fifteen—twenty—twenty-five," she murmured, going on and on, until, suddenly, Peter called out that another mile-post was approaching.

"A hundred and five—a hundred and ten—a hundred and fifteen—a hundred and twenty," Mary continued, raising her voice. At the instant she said "a hundred and twenty," the milestone flashed by, and Peter shouted "Right!"

"A hundred and twenty seconds," Mary exclaimed. "What's that? Why, it's exactly two minutes. So your speedometer is dead right, Daddy, isn't it?"

"That's fine," Father answered. "And now, if you kids can work out how long it ought to take to do a mile, going at forty-five miles an hour, I will accelerate to that speed. We've passed the end of the speed-limit."

"You do it, Mary," said Peter. "You're good at arithmetic."

"Well," replied Mary, "if the car goes forty-five miles in sixty minutes I suppose I must divide sixty by forty-five to find out how long it takes to do one mile. Let me see—sixty minutes divided by forty-five is one minute and fifteen minutes over. What do I do with the fifteen over? Oh, I know—I turn them into seconds and then divide by forty-five again. Well, there are sixty seconds to a minute, so in fifteen minutes there must be sixty times fifteen— er—um—nine hundred seconds; and nine hundred divided by forty-five is twenty. So it takes one minute and twenty seconds to do a mile at forty-five miles an hour. Is that right, Daddy?"

MARY'S 1ST THINK
(WHAT A BRAIN!)

"Quite right," said Father; "but just to make sure that my speedometer is correct at that speed too, I'll go along with it saying forty-five miles an hour, and you can take the time between two milestones."

Mary and Peter timed the car as it ran from one milestone to the next, and found that exactly 1 minute 20 seconds elapsed between Peter's two shouts.

When they had done this, Mary handed back the watch to her father and then leant back in her seat. "Oh dear," she sighed, "I wish we were a jet aeroplane going at six hundred miles an hour. That's ten miles every minute. Only think, one mile in every six seconds."

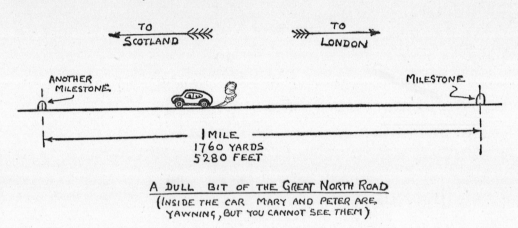

A DULL BIT OF THE GREAT NORTH ROAD
(INSIDE THE CAR MARY AND PETER ARE YAWNING, BUT YOU CANNOT SEE THEM)

"How far is that in a second?" Peter asked.

"A mile is five thousand two hundred and eighty feet," answered Mary. "Divide by six and you get eight hundred and eighty feet—eight hundred and eighty feet in a second. Phew!"

"That is a good figure to remember," interposed Father. "A jet plane does eight hundred and eighty feet in a second; an express train going at sixty miles an hour, or a tenth of the speed, goes one mile a minute, or eighty-eight feet a second, and a motor-car travelling at thirty miles an hour, in a built-up area, say, goes half a mile in a minute, or forty-four feet a second."

"Tell us again, Daddy, how you could find the speed of a train," said Mary. "You told us a long time ago, but I have forgotten what you said."

"Alongside a railway there are posts every quarter of a mile," replied Father. "If you have a watch with a seconds hand, you can find out how many seconds the train takes to run one mile. As there are three thousand six hundred seconds in an hour, all you now have to do is divide three thousand six hundred by the number of seconds you counted on your watch, and your answer is the speed of the train in miles an hour. If you want to do it more quickly and less accurately, you can find the number of seconds taken by the train to run a quarter of a mile and then divide nine hundred by this number. At sixty miles an hour, or one mile a minute, a train takes a quarter of a minute, or fifteen seconds, to run a quarter of a mile. It comes right, you see, because nine hundred divided by fifteen is sixty."

"What is the best speed you have ever done in a train, Daddy?" asked Peter.

"Well," replied Father, "on the famous Western Region express to Plymouth, which leaves Paddington every morning at ten-thirty, I once took the time between quarter-mile posts, and it came to twelve seconds again and again over a long distance. What speed do you make that?"

Peter took an old letter out of his pocket and a stub of pencil. Then he did a division sum, dividing 900 by 12. "It comes to seventy-five miles an hour," he said at last.

"That's right," said Father. "I can just do that speed in this car, but only just, and I should not like to try to keep it up for long. But that train kept it up for half an hour or more several times during that journey. Good going, wasn't it?"

"I say!" Mary exclaimed suddenly. "Do you know where we've got to?"

MARY'S 2ND THINK
(WHAT A TUMMY!)

"Yes," answered her father, "we're half-way, and this is where we stop for our lunch."

"Hip, hip, hooray!" shouted both children together. "Our talk has made the time pass quickly."

CHAPTER TWO

ACCELERATION

ONE day, several months after the holiday, Peter came home from school looking rather cross. He flung his satchel in the corner of the room, and slumped in the big armchair. His father looked up from his book in surprise. "What's the matter, son?" he asked.

"Oh, I've just had the worst of an argument, that's all," replied Peter. "A boy at school said his Dad's car had ripping acceleration, and I said 'So's my Dad's'; and he said, 'What acceleration has your Dad's car got?' and I had to admit I didn't know."

PETER IS CROSS

"Now you come to mention it," said Father, "I don't know what it is either. But we can soon find out. Come on, let's try it and see."

Peter and his father went round to the garage, fetching Mary on the way, and very soon they were bowling along the main road in the car. When they reached a quiet stretch of straight level road, Father stopped the car. "Now then, Peter," he said, "I am going to get the car going again, as quickly as I can, up to a speed of thirty miles an hour. Mary can have my watch, and give me the word 'Go' when the seconds hand is at a good place. You can watch the speedometer, and shout out when the finger points to thirty, and then Mary will sing out the time it has taken us to attain a speed of thirty miles an hour, starting from rest."

Mary looked at the watch and Peter bent over to look at the speedometer. Presently Mary said, "Get ready, Daddy—Go!"

The car bounded forward and, after a very short while, Peter shouted "Thirty!"

"Ten seconds," said Mary, looking up from the watch.

"Well done," said Father; "that means that we have an acceleration of thirty miles an hour in ten seconds, meaning to say a speed increase of three miles an hour in every second, on the average. In a book that would be written three miles per hour per second."

"Would you call that good?" asked Peter.

"No, I can't say I should," replied Father; "I should call it distinctly sluggish, but, you see, the car needs decarbonising, and if I step on the accelerator too hard the engine starts to knock."

"What's a good acceleration?" Peter asked.

"Oh, eight feet per second per second is all right," Father replied.

"What on earth do you mean by that?" asked Mary.

"I mean a speed increase of eight feet a second in every second," replied Father. "You will remember that thirty miles an hour is forty-four feet a second, so that, if its acceleration were eight feet per second per second, a car would reach the speed of thirty miles an hour in forty-four divided by eight or five and a half seconds."

"That sounds pretty hot," said Peter.

"All the same," went on Father, "an acceleration of eight feet per second per second is only a quarter of the acceleration

I can get up a speed of 20 miles per year if you will let me feed on your best lettuces and cabbages

that things have when you let them drop. A stone dropped over a cliff starts to gather speed at the rate of thirty-two feet a second in every second. Terrific, isn't it In three seconds it is going at ninety-six feet a second, or faster than a mile a minute, which, you will remember, is eighty-eight feet a second. In half a minute it is going faster than the fastest jet aeroplane."

"No wonder it hurts to fall from a height," said Mary.

"Yes," agreed her father. "If you drop four feet, your fall will take half a second, and you will hit the ground at a speed of sixteen feet a second. If you drop sixteen feet, your fall will take one second, and you will hit the ground at thirty-two feet a second. The speed at which you will hit the ground will be only twice what it was, dropping from four feet, but the bang you will feel will seem four times as hard, and it is quite likely to break some bones."

"I can jump from a height of six feet," boasted Peter.

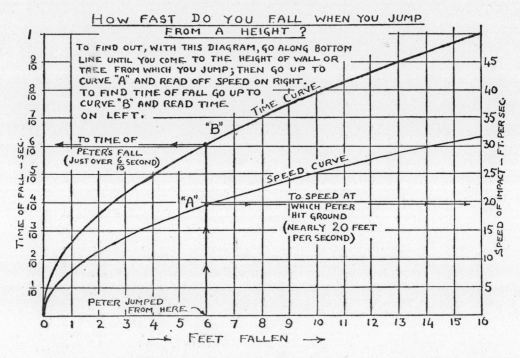

HOW FAST DO YOU FALL WHEN YOU JUMP FROM A HEIGHT?

To find out, with this diagram, go along bottom line until you come to the height of wall or tree from which you jump; then go up to curve "A" and read off speed on right. To find time of fall go up to curve "B" and read time on left.

"B" TIME CURVE

To time of Peter's fall (just over 6/10 second)

"A" SPEED CURVE

To speed at which Peter hit ground (nearly 20 feet per second)

Peter jumped from here

TIME OF FALL — SEC.

SPEED OF IMPACT — FT. PER SEC.

FEET FALLEN

"Well," said Father, "when you do that, you hit the ground at a speed of about twenty feet a second, which is nearly fourteen miles an hour. If I were you, I wouldn't try to do any better than that. And take jolly good care when you climb trees that you don't fall, because it's a certainty that if you fall from a great height you will do yourself some serious injury. Now let's go home."

CHAPTER THREE

THE WELL

MARY and Peter watched the rain tumbling down, as they stood gloomily after breakfast looking out of the sitting-room window. It was Saturday, and they had made up their minds the day before that they would go through the fields to a wood they knew to search for primroses and violets.

" Perhaps it will clear up presently," their mother said cheerfully; " it has been raining all night, and you know the old saying, ' Rain before seven, clear before eleven.' "

" We wouldn't want to go to the wood now, anyway," Mary answered; " think how wet everything would be. We should get our shoes absolutely sopping."

An hour later the sky cleared and the sun came out. But, as Mary had

WET SATURDAY

prophesied, the fields and woods were far too wet to visit without Wellington boots on, and neither of the children had Wellingtons.

" What shall we do? " Peter asked Mary. " Where shall we go? "

" Let's go along the main road to the village and see what they've got in Rawson's shop window," Mary suggested.

" Might as well," Peter assented; "there isn't anything else worth doing."

Half-way to the village, the road went by an old ruined cottage with broken windows and crumbling walls. The garden was just one mass of weeds. The children had passed the cottage many times before, but always they had had pennies to spend and been in too much of a hurry to stop. This morning, however, they were really going to the village just to make the time pass away. They had spent their pocket money earlier in the week.

" I say," said Peter, as they came opposite the ruined cottage, " let's go in and have a look round. I don't mind if we *never* get to the village. I don't suppose Rawson's window's been changed since we saw it on Tuesday."

Mary hesitated, and then stopped. " I don't like the look of the place much," she said.

" Oh, come on," cried Peter, and he pushed aside the rotten remains of the garden gate, and went into the cottage garden. Then he became suddenly excited. " There's a well," he called back to Mary; " come quickly! "

The well was a very deep one, surrounded by a low brick wall. Peter and Mary peeped gingerly over, and far, far away down, at the bottom of the inky-black hole, they saw a tiny speck of light.

"Water," exclaimed Peter shortly. "I wonder how far down it is?"

"Daddy said there was a way of telling the depth of a well by throwing stones in," Mary suggested.

"What do you have to do?" asked Peter doubtfully.

"Let them drop, and then count how many seconds it is before you hear the splash," Mary replied. "I don't know how that helps, but it does. Anyway, let's do it and then ask Daddy at dinner-time."

Peter searched around in the weeds and rubbish of the old garden for a few useful - looking stones. Very soon he was back again by the well. "You throw them, Mary," he said; "do you have to throw hard, or just let them drop?"

"I think you just let them drop," Mary replied. "We'll both do six each, and the time

HOW DEEP IS IT?

ought to come the same for every one. I wish we had a watch with a seconds hand."

Mary let a large stone fall from her hand down the well, and, at the same time, both children started counting slowly, "one —two—three—four—five——" They did not get any farther, because directly they had counted four they heard a hollow-sounding noise from below, which told them that the stone had splashed in the water.

"Four," exclaimed Peter, holding up four fingers. "Now another one!"

The children took it in turns to drop in their stones, and each time they counted up to four before they heard the splash.

"Well, I don't see that we've learnt much," Peter said, when they had finished; "but let's go back and tell Daddy."

On reaching home, Mary and Peter were greeted by their mother, and they told her where they had been.

"I don't like you going near wells," she said when they had finished; "supposing the old wall had been rotten and given way when you leant against it."

Mary and Peter looked glum.

"Oh, well, it didn't, anyhow," mother went on; "only do be careful, and think always how easy it is for accidents to happen. Now go and wash for dinner."

While they were having their meal, Mary and Peter told their father about their experiment of throwing stones in the cottage well. "Can you tell how deep it was, Daddy?" Mary asked at the finish.

"Only if you are sure that the time you counted was really and truly four seconds," her father answered.

"Well, let's suppose it was," Mary said, a little impatiently. "We did our best, but we didn't have a watch."

"All right," her father went on, "I will suppose that the stones took four seconds to fall from your hands to the water at the bottom of the well. Now listen.

"When you let a heavy object like a stone fall in that way, it

HOW DEEP IS IT?

TIME OF FALL OF STONE (SECONDS)	FINAL SPEED OF STONE = 32 × TIME OF FALL (FEET PER SECOND)	AVERAGE SPEED OF STONE = $\frac{1}{2}$ FINAL SPEED	DEPTH OF WELL = AVERAGE SPEED × TIME OF FALL (FEET)
1	32 × 1 = 32	16	16 × 1 = 16
2	32 × 2 = 64	32	32 × 2 = 64
3	32 × 3 = 96	48	48 × 3 = 144
4	32 × 4 = 128	64	64 × 4 = 256
5	32 × 5 = 160	80	80 × 5 = 400
6	32 × 6 = 192	96	96 × 6 = 576
7	32 × 7 = 224	112	112 × 7 = 784
8	32 × 8 = 256	128	128 × 8 = 1024
9	32 × 9 = 288	144	144 × 9 = 1296
10	32 × 10 = 320	160	160 × 10 = 1600

gathers speed, going faster and ever faster the farther it falls. After one second it is travelling at a speed of thirty-two feet in every second, or about the fastest anyone can pedal a bicycle on a level road. After two seconds it is going twice as fast, that is, at sixty-four feet a second. After three seconds it is going three times as fast—ninety-six feet a second, and so on. Your stone took four seconds to reach the water, so it must eventually have plunged in at a speed of four times thirty-two, or one hundred and twenty-eight feet a second. That is the first thing I have to tell you.

" The next thing you ought to know is that when a stone, or anything else, is moving with a speed that increases constantly by the same amount, second after second, you can easily calculate how far it goes because, although its speed is changing all the time, the distance it goes is just the same as if its speed remained *all* the time the same as the speed it had at *half* time. Now your stone started with no speed at all: four seconds later it was going at one hundred and twenty-eight feet a second. At half time—that is, after two seconds—it was going at sixty-four feet a second. So to find out how far your stone went, all you have to do is ask yourself how far a thing moving at sixty-four feet a second will go in four seconds. The answer is four times sixty-four or two hundred and fifty-six feet. Is that clear? "

Mary and Peter looked at one another and gasped: " Two—hundred—and—fifty—six—feet! " said Peter slowly. " Golly! I'm glad we *didn't* fall in."

" I'm going to see if I can work out how deep it would have been if the stones had taken only three seconds to fall in," Mary said.

" Bravo! " exclaimed her father. " Fire away."

" In three seconds," began Mary, " the stone would get up a speed of three times thirty-two, or ninety-six feet a second."

" Agreed," said her father.

" At half time it would have half that speed," Mary went on; " that works out to—forty-eight feet a second—is that right? "

" Quite right," assented her father.

" The stone travels as far as though it went all the time at forty-eight feet a second," Mary continued. " Am I right? "

Her father nodded.

" Well, then," concluded Mary triumphantly, " in that case the well must have been three times forty-eight or one hundred and forty-four feet deep."

" That's splendid," her father cried. " Now you try one, Peter."

" Thanks," replied Peter, " but my mental arithmetic's rotten. I should never get it right. Don't forget, I'm a year younger than Mary."

" Very well," agreed his father, " we'll let you off this time. Now let's go and play ball in the garden."

" Sit down and rest for half an hour first," mother interposed. " You shouldn't rush about directly after a big meal."

" Mother is quite right," Father agreed. " We will amuse ourselves with books for a bit, and go out at two o'clock."

CHAPTER FOUR

PLAYING BALL

WHEN Mary and Peter, accompanied by their father, went out at two o'clock into the garden to play ball, the sun was shining brightly, and nobody would have supposed that the morning had been so wet. The lawn was almost dry.

" How high can you throw a ball, Daddy? " asked Peter.

" Sixty-four feet, my boy," answered Father promptly.

Peter's face expressed surprise. " However do you know that? " he managed to ask at last. " Does the ball go as high as some house or tree that you've measured before? "

" No, nothing like that," Father answered; " give me the ball and I will see if I can still throw to sixty-four feet."

Peter tossed the ball to his father, and both children watched him with interest.

" Here," he said to Mary, "you'd better have this," and he gave her his watch. " What you've got to do is look at the seconds hand; and when it passes a spot that suits you, you give me the signal to throw.   Then you notice how many seconds pass by before the ball comes back into my hand.   You needn't watch it, because you will hear it strike my palms.   Are we ready?"

"Just a moment, Daddy," said Mary; "I'll give you the word when the seconds hand is at sixty; it is getting near now. Ready—steady—THROW!"

As the ball soared aloft, Mary kept her eyes on the seconds hand of the watch.   Then she heard the ball land with a "plop" into her father's hands.

"Exactly four seconds," she cried.

"That means that the ball went up exactly sixty-four feet," her father replied.

"But how can you *tell*?" urged Peter, looking more puzzled than ever by all these mysteries.

"Let's sit in the shade and talk about it," suggested Father, moving over towards the summer-house.

"Now," he went on, when all three were comfortably stretched out in deck-chairs, "there's not much difference between this and the well, really.

"If the ball takes four seconds to go up and come down, it takes half that time, or two seconds, to go up, and the other half, namely two seconds, to come down.   When I send it up it starts losing speed at once and, after two seconds, it just comes to a stand in mid-air, ready to drop down again.   So you have the old problem of a falling body which starts from rest and falls for two seconds."

"Why, it *is* the same as the well!" exclaimed Mary, "the same as when the stone takes only two seconds to reach the water."

"Exactly," agreed her father, "and you can work it out for yourself now, can't you?"

" Let me see," said Mary; " after one second the speed would be thirty-two feet a second; after two seconds it would be sixty-four feet a second. The speed at half time would be half of this, or thirty-two feet a second. It falls as far as if it had this speed all the time, all of the two seconds, I mean. Therefore, it falls two times thirty-two, or sixty-four feet. Is that right? "

" Quite correct," replied Father; " and if it *fell* sixty-four feet, it must have gone *up* sixty-four feet in the first instance, mustn't it? "

" Oh, Daddy! " protested Peter, " don't rub in the obvious; we aren't nit-wits."

" You agree, then," went on Father, " that I must have thrown the ball to a height of sixty-four feet? "

" We agree," assented Peter. " Now, Mary, you time me when I bang this ball up with my racket. Ready? "

Mary followed Peter into the sunshine again, and looked at the watch: " One—two—three—BANG! " she shouted, and Peter banged.

The ball went to a great height, and Peter caught it on his racket as it returned to earth.

" Five seconds exactly," Mary exclaimed

" That means two and a half seconds to come down," Peter put in. " Its speed after one second will be thirty-two feet a second, after two seconds it will be thirty-two and thirty-two, or sixty-four feet a second, and in half a second more it will have increased by a half of thirty-two, which is another sixteen feet a second. Altogether, then, the speed will be thirty-two and thirty-two and sixteen, which is eighty feet a second. At half time its speed will be half of this, or forty feet a second; and its fall will be the same as though it travelled for two and a half seconds at forty feet a second.   Twice forty is eighty and half of forty is twenty, and so the ball must have fallen eighty feet plus twenty feet, which is one hundred feet."

"Very good, Peter," laughed Father; "your mental arithmetic isn't so bad after all!"

CHAPTER FIVE

A RIDE IN THE RAIN

" WELL, of all the rotten luck! " exclaimed Peter in disgust, as he looked out of the window. " Did you ever see a more filthy Sunday afternoon? "

" Peter! " said Mother reprovingly, " how often must I tell you not to use those nasty school-boy expressions in this house—

rotten and filthy, indeed, they are not nice words at all, and they don't apply, anyhow."

" Sorry, Mother," mumbled Peter apologetically. " Only I do feel sore. I hoped we were going out with Dad for a ride in the car."

" And who said you weren't? " put in Father, looking up from his paper.

" Nobody," answered Peter; " only just look at the rain; we can't go out in this."

" Oh, can't we? " persisted Father. " Do you think a little rain would melt your poor old father's car, then? "

" No, Dad," replied Peter, " I don't think that; but it wouldn't be fun."

" Oh, wouldn't it? " cried Father, jumping up from his chair; " I'll just show you. Come along, kids. I haven't had a good skid for months."

" Oh, do be *careful,* George," Mother called out after the retreating figure of her husband, " and don't forget to wear your hat. You've just got over a chill, remember."

" Yes, yes, of course," mumbled Father. " Might as well do the thing decently and wear a crash helmet."

" George! " exclaimed Mother again, " don't *tease* so! "

A minute later Father and the two children were in the car and driving along the main road. Both children had managed to squeeze into the front seat beside their father.

" There won't be much holiday traffic about to-day, Daddy," said Mary.

" No," agreed her father. " That is why I chose to-day for my little experiments. See here, you children, I've told you a lot about speed and acceleration and that sort of thing. Now I want to show you that you cannot have acceleration or, indeed, *any* change of speed, whether to faster or slower, without there being some force to cause it. This car has just been decarbonised, and it is going very well. I'll just step hard on the accelerator and you can tell me what happens."

The car bounded forward as Father spoke.

" Well? " he asked.

" It's going faster now," Peter said dubiously.

" Of course it is, stupid," giggled Mary, " anybody could answer that way."

" Well, what's your answer, then? " asked Father.

" I felt as though the back of my seat was giving me a good old heave behind," said Mary, " and my head, which reaches over the top of the seat, nearly got left behind, because there was nothing except my neck to make it keep up with the car."

" Didn't you feel something like that too, Peter? " queried Father.

" Now you mention it, I did," agreed Peter.

" Well," said Father, " when the car accelerates you accelerate too, but something has to push you to make you do it—every part of you has to be pushed or pulled into going faster somehow. Your seat looks after your body for you, but, as Mary has just found out, her poor old neck has to take care of that great brainy head of hers. Now I am going to step on the brakes; look out! "

The car rapidly lost speed and, as it did so, Peter was thrown forward out of his seat, so that his head narrowly escaped hitting the windscreen. Mary had taken the precaution of leaning back and pressing her feet against the dashboard in front of her.

" Well? " said Father again.

" I felt as if I had been catapulted off my seat," said Peter, unsticking himself from the windscreen at last and sitting down.

" I just felt the need to push myself back all the time with my feet," said Mary.

" That's it," said Father; " your natural tendency is to keep going in a straight line with the same unchanging speed. It needs a force behind you to make you go faster and it needs a force in front of you to make you go slower. Shall I tell you how much force?"

"Oh yes, Daddy!" cried Mary.

"Well, now, what do you think it is that makes a stone accelerate down a well at thirty-two feet per second per second?" asked Father.

Neither child said a word.

"The force of its own weight." Father went on; "and if anyone gives you a butt in the back, equal in force to your own weight, you will shoot forward with an acceleration of thirty-two feet per second per second. But if the force behind the push is only *half* of your weight, then your acceleration will be only *half* of thirty-two, or sixteen feet per second per second."

MARY WORKS IT OUT

"What acceleration has our car got now?" Mary asked.

"I reckon it is eight feet per second per second," answered Father.

"And I weigh eighty pounds," said Mary. "That means the seat must have been giving me a push in the back of twenty pounds, because eight is a quarter of thirty-two, and a quarter of eighty is twenty."

"Oh, gosh," sighed Peter, "I wish I had your headpiece, Mary."

"Well, Peter," said Father, "you can't expect it at your age, but you are shaping just as well as Mary, and in a year you'll be like she is now. Come, the retardation of this car when I put the brakes on was twenty-four feet per second per second; tell me what force it was you needed, but didn't have applied to you, to keep you in your seat."

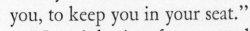

"I weigh sixty-four pounds," said Peter, "and twenty-four is three-quarters of thirty-two, so I suppose I needed a force of three-quarters of sixty-four or—er—um—forty-eight pounds to make me stay put."

"Jolly good, son," exclaimed Father. "I wonder you don't scare yourself sometimes with your own cleverness."

PETER SHOWS WHAT
HE CAN DO

"Any more lessons, Daddy?" asked Mary. "You haven't done any juicy skids yet, remember."

"I'll do a good skid for you," said Father, "and then I'll tell you a true story that will amuse you, sad though it is. Well now, before I get the car going again, to make it skid, I'll tell you what to expect. I am going to get up a good speed and then I am going to lock the *back* wheels with the brakes, quite suddenly. When the wheels are locked they slide along, and do not any longer mind whether they go forwards or sideways. But, of course, the front wheels continue to go in the way they are pointing, so that if the back wheels take the back of the car a little bit sideways, the front wheels just point a little towards the side of the road instead of straight along it. So the whole car edges over towards the bank. But I've already told you that the natural tendency of things moving fast is to go on moving always at the same speed and in the same unchanging direction. The greater part of the car manages to do this, because the locked back wheels will slide anywhere to oblige, and only the front wheels have to obey the direction in which they are pointing. You can see now that, once the back wheels have slipped the least little bit sideways, they will have to slip some more, or the car will follow the front wheels and make for the bank instead of keeping on straight down the middle of the road. And having slipped sideways a little more, they will have to slip sideways again more than ever. To cut a long story short, the back wheels just skid right round until the car is travelling broadside on, and it doesn't stop there, because, finally, the rear wheels go foremost.

"This is a wide road, and there is nothing about, so I will start a

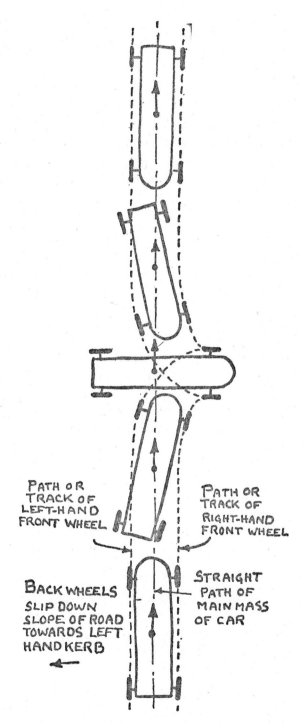

PATH OR TRACK OF LEFT-HAND FRONT WHEEL

PATH OR TRACK OF RIGHT-HAND FRONT WHEEL

BACK WHEELS SLIP DOWN SLOPE OF ROAD TOWARDS LEFT HAND KERB

STRAIGHT PATH OF MAIN MASS OF CAR

good skid going. But as a full skid is rather frightening, and might cause the car to overturn, I will correct it before we get half-way round. That is easy to do, because I merely turn the front wheels the way I want them to take us, namely, straight ahead, not forgetting, of course, to turn them back as the car lines up with the road again. Well, off we go, then."

Mary and Peter held tight to their seats while the car accelerated to about forty-five miles an hour. Then Father made quite sure he had all the road to himself and steered to the centre. The next instant he applied the handbrake, which worked only on the back wheels, and the car, instead of stopping, waltzed in an alarming manner sideways. By clever manipulation of the steering-wheel Father kept the car from reaching the broadside position, and he also avoided hitting either bank. Eventually, he released the brake and pulled up in a normal manner. Both children looked a little pale from the excitement of the last few seconds.

" I wouldn't have done that," said Father, " if I hadn't been a racing driver once. It doesn't do to play about like that unless you've had heaps of experience."

" It went just like you said it would," exclaimed Mary at last; " I suppose the camber of the road decided which way it started to sideslip? "

" That's about it," agreed Father.

" Is what we've seen anything to do with keeping balanced on a bicycle? " asked Peter.

" Why, yes," answered Father; " the theory of balance on a bicycle is quite easy really. You naturally tend to fall over to one side or the other, but if you are travelling along you can make use of your tendency to go in a straight line to hold

① { You are looking down on a cyclist from above, and he is riding straight along, as shown by the arrow A.

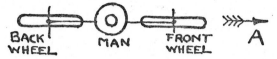

BACK WHEEL MAN FRONT WHEEL A

② { Now the bicycle tries to fall over on the man's left side, as shown by the small arrow B.

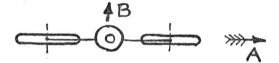

B
A

③ { The man steers to the left and then the force of his own forward tendency, shown by small arrow C, pulls the bicycle the other way and stops its fall

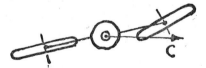

C

④ { If the man starts falling to the right, then he steers to the right'

HOW YOU KEEP UPRIGHT ON A BICYCLE

you up. Supposing you are beginning to fall to the left, you then steer to the left, and your body does not want to follow the direction taken by the front wheel, so it goes straight on.

But to go straight on it must make the bicycle lean over to the right, so it at once stops the lean leftwards and starts a lean the other way. When this gets to be too much, you steer to the right. Your body still tries to keep going straight forwards, so it raises up the bicycle which is now sagging to the right, and makes it incline to the left again. When you are an experienced rider you do not think what you are doing at all, but make imperceptible steering movements automatically, thus keeping your balance. Clever, isn't it? "

" Wonderful! " agreed Peter.

" And to think that a tiny child of three or four years old, or even a monkey, can do it! " exclaimed Mary.

" How about your true story, Dad? " put in Peter.

" Oh yes," said Father. " When I worked at a big omnibus factory many years ago, an inventor came along with a marvellous spring bumper on his car, which he said would make it quite safe for him to hit a tree or concrete wall at thirty miles an hour. He offered to demonstrate, and the Engineer of the company invited him to come and hit the factory wall with his car any afternoon he liked. The inventor promised to come the next day and, in the meantime, I had a look at the sketch he left showing the arrangement of the bumper. I estimated that it would squeeze up about six inches, and that the car would have to stop in this distance if it was to stop at all. I then did a calculation to find what the retardation would be for a stop from thirty miles an hour in a distance of six inches."

" What did it come to? " Mary interrupted.

" Work it out yourself," said Father; " thirty miles per hour is forty-four feet per second; the distance travelled during the time of retardation is the same as if the speed had been half this all the time, namely twenty-two feet per second. The time to travel six inches, or half a foot, when going at twenty-two feet per second is obviously a forty-fourth part of a second; so you have a speed of forty-four feet a second destroyed in one-forty-fourth of a second. This means that in a whole second a speed of forty-four times forty-four or one thousand nine hundred and thirty-six feet per second would be destroyed. So the retardation works out at one thousand nine hundred and thirty-six feet per second per second; terrific, isn't it? "

" I don't see what you wanted to know that for," said Peter.

" Well," said Father, " I wanted to know what sort of a bang the bumper would have to stand. The car was quite a big one, and I took it to weigh a ton. Now, you remember, a ton force, acting on a ton weight, would give it an acceleration (or retardation) of thirty-two feet per second per second. Here the retardation had to be one thousand nine hundred and thirty-six feet per second per second, so the force to be exerted on the car to stop it would have to be one thousand nine hundred and thirty-six divided by thirty-two, or sixty and a half tons."

" Yes," said Peter feelingly, " and I know what you are going to say next. You are going to say that if the driver weighed a hundredweight, eight stone you know, it would need a force of sixty and a half hundredweight, or just over three tons, to make him stay put in his seat."

" Bravo, Peter," cried Father; " you've guessed the object of my calculations. I wanted to save the driver from killing himself on our works, which would have been awkward for us as well as for him."

" Well? " questioned Mary, jumping up and down in her seat with impatience, " what happened? "

"Oh," continued Father, "when the inventor came the next day, we told him we should be quite satisfied if he would hit our factory wall at fifteen miles per hour. So he did."

Father paused.

"Oh, go on, DO, Daddy," cried Mary. "Don't be so exasperating. Did his bumper work all right?"

"No," replied Father, "I can't say it did. The poor man just wrecked the front of his car."

"What did he say?" Mary persisted.

"Say?" echoed Father. "He didn't say anything. He couldn't. He was thrown forward against the steering-wheel and got such a dig in the tummy that he was breathless and speechless for quite five minutes. By the time he was ready to give an explanation everybody else had gone away. So the poor man was left alone to clear up the remains of his car."

"Oh, Daddy," said Mary reproachfully, "didn't you help?"

"Well, no," said Father slowly. "You see, I saved his life by my calculations, and I thought that was enough. The effort of clearing up the mess would teach him a good lesson. Another time he would try out his inventions quietly and carefully by himself before bothering important and busy people to witness his failures."

"What a lovely story!" exclaimed Mary. "But, I say, isn't it tea-time?"

Father looked at his watch. "Gracious goodness!" he cried, "six o'clock; I should just think it is!"

"I knew I was feeling thirsty," said Mary. "Come on, Daddy; let's hurry."

"But no more skids, please," put in Peter.

" We'll take it easy, never fear," said Father as he started the car again.

Half an hour later they were wiping their feet on the mat at the back door of their house.

" Oh, I *am* relieved," said Mother. " I thought you'd had an accident."

" Why, no," said Father, " I didn't need my crash helmet after all."

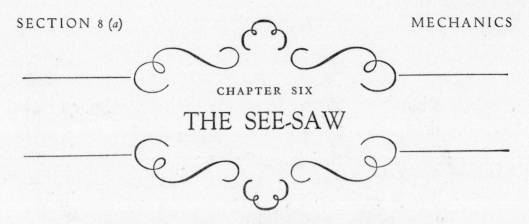

CHAPTER SIX

THE SEE-SAW

"WHO'LL play with me?" fat Percy cried,
"Alone I cannot take a ride."
"I will," said Jill, but oh, dear me,
She's thin as thin as thin can be.

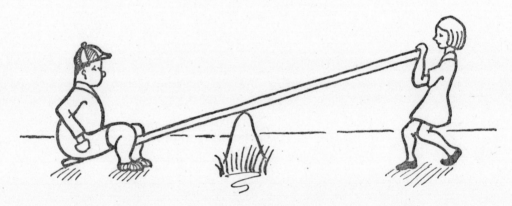

She pulled the plank with all her might,
Stretching to her utmost height;
But all her efforts were in vain,
The plank would not come down again.
At last, bright Jack came to her aid,
And asked how many stones she weighed.
"Why, only four," young Jill replied,
"Ask Percy on the other side."

"Eight stones I weigh," fat Percy said,
And shame made both his cheeks go red.
Then Jack said, "It is plain to me
Young Jill can never balance P.,
Unless he moves his bulk half-way
From end to middle—here, let's say."
And Jack with finger pointed out
Where had to sit that boy so stout.
Fat Percy did as he was told,
And Jill again the plank did hold.

She pulled, and down it came apace
Enabling her to take her place.
And then thin Jill and great fat P.
Were both as happy as could be;
"Thank you, Jack," cried Jill. "It's plain
You've got a really useful brain."

CHAPTER SEVEN

THE LEVER

" HOW can I lift this great big weight? "
Said little Jill to Cousin Kate,
" Just half an inch above the floor
Is all I want, not any more.
If I could only lift one foot
The carpet 'neath it I could put."

Just then came Jack to ask if Jill
Would come to play upon the hill.
By now the girls were tired and hot,
And Jill replied she'd rather not.
" Why, that," said Jack, " is not the way
To lift that thing; you'll strain all day,

And never lift it up at all.
I'll get the plank that's by the wall."
So from the garden Jack did bring
The plank and one more funny thing
That seemed to Jill to be a brick,
It looked about six inches thick.
Jack put the brick a foot or so
From that great thing which had to go

Up in the air a tiny bit
To let the carpet under it.
The plank he rested at one end
Upon the brick, and pushed to send
That end beneath the heavy thing.
A second more, and he did bring
His weight to bear upon the beam;
Then with delight both girls did scream,
For up went what they'd tried to shift;
Jack gave it quite one inch of lift.

In haste Jill pushed the carpet in;
" Oh, Jack! " she cried, " again you win
By use of thought, until at length
You find a way to gain more strength.
This thing's the same as great fat P.,
And you are being little me.
The see-saw plank is here as well,
And what it is you need not tell;

Because to me it's very plain
Your lever sees and saws again,
With you and sideboard having fun,
Each balancing the other one."
At this good Jack did swell with pride—
" What else," he said, " would like a ride?
There's nothing that I couldn't raise,
Resorting to my cunning ways."
" Don't boast, dear Jack," said little Jill,
" Come, let us play upon the hill."

CHAPTER ONE

AN INTRODUCTION TO SOUND

HAVE you ever noticed the big red flaps that so many school-boys have standing out from the two sides of their heads? Those things are called ears. Girls have them too, but usually they are more dainty, something like pretty little sea shells, and they are often hidden behind silky curtains of hair.

Mary and Peter have ears, of course, and they show very distinctly in the photo Mother had made of them last Christmas to be a present for all their aunties and uncles. One of these photos Mother kept for herself, and it stands on the mantel-piece in the dining-room. Often, when Mother comes into the room, she finds it turned with its face to the wall. She cannot think who could be so unkind as to turn it thus, but she has noticed that it happens mostly at week-ends and at holiday time.

Wishing you a
Merry Christmas
from :—
Mary × × ×
Peter × + +

What are ears for?

Are they for ornament?

Whenever this question is asked, Mary looks at Peter and says, " No! " and Peter looks at Mary and says, " Certainly not! "

Are they for amusement?

Mary once thought they were. She was sitting in her high chair when she was two years old and she suddenly discovered that in each ear there was a little hole into which she could put her finger. So she started putting her breakfast inside, and the more Mother chided her, the more often did she lift her bread and marmalade to her ear. You can see from this what sort of a girl Mary was!

Later on, of course, both children discovered that the little holes had something to do with their hearing. If they put both fingers in they could hardly hear at all.

It was very useful not to be able to hear sometimes, especially during a quarrel. Mary would call Peter a " mean pig," and Peter would stuff his fingers in his ears and say, " I'm not." Then Mary would stuff her fingers in her ears and start singing " You are, you are, you are——," while Peter, to drown the noise, would go stamping round the room, still keeping his fingers in his ears, and shouting " I'M not, YOU are, I'M not, YOU are, I'M not, YOU are——" Neither would hear Mother come into the room, or notice her presence, until she knocked their heads together.

It was Father who told them how their ears worked.

" You see," he said, " the air is full of tiny, tiny movements and flutterings, caused by things vibrating, and these air movements enter our ears and make us conscious of the vibrations.

We say that we can hear a sound. What really happens is that the air movements cause a sensitive mechanism inside our heads to start fluttering or vibrating in unison, so that it imitates the vibrations that were the first cause of the air movements. When somebody twangs a piece of stretched elastic, a stretched membrane, something like the elastic but differently shaped and situated inside our head behind our ear, starts to vibrate in the same way. This membrane is called a diaphragm, and there is one for each ear. The air is made to vibrate by the elastic, and the diaphragms in our ears are made to vibrate by the air. If it were not for the air we should be unable to hear anything.

" Steel wires behave like elastic and can be set vibrating, and so can strings of catgut. You find steel wires in a piano and in other musical instruments, and you find strings of catgut in a violin. The musical sounds made by these instruments come from these wires and strings.

" The sounds from a gramophone or a wireless receiver come from a vibrating diaphragm—a disc or cone made of metal or some other material. In a mouth organ, or an accordion, the vibrating members are little brass strips, or fingers, called reeds. In flutes, organs and some other wind instruments the air imprisoned in a long pipe is caused to vibrate on its own without there being any solid wire or reed or diaphragm to start it off."

So you see sound is all a matter of vibrations, and the study of sound is a study of vibrations. You will find this out if you read the stories which follow. Here you will see that vibrations are often spoken of as waves. A wave is what you behold when you throw a stone into water. Little waves are called ripples, but they are still waves. They spread in ever-widening circles round the place where the stone went " plop." It looks as though rings of water are stretching and stretching and stretching, but this is not what really happens. If there is a cork or a piece of stick in the water, you will see that it does not get caught up and carried along by a wave: it just rises and falls while the wave passes underneath. As a matter of fact, that is all the water does: it just rises and falls, passing on the hint to neighbouring areas of water to do the same.

Imagine two long lines of children, as in a school crocodile, holding hands and standing still awaiting the order to march. Now imagine that a mischievous boy dives under the clasped hands of the pair at the back, pushing them up in so doing. Imagine that he forces his way to the very front by squeezing under the children's hands as he goes along. You would see hands and arms go up to let the boy pass under them, and then you would see them fall again. The boy's back would send a sort of hump or wave in the children's arms right the way up from the back of the crocodile to the front. A wave in water is just a travelling humpiness like that made by the boy going under the children's arms.

You can see another quite good imitation of a wave when Baby gets under the floor carpet and crawls from one end of the room to the other. The carpet does not move across the room, but the hump in it does.

Sound goes from place to place as waves in the air, but they are invisible waves. They may start as visible waves in a vibrating piece of elastic; but once the air has taken up these waves, they spread as invisible ripples, and only your ears can tell you of their presence. Your eye cannot see them nor your hand feel them.

In order to know anything useful about sound you must

know quite a lot about waves. The next story tells you about the waves you can make in a stretched wire or rope or piece of string. If these move fast enough they give you a sound you can hear. To study them closely, however, you need to make slowly moving ones that are soundless. What you learn about the slow soundless ones is equally true of the quick audible ones, so please read on and take as much interest as you can in these slow waves.

CHAPTER TWO

THE CLOTHES-LINE

"THIS is the sort of Monday I like," said Mother, looking out of the window at breakfast-time one sunny spring morning; "plenty of sun and a nice fresh breeze. Real drying weather, this!"

Of course Mother was thinking of her washing, and by eleven o'clock this was all hanging out to dry on the long line that stretched from the kitchen window to the wall of the potting-shed.

During the day the wind freshened, and at 11.30 a.m., to be precise, a sudden anguished cry was heard from Mother:

"All hands to the rescue—my clothes-line has broken."

Father, at work in his study, rose from his seat to see what had happened. Mary and Peter, not yet back at school after the Easter holidays, ran out from the summer-house at the same moment. All Mother's beautiful clean washing lay in a straggling line across the lawn.

"The rope was old and rotten," said Mother; "I knew it couldn't last much longer. Help me gather up these things before they are dirtied any more than they are now. Oh dear! I suppose half of them will have to be washed all over again."

But things were not so bad as Mother feared. The lawn was dry and clean, and the clothes showed hardly any trace of having lain on the ground. Mary and Peter helped Mother to pack them into a big basket, while Father busied himself untying the two broken pieces of clothes-line.

A few moments later Peter rode off on his bicycle to visit the ironmonger, where he had been sent to buy a new clothes-line. When he returned, Father fastened one end of the strong new rope to the hook near the kitchen window, and Mary ran off down the garden with the other end.

"What a lovely skipping-rope this would make," she said,

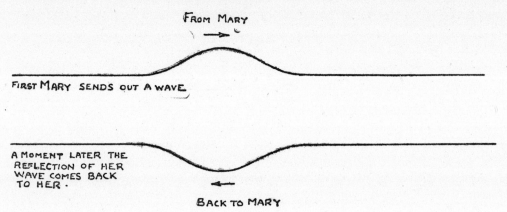

pulling the rope so that it hung in a graceful curve, and giving the end a shake.

To Mary's surprise, the long rope refused to be turned. When she moved the end up and down, she merely made a hump or wave in the rope which travelled swiftly from where she was standing towards the kitchen window and then came as swiftly back, upside down, to give her hand a violent shaking. Father saw what was happening and called out to Mary, "Do it again, and let Peter see."

A moment later he came out of the house and took the free end of the rope from Mary. "The best instance of this I have ever seen was among the mountains in southern Switzerland and northern Italy," he said. "There the peasants stretch wires for half a mile or more from the summits of wooded slopes down into the valleys. They use them as a means of transport for cut faggots and timber. Bundles of stuff are sent sliding down a wire far more easily and cheaply than they can be carried by mule or donkey down twisty and slippery mountain-paths. If you stand at the bottom or top anchorage of the wire, you can send a wave from one end to the other, and because the wire is so long, it takes quite a while for the wave to reach the far end; in fact, you can watch it go out of sight. Then, some seconds later, you see it coming back again in reverse, or upside down. At first the reflected wave looks very tiny, but as it rushes towards you you can see that it is nearly as big as the wave you made in the first place. Presently it reaches the anchorage where you are standing, and here it is reflected a second time. It goes away from you, reversed again, and looking almost exactly the same as the wave you made in the first instance. To cut a long story short, the wave travels backwards and forwards many times before it becomes too slight for you to see. And if you sent out a hump to begin with it comes back a hollow, only to go forth as a hump again after the second reflection. Each time thereafter it goes from you as a hump and comes back towards you as a hollow. This clothes-line is long enough to let you see the hump travelling along to the far end and coming back as a hollow, but the events happen rather quickly, and you need to be sharp to see what occurs. The second reflection, which ought to take place at my hand, is not very distinct, as my hand is not a sufficiently firm support.

"If I keep on sending waves out I shall get a whole series of reflected waves coming back, and the reflected waves interfere with the outgoing waves to give the rope a combined movement. This combined movement is very peculiar. Certain points on the rope go quite still: these are called nodes; other points on the rope oscillate from side to side: these are called anti-nodes. The odd thing is that you cannot any longer see waves going out or coming back. The displacements at the anti-nodes appear always in the same places, and for this reason they are called stationary vibrations, or standing waves.

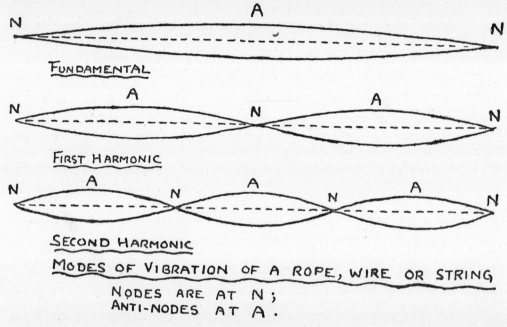

MODES OF VIBRATION OF A ROPE, WIRE OR STRING
NODES ARE AT N;
ANTI-NODES AT A.

"By moving my hand very slowly to and fro, I can get the rope to vibrate as a whole, with a node at the far end and another close to my hand here. You did not go slowly enough, Mary, when you tried to get the whole rope to obey you and turn like a skipping-rope. Now that I have got it vibrating in unison, or in the fundamental manner, as it is called, I can easily turn the vibration into a rotation, and after this I can speed it up to any desired rate.

"If I move my hand up and down faster, I send out shorter waves; and if I get the length of these just right the interference between outgoing and returning waves will cause the rope to divide in two. There will be a node in the middle as well as at each end, and there will be anti-nodes at one-quarter and three-quarters of the way along. By sending out shorter waves still I can produce two intermediate nodes and three anti-nodes."

While he was speaking, Father made the rope fulfil his predictions. He went farther than this and turned it into a wonderful skipping-rope in three loops.

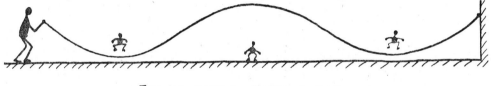

THE WONDERFUL SKIPPING ROPE
(See if you can turn one like this)

Then Mother intervened. "When you have quite finished playing," she said, "I would like to hang up my washing again."

Father quickly tied his end of the rope to the hook in the potting-shed wall. "There you are, Mother," he said. "Carry on with the good work. Come along, Mary and Peter, we will finish our talk about waves indoors.

"When Mother takes in her washing this evening we will make the rope vibrate in all possible ways once again, and you can have my watch to see how many vibrations it does to the minute. You will find that when it is vibrating in the second manner, that is with one intermediate node, it makes exactly twice as many vibrations per minute as when it is vibrating in the fundamental manner. When it is vibrating in the third manner, that is with two intermediate nodes, its frequency of vibration is three times the fundamental frequency.

"If the vibrations occur very quickly, as in a thin, tightly stretched string, they make a pretty musical sound. Advantage is taken of this by makers of musical instruments. The harp, the piano, the violin, the banjo and lots of other instruments all produce agreeable sounds by means of vibrating strings. It is enough to pluck, or strike, or rub one of these strings to set up standing waves in them. And every string has its own

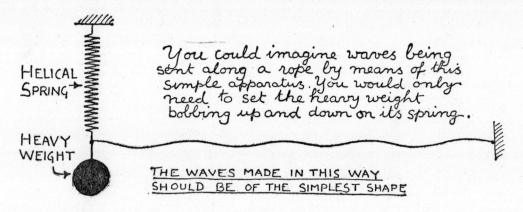

HELICAL SPRING→

HEAVY WEIGHT↳

You could imagine waves being sent along a rope by means of this simple apparatus. You would only need to set the heavy weight bobbing up and down on its spring.

THE WAVES MADE IN THIS WAY SHOULD BE OF THE SIMPLEST SHAPE

fundamental note. When it is vibrating in the fundamental manner it has a definite frequency of vibration, and it gives out a definite note that can only be changed by making the string tighter or slacker. Instruments are provided with means for altering the tightness or tension in the strings, and they are 'tuned' by having these tensions correctly adjusted. A string can, with some trouble, be caused to vibrate in the second, third and other manners, and then the note given out is one corresponding to tmo, three or four times the fundamental frequency. These notes are higher octaves of the fundamental, and are called the first, second, third and so on harmonics of the fundamental."

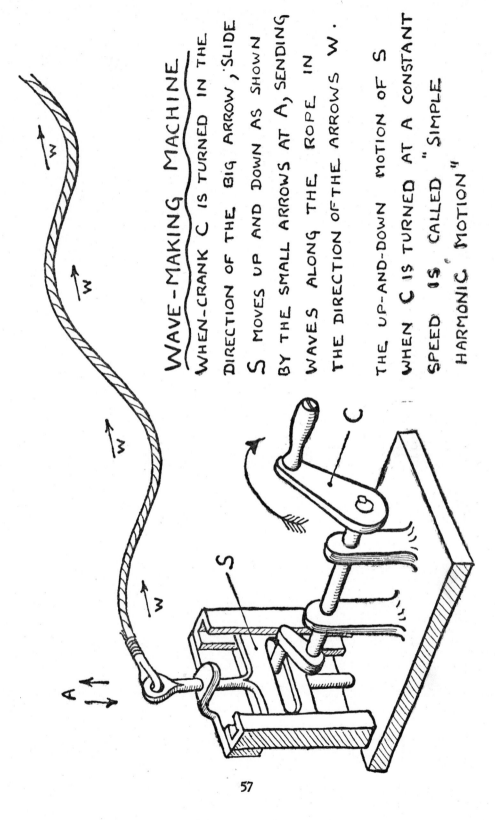

WAVE-MAKING MACHINE

WHEN-CRANK C IS TURNED IN THE
DIRECTION OF THE BIG ARROW, 'SLIDE
S MOVES UP AND DOWN AS SHOWN
BY THE SMALL ARROWS AT A, SENDING
WAVES ALONG THE ROPE IN
THE DIRECTION OF THE ARROWS W.

THE UP-AND-DOWN MOTION OF S
WHEN C IS TURNED AT A CONSTANT
SPEED IS CALLED "SIMPLE
HARMONIC MOTION"

" What is the shape of a wave, Daddy? " asked Mary.

" The simplest and purest wave shape is the one made naturally by any springy or elastic body when it is vibrating in its fundamental manner. If a heavy weight on a spring is set bobbing up and down, it might be used to send waves along a cord or rope just as my hand did; but whereas my hand may have moved according to almost any rule, and sent out waves of any shape, the weight on the spring is bound to move up and down in accordance with natural law, and send out waves of the purest and simplest shape. Its movement is what scientists call ' Simple Harmonic Motion.' It has its own frequency of vibration, which depends on the mass of the hanging weight and the stiffness of the spring. It will produce standing waves in the cord if the latter is tuned to have one of its natural modes of vibration corresponding in frequency with that of the oscillating weight.

" You could imitate the natural motion of the weight on the spring by using the crank-and-slide mechanism I will sketch for you. By turning the handle at different speeds you can vary the frequency of the vibration of the slide.

" You can easily draw the shape of a pure wave. First you make a circle and find on it four points equidistant from one another. I have numbered them 0, 3, 6 and 9 on the circle I am drawing. Now, keeping your compass set to the radius of the circle, you put its point at 0 and you mark the circle on either side of 0, thus obtaining points 2 and 10. Now, with centre 3 and the same radius, you mark the circle at points 1 and 5. You go in the same way to point 6 to find points 4 and 8, and to point 9 to find points 7 and 11. The purpose of all this is to divide your circle up into twelve equal segments.

Now you prolong the horizontal diameter o–6 of your circle to the right and along this prolongation you mark off twelve equal distances by points which are most conveniently numbered o′, 1′, 2′, 3′ and so on. All you have to do now is draw a horizontal line from 1 on the circle to meet, at 1″, a vertical from 1′ on the prolonged diameter; another horizontal line from 2 on the circle to meet, at 2″, a vertical from 2′ on the prolonged diameter; another horizontal from 3 on the circle to meet, at 3″, a vertical from 3′ on the prolonged diameter and so on. In

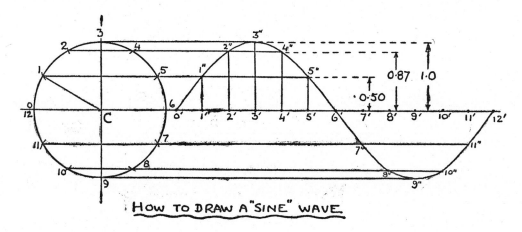

HOW TO DRAW A "SINE" WAVE

the end you join up points o′, 1″, 2″, 3″, 4″ and so on, thus obtaining the shape of your wave.

" The circle 1, 2, 3, etc., is really the circle described by the pin of your crank in the crank-and-slide machine. The crank-pin in the slide occupies the positions o, 1, 2, 3, etc., in turn as the crank takes up the positions C1, C2, C3 and so on. The height of the slide above its central position at every instant is the distance from 1, 2, 3 and so on down to the horizontal diameter, and lengths 1′ 1″, 2′ 2″, 3′ 3″, etc., are made the same.

" When I want to draw a wave I am always in too much of

a hurry to draw the circle and rule all the necessary lines. Instead, I remember that if the radius of the circle is 1 unit long, then line 1′ 1″ is 0·5 unit long, line 2′ 2″ is 0·87 unit long, line 3′ 3″ is 1·0 unit long and so on. The reason why I have memorised these figures is that I have met waves of this shape not only in studying sound or acoustics, but also in studying mathematics and electricity. If you study the sciences closely in your later years you will constantly encounter this

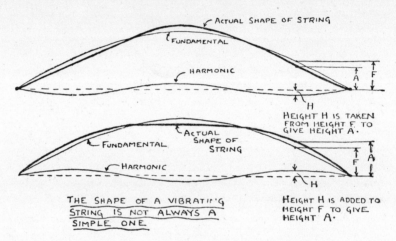

ACTUAL SHAPE OF STRING
FUNDAMENTAL
HARMONIC
A F
H
HEIGHT H IS TAKEN FROM HEIGHT F TO GIVE HEIGHT A.

ACTUAL SHAPE OF STRING
FUNDAMENTAL
HARMONIC
F A
H
HEIGHT H IS ADDED TO HEIGHT F TO GIVE HEIGHT A.

THE SHAPE OF A VIBRATING STRING IS NOT ALWAYS A SIMPLE ONE.

interesting wave shape. Scientists and engineers call it the 'sine wave.'

"Often you get a string vibrating in two or three ways at once. On top of the fundamental vibration there may be a first or second harmonic vibration. In fact, if you pluck or hit a string in the centre, you are almost certain to induce second harmonic vibrations as well as the fundamental. In the sketch I am making now, you can see a big sine wave for the fundamental and a triple-frequency one of smaller height or amplitude for the second harmonic. If I add the vertical displacements together I obtain the actual shape of the string. In one case it is more pointed at the centre and flatter towards

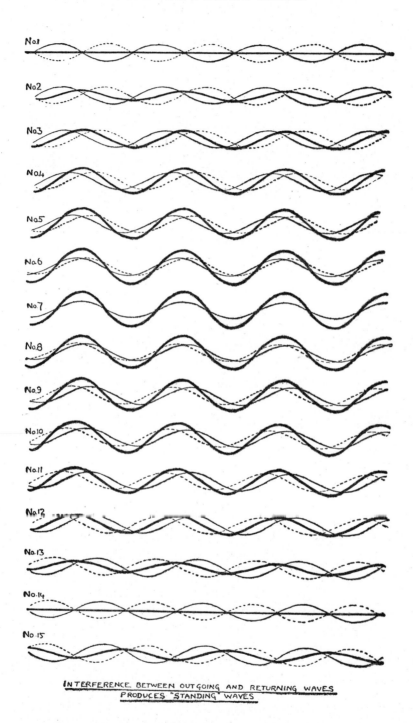

No.1
No.2
No.3
No.4
No.5
No.6
No.7
No.8
No.9
No.10
No.11
No.12
No.13
No.14
No.15

INTERFERENCE BETWEEN OUTGOING AND RETURNING WAVES
PRODUCES "STANDING" WAVES

the ends; in the other case it is more bowed near the ends but
very flat at the centre. In different instruments the string is
vibrated by different methods as, for instance, by the fingers,
by hammers or by a bow. In whatever way the exciting is
done, you are almost sure to get harmonics, and in no two
instruments will those harmonics be the same ones. The
difference between the harmonics gives you the difference in
tone or ' timbre ' that you notice when different instruments
are compared."

" What I don't understand, though, Daddy," Mary interrupted, " is how stationary vibrations are caused by moving
waves going along the string in opposite directions. That's
puzzling to me."

" The only way to convince yourself that it must happen is
to draw out the two sets of waves going opposite ways and
add up the displacements they cause at each spot in the string
to find out the resultant displacement. You will have to draw
something like a dozen of these pictures, showing how the
waves move relative to one another from instant to instant.
In picture No. 1 you can draw the waves opposite to each other
and thus neutralising each other to leave the string straight. In
picture No. 2 you can show the outgoing wave moved a small
way to the right and the returning wave a corresponding
distance to the left. In picture No. 3 the movements to right
and left will be rather more. In picture No. 4 more still, and
so on.

" When you have drawn the waves at twelve or more instants
of time, the next thing to do is to combine their effects, adding
the displacements caused by one to those caused by the other,
or subtracting if the effects are opposite to one another. When

you have done this combining, you will find that you have a third wave, which you can distinguish from the others by drawing the line more thickly. This third wave shows the actual displacement of the string. You will notice that as you go from instant to instant the string displacement increases or decreases at particular places, but that the waves as a whole stand still—they do not move along the string. You get nodes where the string does not move at all, and anti-nodes where it displaces to the maximum extent. The drawings take a long

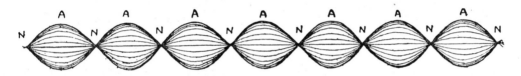

COMBINATION OF DIAGRAMS I TO 14 AND A SIMILAR SET FOR THE NEXT HALF-VIBRATION

time to make and have to be done with great care. When I did this work in my school days I drew twelve pictures in between those representing the string as a straight line, and these showed the progress of only half a complete vibration. Another twelve would have been needed to show the progress of the other half. Of this second twelve I did only one to prove that the whole would be just a repeat of the first twelve but drawn upside down. In the end I transferred all my ' actual shape ' diagrams to one sheet, putting in those for the second half of the vibration as well as those I had obtained for the first half. It made a funny-looking picture—like a string of onions—but it showed nodes and anti-nodes very clearly."

CHAPTER THREE

WAVES THAT SPEAK

" WHERE is my clothes-horse; has anybody seen my clothes-horse? "

Saying these words, Mother burst into the front room in a great flurry. What she saw there was Father busy tying a sort of wire serpent to her clothes-horse by means of dozens and dozens of pieces of cotton. Mary and Peter were helping.

" Well, of all the——! " Mother was too indignant to finish her sentence. Then she remembered what had happened a day or two before, and she started to laugh. " First you take my clothes-line for your experiments, then you go running off with my clothes-horse. Here, can you make any use of these?"

Saying these words Mother threw an armful of wet towels over Father and bounced out of the room, still laughing. Father peeled the wet towels from his head and shoulders, and at the same time explained to Mary and Peter that many people considered such things helpful to the brain worker. " Students are said to wrap wet towels round their heads when studying extra hard," he said; " but this is the first time I have ever had them round my head. I must say I found them soothing."

" But what shall we do about the clothes-horse? " Mary asked ruefully. " Mummy wants it."

" I will go and explain," answered Father, and he went,

taking with him a sketch showing the thing he had been trying to make for the children.

"I wanted two parallel rods or bars about six feet long," he said to Mother, "and although your clothes-horse isn't six feet high, it was the best thing I could think of as the basis of our longitudinal-wave apparatus."

"So that was it, was it!" said Mother grimly. "Because I give you a bit of latitude to do as you please in this house, you

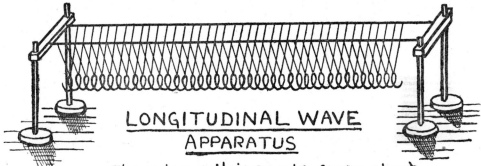

LONGITUDINAL WAVE
APPARATUS

The wire coil is made from about
20 yards of 14-gauge copper wire
wound round a tin or bottle about
3 inches in diameter; it is then
stretched to about 6 feet in length
Every turn is supported by a thread
3 feet long.

must needs go in for a bit of longitude too. And will the thing put curls in my hair or Mary's when it is made?"

"No, it won't," answered Father; "it will make *travelling* waves, or *standing* waves, but it won't make *permanent* waves."

'Well, then," said Mother grudgingly, "I'll let you keep the horse until next Monday, but not a day more. That gives you three whole days, starting from to-morrow. If I find your wire snake tied to it on Monday morning, I'll wring its neck and put it in the dust-bin. Oh, and what about my towels?"

"We are keeping those too," said Father, skipping quickly

out of the kitchen as he said so. "We are putting them round our heads to help us think better."

The old cookery book that Mother threw after him missed him by six inches, and hit Peter instead.

"I say," grumbled Peter, "do be careful; I'm not in this joke, you know."

Mary was putting on the last piece of cotton as Father and Peter rejoined her in the front room.

"Splendid," cried Father; "now we can try it." He gave one end of the spring or coil a smart tap, causing the coils near his hand to bunch up more closely together. The bunchy

FALLING SKITTLES

appearance of the coils instantly started to travel along the spring towards the far end. "That is a wave of compression," said Father; "when I hit the near coils they squeeze together and push the ones in front, but it takes time for the front ones to bunch up, and it is not until they have done so that the ones still farther on begin to feel the push. The coils behave rather like a line of skittles when the one at the end is knocked over. No. 1 knocks over No. 2, No. 2 knocks over No. 3, No. 3 knocks over No. 4, and so on. You only have to knock one down in order to have the whole line knocked over. The wave I have just sent along our spring is called a longitudinal one, because the coils making it move to and fro along the direction in which the wave is transmitted. In a rope, you will remember, the particles of rope move from side to side, or up and down, the direction of their motion being at right angles to the direction of propagation of the wave, which is along the rope. Waves in a rope or string are called transverse waves to distinguish them from the ones I am making in this spring. Now I will send a wave of rarefaction along the spring."

As Father stopped speaking he gave the end coil of the spring a sharp tug, opening out the end turns. This extra wideness between the turns was passed on from turn to turn, and as fresh turns separated, the ones behind closed up again. The action was rather rapid and therefore difficult to follow, but the children distinctly saw a disturbance of the coils rush from

WAVE OF
RAREFACTION
→

WAVE OF
COMPRESSION
→

A   B

APPEARANCE OF LONGITUDINAL
WAVES IN A SPRING

THE NORMAL DISTANCE
BETWEEN COILS IS IN-
CREASED AT A AND
REDUCED AT B.

Father's end to the far end. In fact, they saw more than this, and said so.

"It comes back again when it reaches the end!" exclaimed Mary.

"I was wondering if you would notice," said Father. "The wave of compression is returned by reflection from the free far end as a wave of rarefaction, and the wave of rarefaction is returned as a wave of compression. You see, the compressed coils at the far end push against nothing and over-shoot themselves, causing a stretch behind themselves. This stretch goes rushing back to me. That is why a compression is reflected as a rarefaction. A rarefaction is really a pull on the coils in front. When the pull reaches the far end there is nothing to pull against. The last coil is like the boy in front of a tug of war when the rope breaks. The boy falls back and pushes the one behind him, all get the push in turn and all fall over. What was a state of tension is turned into a state of compression, which goes rushing back."

WAVE OF
COMPRESSION
→

WAVE OF
RAREFACTION
→

←
WAVE OF
RAREFACTION

←
WAVE OF
COMPRESSION

By reflection at free end, a wave of compression is turned into a wave of rarefaction, and —

— a wave of rare-faction is turned into a wave of compression.

The children sent waves of compression and rarefaction along the spring, and watched how, each time, the reflected wave was of the opposite kind to the transmitted wave.

"If I block the far end with my hand by holding the last coil, you will see that a wave of compression is reflected as a wave of compression," said Father, "and a wave of rarefaction as a wave of rarefaction. That is because the blockage, in this case my hand, is able to return push for push and pull for pull."

TUG-OF-WAR

The children experimented for some time to make sure that all was exactly as Father said it was; and then Father spoke again: "If I had a wave-making machine of the crank-and-slide kind, I could use it to make longitudinal as well as transverse waves. I should just turn it on its side so that the slide moved to and fro along the axis of the coil."

"I can make a wave-making machine with my Meccano," said Peter; "I will go and do it now."

So saying, Peter scrambled to his feet and ran to his own

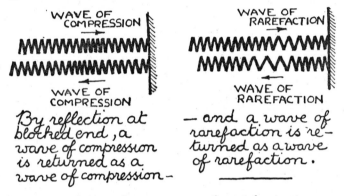

WAVE OF COMPRESSION

WAVE OF COMPRESSION

By reflection at blocked end, a wave of compression is returned as a wave of compression —

WAVE OF RAREFACTION

WAVE OF RAREFACTION

— and a wave of rarefaction is returned as a wave of rarefaction.

room. An hour later he returned with quite a well-made crank-and-slide machine. In the meantime, Father had been explaining to Mary how it was possible to draw a longitudinal wave. First he had drawn a transverse wave, making the height of this equal to the greatest displacement occurring in the longitudinal wave. Then, with a compass, he had swung the displacements round at right angles so that transverse distances became longitudinal ones.

"If I showed each coil of our spring by a straight line, you would get the spring showing at first as a succession of equally spaced lines," Father said. "After displacement by wave action, the lines would appear bunched in the region of a compression and opened out in the region of a rarefaction.

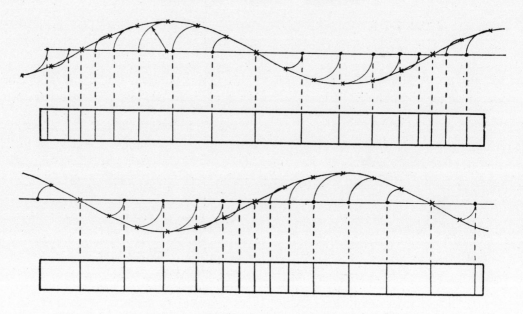

TRANSVERSE AND LONGITUDINAL WAVES

" Ah, here is Peter and his machine. Now we can make truly harmonic waves if we wind the handle of the machine at a constant speed."

Father took the machine from Peter and, after bending the end coil of the spring into a hook, he sat with the machine against his chest and duly attached to the spring.

" Now," he said, " if I send out a series of waves by turning this handle, I shall get a series of reflected waves; and the interference between outgoing and returning waves when these

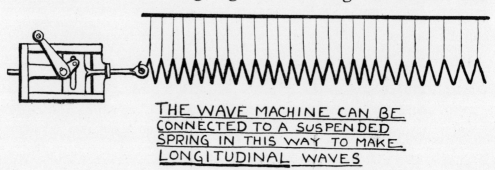

THE WAVE MACHINE CAN BE
CONNECTED TO A SUSPENDED
SPRING IN THIS WAY TO MAKE
LONGITUDINAL WAVES

Harmonic-motion machine made from Meccano.
(See also page 57.)

Longitudinal-wave apparatus.

are of a particular length will set up standing waves in my spring. At what is called the condition of resonance, that is, when I turn the handle at exactly the right speed, I shall get the spring vibrating merrily, with nodes at some points and anti-nodes in between. The spring has its own natural frequencies of vibration, like a stretched wire, and I must find these by varying the speed of Peter's machine until it gets all excited."

Saying these words, Father started to turn the machine slowly. Very gradually he increased the speed until, quite suddenly, the whole spring started to surge to and fro from a point just in front of the machine. "There's the node!" exclaimed Father, putting his finger on this point; "the anti-node is at the far end. Now I will go faster."

As Father accelerated the machine the spring went relatively quiet again. Then, as he reached twice the original speed, it became more active, the two ends moving in and out together while the centre remained stationary.

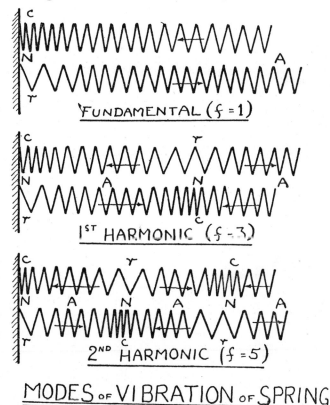

FUNDAMENTAL ($f = 1$)

1ST HARMONIC ($f = 3$)

2ND HARMONIC ($f = 5$)

MODES of VIBRATION of SPRING

(HELD AT ONE END)

T = RAREFACTION
C = COMPRESSION

"The node is now at the centre and the two ends are anti-nodes," said Father. "You see that the end attached to the machine behaves first like a fixed end (although it isn't really fixed) and then like a free end. At three times the first resonant speed it will behave like a fixed end again and give me a node close by. There, now I've got it vibrating with a node just near me, and another one two-thirds of the way along. The anti-nodes are a third of the way along and, of course, at the far end, this always being an anti-node, because it is free. Remember that nodes are places where pressure rises and falls but no movement occurs, whereas anti-nodes are places where there is a lot of movement but no alteration of pressure. The coils at anti-nodes stay the same distance apart, however agitated their movement may be."

After this Father wound the handle of the wave-making machine faster still, and he obtained resonance at 4, 5 and 6 times the first resonant speed.

"I cannot wind it any faster," he said.

FUNDAMENTAL (f = 2)

1ST HARMONIC (f = 4)

2ND HARMONIC (f = 6)

MODES of VIBRATION of SPRING
(FREE AT BOTH ENDS)

r = RAREFACTION
c = COMPRESSION

"Let me rest now and I will sketch for you all the different modes of vibration we have discovered so far. They correspond to the two states of both ends free and only one end free."

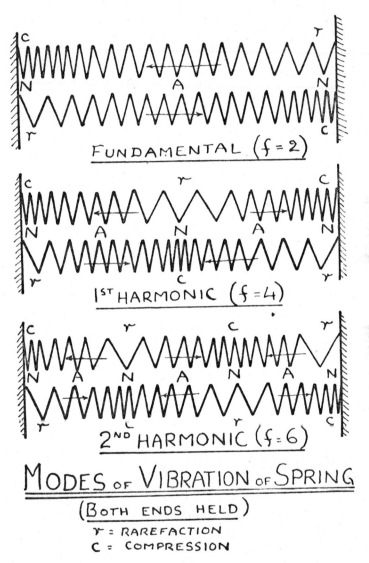

FUNDAMENTAL ($f = 2$)

1ST HARMONIC ($f = 4$)

2ND HARMONIC ($f = 6$)

MODES OF VIBRATION OF SPRING

(BOTH ENDS HELD)

r = RAREFACTION
c = COMPRESSION

The first diagram drawn by Father showed the spring with one end held. For each mode of vibration (and there were three of them) he drew two sketches showing the spring when it was momentarily at rest at each end of its to-and-fro travels. The vibration frequencies he indicated as 1, 3 and 5 (page 71).

The second diagram was made in the same way but for the spring vibrating with both ends free. The frequencies this time were 2, 4 and 6 (page 72).

"We have not tried the effect of having the far end held yet," said Father; "but I can predict what it will be. It will make that end definitely into a node, but, as you will see, we shall not get any new frequencies out of doing this."

Father made sketches for the condition "held at both ends," and the children saw for themselves that the spring was divided up by nodes and anti-nodes into the same lengths as when both ends were free. Thus the vibration frequencies were also the same, namely, 2, 4 and 6 (page 73).

"We will verify that," said Father, and he turned the machine while Peter held the far end of the spring. At each resonant speed Peter let go and the spring continued to vibrate, but changing its mode of vibration so as to make the far end an anti-node instead of a node.

Some of the effects obtained with the spring were not seen without difficulty.

"It helps to know what you are looking for," said Father. "I can tell beforehand what should happen, and by persevering I can *make* it happen; but if somebody quite ignorant was given this spring to play with, he might joggle it for hours without ever learning anything from it."

"Do we need the wave-making machine to set up the standing waves?" Mary asked.

"By no means," answered Father. "You can get all the resonant effects by moving the end coil to and fro in your hand;

but you need to be a little skilful to move your hand in the simple harmonic manner, more especially as the spring sometimes tries to hustle you and at other times does not seem to give you any help at all."

"You have forgotten to tell us what all this has got to do with sound," put in Peter; "even at its fastest this old spring does not make any noise at all."

"It doesn't vibrate fast enough," Father answered. "You do not hear any noise until the vibrations are eighty or ninety a second, and then it is a very low note. Ordinary notes that you can sing average two hundred to three hundred vibrations a second, but you can hear shrill notes of more than twenty thousand vibrations a second. The squeak of a bat is even shriller than this, and old people do not hear it at all. Dogs can hear the shrillest sounds, and you can buy whistles to call them that give a note above the limit of human audibility. The dog can hear it and answer to it, but nobody human hears any sound at all."

"Does the shrillness of a note depend only on the number of vibrations a second?" asked Mary.

"Yes," answered Father! "the pitch, as it is called, is determined by the number of vibrations a second. An orchestra with drums, violins and piccolos and all the other instruments makes notes ranging from thirty vibrations a second or so up to ten thousand a second and more. You get longitudinal vibrations from the wind instruments and transverse vibrations from the string instruments. Drums give transverse vibrations too, the vibrating object being a stretched-skin or parchment diaphragm.

"A simple length of tubing about a quarter of an inch in diameter and a foot long will make a primitive whistle. It will give you vibrations in the air exactly like those produced by our spring, but they are rapid enough to make a musical note, and, of course, the movement of the air is invisible. You get the lowest note by putting your finger over the bottom end and blowing across the top. The node is then at the bottom and the anti-node at the top. The air against your finger is being alternately squeezed and rarefied by the movement of the air above it, and the greatest movement of air up and down the tube is at its mouth, where the anti-node is situated."

While Father was speaking, Peter was rummaging in a corner for something, and presently, with a cry of triumph, he produced a paper pea-shooter he had made some months before. It was just about the right size.

"We will put this to a more intelligent use than that for which it was made," said Father; "we will turn it from an instrument of war into—into——"

"An instrument of torture," giggled Mary, remembering what a nuisance Peter had made of himself with his last whistle.

Father put a finger over one end and blew across the other. It could hardly be said to whistle clearly, but it gave forth a hollow hiss, the note of which rose a full octave when he took his finger away.

"With my finger away and the bottom end open, you get double the frequency of natural vibration," said Father, "and the node is at the centre. If now I made a hole in the middle, there would have to be an anti-node there, because the pressure there could no longer rise above or fall below that of the atmosphere. Two nodes would then appear, one a quarter of the way down and the other three-quarters of the way down. The vibration frequency would then be four times the lowest."

With a penknife Father quickly pierced a small hole in the side of the tube half-way along its length. He then put one finger over this hole and the other over the bottom end. While blowing, he removed the finger over the bottom end, causing the note to rise one octave; then he removed the finger over the

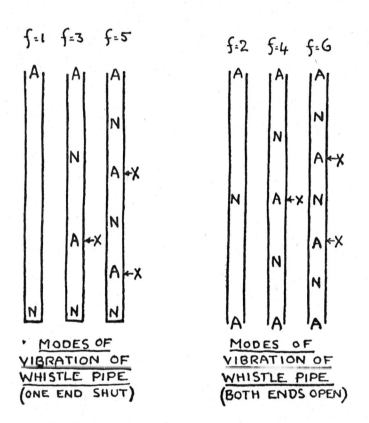

central hole, and the note jumped up another octave. Finally, he made sketches to show the several modes of vibration of the tube, first with one end stopped up and then with both ends open. Over the top of each sketch he wrote numbers to indicate the relative vibration frequencies, starting with 1 for the lowest note. The positions of the nodes and anti-nodes agreed with those for the vibrating spring.

" You can make sure of getting the right mode if you cut holes in the tube at the right places," Father said. " Already I have told you that you must have a hole in the centre to get frequency four. To get frequency three you must stop up the bottom and open a hole one-third of the way up. Of course you close the hole half-way up while you are trying to get frequency three. Frequency five calls for holes a fifth and three-fifths of the way up—either or both; frequency six calls for an open end and holes a third and two-thirds of the way up—either or both. Your ear should tell you if you are rising a whole octave each time I say you should; but unless you begin with a long tube, giving a very low fundamental note, you may find it hard to hear frequencies five and six properly."

" Does the length of the tube matter, then? " Mary asked.

" Of course it does," Father answered; " I will nip off an inch of this pea-shooter and you will hear the fundamental note go higher."

It was as Father said. He nipped off a second inch and the note went higher still. He went on nipping off inches until even the lowest note was very shrill indeed.

" The best way of doing that experiment is to blow into an old empty medicine bottle till it gives a clear note (it works better than a paper tube), and then do the same thing with ever-increasing quantities of water in it. As the water level rises the pitch of the note rises too until it is really shrill.

" I once fixed an old bottle with its mouth close to a keyhole through which a fierce draught blew on windy nights. It made a moaning noise that filled the whole house, and for a long time my mother (that is, your old Grannie, you know) wondered whatever it could be, until she went to investigate."

"Oh, Daddy, you shouldn't have said that!" cried Mary reproachfully. "Now Peter will be trying it."

Peter made a dash at Mary and pushed her indignantly; then, seeing Mary about to retaliate, he rushed from the room into the garden. Mary followed at lightning speed.

"That's the end of science for to-day," said Father sadly, and he started to dismantle the longitudinal-wave apparatus so that Mother could have her clothes-horse back.

CHAPTER FOUR

HOW TO MEASURE THE PITCH OR FREQUENCY OF A NOTE

IF you put the edge of a card against the teeth of a revolving cog-wheel you will hear a musical note. This note becomes more and more shrill if the cog-wheel be made to revolve faster and faster. The number of vibrations per second corresponding to the given note is equal to the number of teeth hitting the card in a second, so, if you knew the speed of rotation of the wheel, you could easily calculate the pitch or vibration-frequency of the note. If you have an old broken clock with the mainspring still intact, you can make a pitch - measuring machine out of it.

SIMPLE WHEEL VIBRATOR

The part broken in a clock that has been dropped is nearly always the "escapement." Very often the balance-wheel is jerked out of its pivots, or the hairspring is twisted up. Sometimes you can easily mend a clock that has been dropped; but if it is really damaged beyond repair, all you have to do to make it useful in a new way is take out the balance-wheel with the attached hairspring and also the lever. Do not forget to begin by detaching the hairspring at its anchorage. You will find it secured by a little taper pin that you must pull out with pliers. To remove the balance-wheel you must unscrew one of the pivots. To get the lever out you will have to loosen the nuts holding the back mechanism plate of the clock in position. Do the loosening a little at a time and pull back the mechanism plate very carefully until it comes back only just far enough to let the lever spindle drop out of its bearing holes. If you pull it too far, all the other wheels will drop out of position too, and then you will have difficulty putting them all back. Once it is free to revolve, the scape-wheel will fly round at a great

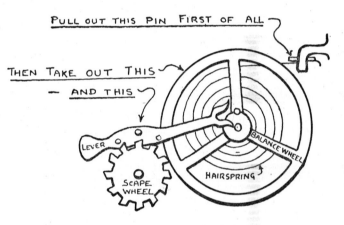

WHAT TO REMOVE FROM AN OLD CLOCK

rate. The hands will go round fast too, but not so fast that you cannot count the revolutions they make. If you press a card or piece of paper lightly against the scape-wheel teeth, you will get a note. By pressing harder you will slow down the wheel and get a lower note. With a little practice you will be able to adjust the pressure until the note is in tune with any note you like to play on the piano.

When you have your old clock sounding the right note, you

must get a friend to count the number of turns that the big hand makes in, say, a quarter of a minute. He will use a watch with a seconds hand to do this. Now you must find out how many turns the scape-wheel makes for each turn of the big hand. To do this it is best, first of all, to mark one of the scape-wheel teeth very clearly, with ink, or with chalk. With your finger you then turn the next wheel to it, and count how many times the scape-wheel goes round for each turn of the big hand. This is rather a slow business: in an old French alarm clock I used for this purpose the scape-wheel made four hundred turns for each turn of the big hand. It had fifteen teeth, and so I knew that each turn of the big hand corresponded to $400 \times 15 = 6,000$ vibrations of the card. When I tuned my machine to give me middle "C" on the piano, I found that the hour-hand took twenty-four seconds to make one revolution. The note, therefore, was one of 6,000 vibrations in 24. seconds, or $6000/24 = 250$ vibrations in each second. As a matter of fact, middle "C" is given by 256 vibrations a second, so my measurement was not quite accurate. But it was very good considering how simple were the means used to make it.

CHAPTER FIVE

AN INSTRUCTIVE TOY OF CARDBOARD

NATURAL waves travel at their own speed, and often go too fast for you to be able to watch what happens in any detail. There is, however, a toy that you can make which enables you to produce imitation wave effects, and you can turn the handle of this toy so slowly that you can easily follow exactly what happens. The toy can be made in two ways, and I shall describe both. Made in one way it helps you to understand the propagation of a travelling wave; made in the other way it gives you a good imitation of a standing wave. In each toy there is a disc of white cardboard

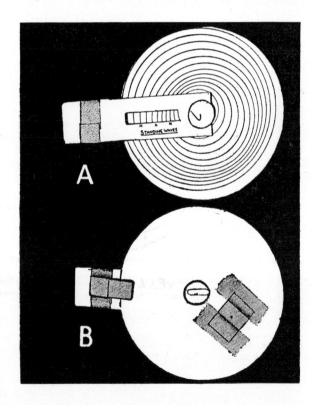

about eight inches in diameter, and the only difference between the two toys is in the way the disc is marked. Sketches A and B show both sides of a completed toy.

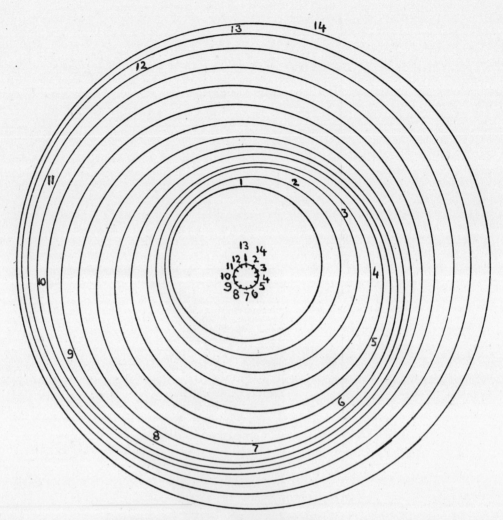

TRAVELLING WAVE DISC

The small circle at the centre is drawn with a radius of an eighth of an inch and is divided into 12 parts by points numbered 1 to 12. Circle 1 is drawn from centre 1 with radius $\frac{3}{4}$ inch; circle 2 is drawn from centre 2 with radius $\frac{7}{8}$ inch; circle 3 is drawn from centre 3 with radius 1 inch, and so on, the radius getting $\frac{1}{8}$ inch bigger every time

For the travelling-wave disc you must begin by drawing a tiny circle at the centre with a well-sharpened compass pencil. The radius of this circle is only ⅛ inch, and you must divide its circumference into twelve equal parts. The way to do this is described on page 58. You must number the points of division 1 to 12. Then, with centres 1, 2, 3, 4, 5 and so on, you draw circles having radii of ¾ inch, ⅞ inch, 1 inch, 1⅛ inch, 1¼ inch and so on, making the radius ⅛ inch bigger each time. To avoid making any mistake, it is as well to number each circle as you draw it. When you have drawn the circle with centre 12, you begin again with points 1, 2, 3 and so on, and, of course, you continue making the circles larger and larger. Altogether you need about 24 circles. When you have drawn all of them you should rub out the numbers. If you have a compass that will draw with ink you can go over the circles in ink to make them clearer and less easy to smear, but be careful to choose the right centre for each circle or you will make a mistake and spoil your disc.

The disc for standing waves is made in much the same way, only the circles are drawn with centres spaced out along a diameter of the tiny circle at the centre instead of around the circumference. When you have completed the disc part of your toy, you must prick the centre through with a fat pin or darning-needle. The holder is made from a piece of cardboard about 2 inches wide and 8 inches long. Half an inch from one end of this, and in the middle, you prick this through. The axle for your disc will go through this pin-prick. Now you must cut a long narrow window in the holder; this is best done with a sharp pen-knife. The window should be ½ inch wide and 2¾ inches long, and begin 1 inch from the pin-prick.

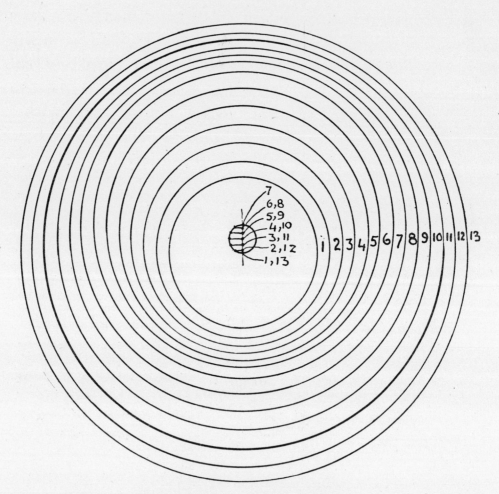

STANDING WAVE DISC

The small circle at the centre is drawn with a radius of an eighth of an inch and one half of it is divided into six equal parts. From the points of division horizontal lines are drawn to the vertical diameter to give points 1, 2, 3, 4, 5, 6. Circles 1, 2, 3, 4, 5, 6, etc are drawn from centres 1, 2, 3, 4 5 6, etc, respectively, the radii being $\frac{3}{4}$ in., $\frac{7}{8}$ in., 1 in., $1\frac{1}{8}$ in., $1\frac{1}{4}$ in., $1\frac{3}{8}$ in. etc. Note that the radius gets $\frac{1}{8}$ in. bigger every time.

Make three cardboard washers 1 inch in diameter and prick each one through. Now straighten out one half of a wire paper-clip and make it stand up at right angles to the bent half. On this straightened part thread (1) a washer, (2) the disc, (3) another washer, (4) the holder, (5) the last washer. Bend over the projecting part of the paper-clip so that it lies flat on the washer, and then bend again in the middle of this

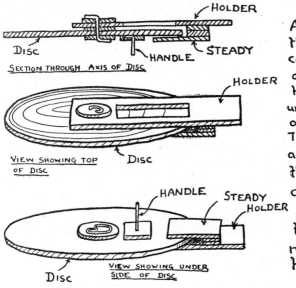

A wire paper clip makes the axle for the disc; a cardboard washer is put on top of the holder; between holder and disc and also under the disc. The steady is made of 3 pieces of cardboard. The handle is made of another paper clip pushed through a small piece of cardboard which is stuck on the under side of the disc. Note the long narrow window in the holder.

HOW TO MAKE A WAVE-IMITATING DISC

flat part. Your disc is now ready for use, but it will work better if you put a handle on the back, as this will enable you to turn it steadily. The handle consists of another paper-clip, half straightened, pushed through a small square of cardboard. As this square must be stuck on the back of the disc, it is advisable to hollow out a place in it to take the curly half of the paper-clip. You can do this with a sharp pen-knife. If this is not done, the wire prevents the square from touching the disc properly and you may be unable to make it stick.

Another improvement is a steady to keep the disc close up against the window in the holder. The steady itself is a strip of cardboard that overlaps the disc on its under side. This strip is pasted to the holder with two thicknesses of cardboard to hold it the required distance away. As paste takes rather a long time to dry, you can, if you like, put sticky brown-paper tape round the parts you are trying to hold together.

With your two toys completed you can watch the progress of both kinds of waves—travelling waves and standing waves. You will notice that each of the lines seen through the window merely moves backwards and forwards. The lines that make a travelling wave move backwards and forwards the same amount, but they do not keep time with one another—they are out of step or out of phase with one another. What travels from one end of the window to the other is the condition of "bunchiness" or "compression" and also the condition of scarcity or "rarefaction."

The lines that make a standing wave move backwards and forwards by different amounts, but they keep in time or in phase with one another. At intervals along the window are lines that do not move at all. The other lines crowd in upon these stationary ones and then separate from them, only to crowd in again a little later. These points of little movement but of greatest variation in the density of the lines are the nodes. The intermediate points, half-way between the nodes, where the lines move backwards and forwards the greatest amount, but do not vary their distance apart, are the anti-nodes.

CHAPTER SIX

SOUNDS FROM AFAR

MARY and Peter were standing on top of a high hill with their father. The day was fine and clear, and they were watching a train in the distance far below them. Without the help of binoculars it looked very tiny, and although its speed was very fast, its progress seemed little better than a crawl. Father looked at his watch. "That'll be the nine-thirty morning train from London," he said. "It will stop at the junction, and from here we can watch it starting again. The engine always gives a sharp whistle before the train starts, and if you watch closely you will see the plume of steam come from the whistle quite an appreciable time before the sound reaches you. We will use my watch to find out just how long the sound takes to come from the junction to here. Our map shows the distance to be two and a quarter miles."

Peter watched the train with the binoculars, and Mary kept her eyes on the seconds hand of Father's watch, waiting for Peter to say "Right," which word was to signify that he had seen the plume of steam. Directly he said "Right," Mary started to count seconds: "One, two, three, four, five, six," she said, "seven, eight, nine, ten, elev—nearly eleven."

"Say eleven seconds," said Father. "Two and a quarter miles is 1,760 yards twice and 440 yards more—that is, 3,960 yards, or 12,000 feet all but 120 feet, meaning to say 11,880 feet. That divides by eleven very nicely, giving the speed of sound as 1,080 feet a second. This speed is generally agreed to be about 1,100 feet a second at ordinary temperatures. If you see a flash of lightning you can reckon it to be about one mile away for every five seconds elapsing before you hear the thunder, a mile being 5,280 feet."

" I once watched a man hitting a stake with a big hammer," said Mary, " and the funny thing was that he did not make any noise at all on the down stroke of his hammer, but only on the up stroke. It sounded as though the sky was made of something hard, and not the stake! "

" That," said Father, " was only because he was some distance away. By the time the sound of hitting the stake reached you, the man had had time to lift his hammer for the next blow."

" What sort of waves bring sounds to us from a distance? " Mary asked.

" They are longitudinal waves in the air," answered Father; " and they are travelling waves, not standing ones. Standing ones, you will recollect, are formed by the interference between waves going in opposite directions, as when reflections occur, and returning waves meet outgoing waves."

" How long are the waves? " asked Mary. " I mean, how far is it from one compression to the next? "

" The wave length varies enormously," answered Father; " you see, it depends on the pitch of the sound. A shrill sound corresponds to thousands of very short waves being sent out every second, but a low rumbling sound corresponds to something fewer than a hundred quite long waves in a second. The total length of all the waves emitted in a second amounts to

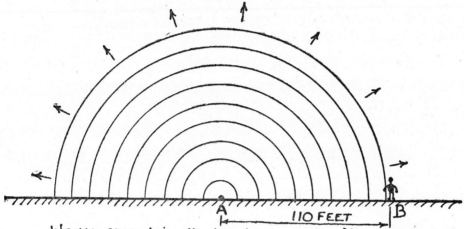

A   110 FEET   B

Waves spread in all directions from the sounding body at A. Each compression is shown by a semicircle, but in space it is a hemisphere. The sound is one of 90 vibrations a second, and it takes 1/10 second to reach the listener at B, who is 110 ft. from A. The wave length is 12 2/9 ft.

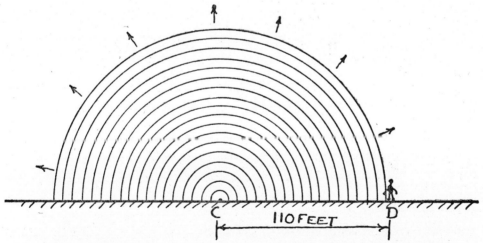

C   110 FEET   D

Here the sound comes from C, which emits 180 vibrations a second. Twice the original number of waves must occupy the same space because the speed of propagation is still 110 ft. in 1/10 second. The wave length is thus 6 1/9 ft.

HOW SOUND REACHES US

1,100 feet in each case, so you see there must be a definite length of wave for each musical note. If you divide 1,100 feet by the pitch or vibration frequency of the note, you will get the exact wave length. For the low note of one hundred waves a second, the wave length is 1100/100, which is 11 feet. For a shrill note of say, five thousand waves a second, the wave length is 1100/5000, which is little more than a fifth of a foot, about 2⅝ inches. Middle 'C' on the piano, which has a frequency of 256 vibrations a second, has a wave length of 1100/256, or 4 feet 4 inches. When people are building an organ or any other wind instrument, they are able to make the pipes of exactly the right length to produce the notes they require. Standing waves have the same length as that of the travelling waves which produce them, and the wave length of a standing wave is the distance from one node to the next but one. The distance from node to anti-node is a quarter of the wave length. So if you want a pipe closed at one end and open at the other to give middle 'C' for its lowest, or fundamental, note, you must make it a quarter of 4 feet 4 inches in length—that is, 1 foot 1 inch."

The children were so interested in what Father was saying that they scarcely noticed where they were going, and it was with surprise that Mary realised some minutes later that they were now at the foot of the hill, quite near the railway. Just here the line was level with the fields; a little farther on it dived into a deep cutting and then into a tunnel.

"Let us wait to see a train," said Peter, going to the railing only a few feet from the track.

"Oh, need we?" said Mary; "they aren't very interesting."

"Indeed?" said Father. "I am surprised to hear you say so,

Mary. I should have expected you to find trains quite as interesting as Peter does."

"Listen," cried Peter; "I think I can hear one coming."

Peter was quite right, and a moment later they saw a train approaching at full speed. When it was quite near it started to whistle in order to give warning of its approach to any men who might be working in the tunnel. The note of the whistle was very shrill; but as the engine rushed past, and plunged into the tunnel, the note seemed to drop a tone and become "flat." Father asked Mary if she had noticed the fall in pitch of the sound of the whistle.

"Yes," answered Mary; "I noticed it, and I have noticed the same thing happen to the buzz of a low-flying aeroplane when one goes past. The buzz seems to change and become lower as the plane zooms by. Why is it?"

"The explanation is quite simple," said Father. "Suppose that the engine whistle is giving out a note of 5,500 vibrations a second, and suppose that the engine is standing still. You will then have 5,500 waves passing you in a second, each of wavelength 1100/5500, or a fifth of a foot, and you will hear the true note of the whistle. Now suppose that the engine is coming towards you at a speed of 100 feet a second. In each second the whistle will send out 5,500 waves, as before, and these waves will travel towards you at 1,100 feet a second, as before, but the distance occupied by 5,500 of them will no longer be 1,100 feet because the engine will be 100 feet nearer to where you are standing when its whistle is sending out the last of the 5,500 waves. In other words, the 5,500 waves will be crowded into a space of 1100 − 100 = 1,000 feet, and the length of each individual wave will be shorter than a fifth of a

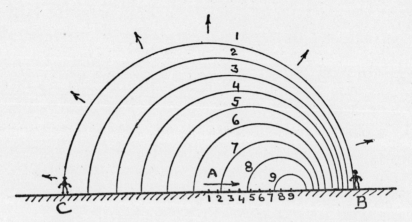

Waves emitted by a moving body A are obliged to travel like all others at 1100 ft. a second, and so they become crowded together in front of the body and attenuated behind it. Waves 1, 2, 3, 4, 5 etc. are made when the body is passing points 1, 2, 3, 4, 5 etc. By the time wave 1 reaches the listeners at B and C, the sounding body will have reached point 9. Plainly waves travelling at 1100 ft. a second will be more frequent passing B than passing C, and so B will hear a higher note than C

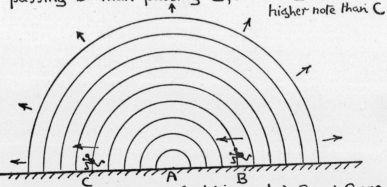

The sounding body A is stationary but B and C are running near it. Plainly B, running towards A, will be passed by more waves than C, who is running away. Consequently he will hear a higher note.

DOPPLER'S PRINCIPLE

foot. Behind the engine it is different. The waves of sound travel back at 1,100 feet a second while the train goes forward at 100 feet a second, and so the sound-waves behind the train will be spread out at the rate of 5,500 to every $1100 + 100 = 1,200$ feet. The length of each wave will be more than a fifth of a foot. I think now you will see why there is a drop in the whistle's tone as the train passes you. When the engine approaches you hear the note higher than it really is because, in 1,100 feet of air in front of the engine, there are $\frac{1100}{1000} \times 5500$, or 6,050 waves, whereas in 1,100 feet of air behind the engine there are $\frac{1100}{1200} \times 5500$, or just over 5,041 waves, giving you a note which is lower than the true note of the whistle.

"Sometimes you get the same effect produced in rather a different way. You might be in a train moving at 100 feet a second towards a stationary train, the engine of which is whistling. As you rush to meet the sound the effect is similar to adding 100 feet a second to the normal speed of sound, which is 1,100 feet a second. You encounter waves at the rate of 5,500 for every 1,100 feet, and consequently you hear a note of $\frac{1200}{1100} \times 5500$, or just over 5,909 vibrations a second. After passing the standing engine you still hear the sound of the whistle, because the sound is able to overtake you. Your speed is 100 feet a second, but the sound-waves travel at 1,100 feet a second, and therefore they pass you by at 1,000 feet a second. You do not get 5,500 of them passing you in a second because there are 5,500 of them in 1,100 feet and rather fewer in 1,000 feet. In 1,000 feet there are only $\frac{1000}{1100} \times 5500$, or

5,000 of them, so the note you now hear is one corresponding to 5,000 vibrations a second.

"It was a scientist called Doppler who first explained why you could not hear the true note emitted by instruments if they or you were travelling at speed through the air."

Just then there was the sound of a rapidly approaching aeroplane.

"Why, it is one of those new jet planes," cried Peter excitedly.

With a scream the machine tore overhead and receded into the distance at a rate of about one mile in every six seconds. The children watched it and saw it turn.

"I believe it is coming back," Peter said.

The machine did come back, but it made the return journey some distance west of where the children were standing.

"Do you notice how it seems to be ahead of its sound?" Father said. "You might think that it was a perfectly silent plane being followed some way behind by an invisible but very noisy pursuer. The sound-waves reaching you are always those that were originated by the machine some seconds before, when it was anything up to half a mile behind the position where you see it; that is why the sound seems to come from behind the machine."

On the way home, Father led the children along a path that wound its way between the hills. At one place the hills on their right had been cut away to make a chalk pit. Two hundred yards away the cliff of white chalk rose perpendicularly to a height of about one hundred feet.

"If you shouted here you ought to hear a good echo from that cliff," said Father.

"Hip, hip, hooray!" shouted Mary.

" Hooray!" the cliff answered back with Mary's clear voice.

" Rule, Britannia! " yelled Peter.

" Britannia! " the cliff answered back.

" You only hear the last two or three syllables repeated, because we are too near to hear any more," said Father. " Two hundred yards there and back makes four hundred yards in all

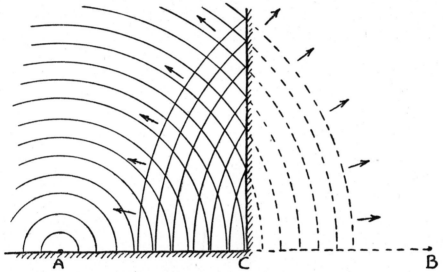

HOW AN ECHO IS CAUSED

The sound made at A produces waves that are reflected by the cliff C . The reflected waves seem to have their origin at B , which is as far behind C as A is in front

—that is 1,200 feet, or just over one second's journey for the sound waves. All you can hear repeated complete is what you can say in one second. If you say anything that takes longer, the echo starts coming back to you before you have finished speaking, and so, when you stop speaking, to start listening, only the last bit of the echo reaches you. In mountainous countries like Switzerland, there are places where you can get echoes to quite long sentences, and the peasants yodel for the fun of hearing an answering yodel from inaccessible crags and cliffs. It sounds rather weird—as though there were mountaineers up there, answering back. The peasants have also a mournful-sounding horn or trumpet about ten feet long with which they blow dismal notes you can hear echoed from the mountains in the same way. For this pleasure you are expected to pay a small fee to the horn blower."

"How much more are you going to tell us about sound?" Mary asked.

"Only one thing more," answered Father. "When two notes of almost the same frequency are sounding, you get a

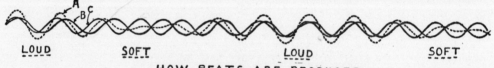

LOUD   SOFT   LOUD   SOFT

HOW BEATS ARE PRODUCED

WHEN ONE WAVE IS SLIGHTLY LONGER THAN ANOTHER (B IS LONGER THAN C) THE TWO WAVES TOGETHER PRODUCE A RESULTANT WAVE (SHOWN DOTTED AT A) THAT IS ALTERNATELY OF LARGE AMPLITUDE (AS WHERE IT SAYS LOUD) AND SMALL AMPLITUDE (AS WHERE IT SAYS SOFT). A THROBBING NOTE OF PITCH EQUAL TO THAT OF THE SHORTEST COMPONENT WAVE C IS WHAT YOU EVENTUALLY HEAR.

throb effect. The two sounds combine to give you a loud sound one instant and hardly any sound at all the next. The engines of a twin-engine aeroplane do not always turn at exactly the same speed, and you hear a throbbing sound. If one of the engines is going a revolution a second faster than the other, you will hear the sound throbbing loud and soft once in every second. The tremolo effect you get on a good accordion is produced by arranging for each key to let the wind blow past two little brass reeeds, one of which vibrates a little faster than the other. You can understand the effect very easily if you will draw out two sets of sine waves, one with a shorter wave length than the other, and then add up their effects. The resultant or combined wave waxes and wanes; that is to say, it is very peaky at some instants and very flat, almost non-existent, between whiles."

"People used to tell the German bombers from our own by the throbbing noise they made," said Peter.

"I know," answered Father; "but it wasn't a very sure indication. Some of the German machines didn't throb, and on the other hand, some of ours did. People used to say cheerfully, ' That's only one of ours,' and the next instant there was a crash that sent them scuttling for their shelters. But it is pleasanter to think of the gentle pulsations of note given by a good musical instrument. They seem somehow to give the note more feeling, possibly because good singers make their voices pulsate. When the pulsations are caused by two vibrations of different frequency, scientists call them beats. It isn't a very romantic name for them, but I tell it to you in case you should meet it in a book one day. Another unromantic word is ' acoustics.' All that I have been telling you is referred to sometimes as the science of acoustics. The old type of gramophone, in which the sound record transmits vibrations by way of a needle to a diaphragm of metal or mica, and thence to a column of air in a big trumpet, is sometimes called the acoustic type of gramophone to distinguish it from the electric type, in which the vibrations of the needle are converted to electric impulses these, in turn, being amplified and then passed to the coil of a moving-coil loud speaker, the essential part of which is a very large vibrating diaphragm."

CHAPTER ONE

EVENING AT A COUNTRY COTTAGE

MARY and Peter sat with their father on a fence, watching the sun go down behind some distant hills. They had spent the whole day together tramping in the country, and now they were on their way home.

"What a glorious day it has been," said Mary; "the sun has not left off shining for one single minute. Good-bye, sun, until to-morrow, and thank you for making our half-term holiday such a lovely one."

As Mary spoke, the last tiny part of the sun's rosy disc slipped down behind the hills and disappeared from sight.

Peter slid down from the fence into the roadway. "Come along," he said, "I'm ready for my tea."

"Not so fast, young man," said Father, getting down in his turn, and giving a hand to Mary; "we have a call to make before we can go home. Old Mr. Parker has been ill, and I want to ask how he is getting on. We shall be coming to his cottage in a few minutes."

"Who is Mr. Parker?" asked Peter.

"Mr. Parker is a very old friend of mine," answered Father. "He keeps poultry, and every Christmas we get our turkey from him. We buy other things from him too, but perhaps you never stop to wonder where all our nice butter and eggs come from. You just gobble and gobble and——"

Watching the sun go down.

"Like a turkey yourself," interposed Mary in a teasing tone.

"I can see the cottage now," Father went on hastily, to avert a quarrel. "Look, that is its chimney you can see peeping through those trees."

Mary and Peter looked towards where their father was pointing and saw a column of grey smoke rising lazily into the still evening air. A moment later they came to a little white gate set in a low stone wall. They opened it and walked up a narrow path flanked on both sides with beds of fragrant flowers. The air was laden with the scent of stocks and sweet brier, and countless gnats danced in the twilight. Father had to stoop when he reached the cottage door, so low was the porch. He gave a knock on the door with his knuckles, and a moment later it was opened by an old lady with white hair, who was wearing a white apron over a lavender-coloured dress.

"I've called to ask how Mr. Parker is," said Father.

"He is making very good progress," answered the little old lady; "but do come inside, all of you, and I will tell him you are here."

Father followed the little old lady into a neat parlour with a low whitewashed ceiling and a red-brick floor. A wood fire was burning cheerily in the grate and sending up volumes of the grey smoke that the children had seen from afar.

"I was just making a cup of tea," said the little old lady; "you and the children would like one, I daresay."

"It is very kind of you to ask us, Mrs. Parker," said Father. "A nice warm cup of tea would be very welcome, if it is not giving you too much trouble."

"No trouble at all," replied Mrs. Parker. "The kettle will be boiling in a moment, and when we've had tea I'll take you to see Mr. Parker. He'll be feeling more like himself after his tea; he always does."

The cottage parlour was a dim place, with only the fire to light it, but Mrs. Parker fetched an oil lamp from the dresser and put it in the middle of the table. This she proceeded to light.

Peter had never seen an oil lamp before, and he was so curious that when Mrs. Parker removed the glass chimney and touched the wick with a lighted taper he nearly burned the end of his nose. Mrs. Parker laughed. "It's easy to see that you've never set eyes on the likes of this, Sonny," she said. "Well, we're old-fashioned folk hereabouts. No gas, no electricity, no water laid on, no drains, no nothing."

"Why doesn't the rag, or whatever it is you've lighted, just burn up and go out?" Peter asked.

"The wick?" queried Mrs. Parker; "oh, that goes down into the glass body of the lamp where you can see there is a pint or two of paraffin oil. The oil runs up the wick and keeps the top nice and moist. It's the oil that burns, not the wick. Look, I can make the flame small or big by turning the wick down or up."

Saying these words, Mrs. Parker turned the wick down so that the flame became small, then she turned it up so that the flame became big and smoky.

"Now, Master Peter," she went on, "if you will mind your nose, I will put on the chimney. See, I turn the flame very low to begin with. That is because the chimney would crack if it were heated too quickly. It goes all steamy at first, then it goes clear, and after a minute or two I can turn the flame up nice and bright, so."

At that moment the kettle boiled over, and Mrs. Parker left Peter gazing at the wonderful oil lamp while she went to make the tea.

All through tea, Peter gazed at the lamp. Presently he started to sniff.

"It smells, doesn't it?" he broke out at last.

"Eh, what's that?" said Mrs. Parker. "Oh yes, the lamp, you mean. Yes, it smells a bit when it gets hot, and it makes the room hot too. You can always tell the place where they have oil lamps. Now I daresay your gas and electric lamps don't smell at all, nor yet heat the room."

"You get some heat from the gas," said Father, "but nothing to speak of from electric lamps; and of course the electric lamps are clean and quite without smell."

"This old lamp of mine is apt to run up," said Mrs. Parker. "It hasn't got the virtues of Aladdin's lamp; on the contrary, it is an old demon. If I leave it for half an hour, sure enough, when I come back, it is flaring up the chimney and pouring out the dirtiest of black smoke. It covers everything with black smuts if you give it half a chance. I always turn it down low when I go out of the room to save it from doing that. I'll turn it down now, as we'll be going along to Mr. Parker's room directly."

So saying, Mrs. Parker turned down the oil lamp. Then she reached up to a high shelf on the dresser, and brought down a beautiful blue candlestick.

"My!" exclaimed Peter, "I didn't think anyone used those things nowadays. It's a candle, isn't it? I've read about them in books. They are made of tallow, aren't they?"

Mrs. Parker made a spill of paper, which she lighted at the

fire. Then she touched the wick of the candle with it. "We country folk wouldn't be without our candles," she said. "We all use them still. Not many of us have oil lamps for upstairs use."

Putting her hand round the flame of the candle to shield it from draughts, she led the way to the passage and then up the stairs.

Father was soon engaged in discussion with old Mr. Parker, who said he would be well enough to get up in two or three days' time. The children did not pay much heed to the conversation, but watched the candle. The flame waved from side to side, and every now and then it did a little dance, bobbing up and down in a steady rhythm. Presently the cup of melted tallow at the top of the candle overflowed and tears of grease poured down the side, where they congealed and formed blobs.

After awhile Father got up to go. Mrs. Parker took up the candle and led the way downstairs. Reaching the parlour again, she blew out the candle. The wick smoked for a second or two afterwards, filling the room with a strange new smell. "Well, now," she exclaimed, "my mother always told me *never* to blow out a candle but always to pinch the wick. It stops the smell. That's nigh on fifty years ago, and I've never remembered to do her bidding yet—except when it's too late!"

She turned the oil lamp up again and put the candlestick back on the dresser. "You children must have seen candles before, I feel certain," she went on. "Don't you have them on your birthday cakes—one for each year of your age? Haven't you ever had them on a Christmas tree?"

"We have electric fairy-lights on our tree," answered Mary; "and Mother tried to get tiny candles for putting on my birthday cake last year, but the shopman said that he had stopped stocking toy candles—because there was no demand for them. He said everyone used imitation ones worked by electricity."

"Well, I prefer the old-fashioned ways of doing things myself," said Mrs. Parker; "but then, I daresay I am a back number."

"Mother said the toy candles were all different colours and made with twisty bodies," said Mary.

"So they were, so they were," mused Mrs. Parker; "but it's a long time since——" She suddenly stopped speaking and sat up very straight. "Why, bless me!" she went on, hitting her knees and laughing, "I believe I've got a boxful tucked away somewhere. Ten years ago my son was going to celebrate his twenty-first birthday here, and I got everything ready, and then a telegram came to say he couldn't get leave. He's in the Navy, you know. If I can find that old box of candles you're welcome to them."

Saying these words, Mrs. Parker went to a corner cupboard and rummaged among the packages and oddments that lay inside.

Presently she gave a cry of triumph and brought out a dusty cardboard box that contained an assortment of little coloured candles. They had twisty stems, just like Mary had imagined, and besides white and yellow ones, there were red, green and blue ones.

"For your next birthday cakes, dears," said kind old Mrs. Parker, handing the box to Mary.

"Oh, thank you, *thank* you," cried Mary, putting her arms round the old lady, and giving her a rapturous kiss; "oh, what fun, Peter! Do hurry and have your birthday. Yours comes before mine."

Father rose to go. "Thank you very much for your lovely cup of tea, and for your kindness to the children," he said; "I'm delighted to know that Mr. Parker is on the way to recovery. I'll send him a tin of that stuff we were speaking about upstairs. It did me a lot of good after my last illness, and I am sure he will benefit by taking it. Come along, children."

Father led the way out of the cosy little cottage, which now looked bright and comfortable compared with the outer darkness. Mrs. Parker bid them all good night, and held the door open to light their way down to the wicket. The air still smelt strongly of stocks.

Once in the road, Father and the two children walked briskly the long distance homewards, but to Mary the journey seemed very short indeed, as her mind was not on the walk at all but on the fun she and Peter were going to have with the precious box of coloured candles that she hugged so closely to her breast.

"Quite a lesson you've had in old-time methods of domestic lighting," said Father, breaking the silence at last.

"Yes," agreed Peter, "awfully interesting I thought it was. If anybody wants to know what I'd like for a birthday present, tell them I'd like an oil lamp. I think it's better than the electric ones, because you can make it dim or bright and you can move it about so easily."

"You're a queer boy, Peter," said Mary in a patronising tone; "you ought to have lived in the Dark Ages."

"Queer yourself," snorted Peter; "you and your old box of candles!"

"Now, now, children," warned Father. "We all like a

change sometimes, and it is nothing to be ashamed of. All the same, an oil lamp is a dangerous thing. I read once of a cat upsetting a lamp over itself on a farm. The oil soaked its fur and caught alight. Poor flaming pussy rushed through the farmhouse, setting fire to everything on her way. Then she dashed out into the farmyard, setting fire to barns, ricks, chicken-houses and everything else. The whole place was ablaze in no time. Pussy had the sense to jump into a river nearby and was saved, but the farm was doomed. I'll let you have a lamp, Peter, on condition that you keep it in a safe place."

" Thanks, Dad," answered Peter.

" Why, we are at the end of our road! " cried Mary suddenly, " I'm going to run on. Catch me, Peter! "

CHAPTER TWO

NEW LAMPS FOR OLD

PETER'S birthday party was over and all his little guests had gone home. The birthday cake, or what was left of it, stood on the sideboard with ten candles still proudly surmounting it. Standing by the cake was a beautiful shiny oil lamp, which Father had given him for his present. It had been burning ever since breakfast time, but Peter had not yet had a chance to try it in the dark.

"Can we switch off the electric light now, Daddy?" Peter pleaded.

Father nodded assent, so Peter ran to the light switch and turned it off. Then he proudly carried his new oil lamp round the room and admired all he could see by its rather dim light. Big shadows rose and fell as he moved; they seemed to be following him round the table in a sort of procession. At last Peter set the lamp down in the centre of the table and moved to a place near the fire, beside his father. Mary sat on a stool at his other hand.

"When I was young I was just as fascinated as you are by light of various kinds," said Father meditatively. "I suppose we are all born with the same instinct that plants and insects have. Like moths, we are attracted by anything bright. I used to live in a country cottage, much the same as the one Mrs. Parker has, and the only light we had there came from oil lamps and candles. At Christmas time I used to be invited to stay with my old Grannie and Grandpa in London, and I loved every minute of my stay for many reasons, but what I remember liking most were the gas lamps in the house, and all the strange lights in the busy shopping street."

"Tell us about your visits," cried Mary.

"I can remember morning time and evenings best," said Father. "The front door of the house had glass in it of many colours. All round the edge were little strips of ruby red. If I stood on tiptoe I could look out at the garden through one of the lowest strips. It seemed lovely to me. The morning sun used to come streaming through that glass window, and to this day it gives me a thrill when I see the glitter and sparkle of sunshine through a window of many-coloured pieces of glass. The dining-room windows had coloured lights too, at the top. There were great bull's-eyes of rose-pink glass, like magnifying glasses, only wrinkled instead of smooth. They too sparkled in the morning sunshine."

"Tell us about the evening," said Mary.

"My Grannie used to pull a white china knob beside the fireplace when she wanted tea. Sometimes she would let me do it. The knob started a big bell clanging in the kitchen a long way away, down two or three flights of dark twisty stairs. Clara the maid came up to see what was wanted, and my Grannie said, 'Please bring in the tea now, Clara,' and then Clara went away to put the kettle on and cut the bread and butter and toast the scones. While all these lovely preparations were going on, I would run to the sofa by the window and kneel upon it to watch for the lamp-lighter. Just outside the house was a gas lamp on a yellow post which was shaped like a school pencil, not round, but with six flat sides. I loved that lamp with its little glass house at the top. I used to think it would be fun to be small enough to live inside. It had a pointed roof with crinkly eaves, and a great chimney in the middle. The lamp-lighter had a long pole, which was black at the top end. He carried it over his shoulder, and when he got to my lamp he poked the black end up through the floor of the little glass house and, hey presto, the most wonderful greeny-white light appeared, right in the middle of the little house. Then the man pulled out his pole and went away. When I turned round I found that the greeny-white light was shining into our room and making shadows on the wall opposite to the window.

" Presently Clara came in with a lighted taper. She stretched up over the table to pull a little chain on the lamp hanging from the ceiling, and when it started hissing she put the taper over the glass globe. The light gave a tremendous pop and then shone out with the same greeny-white light as the lamp in the street. Clara turned it low to begin with, to prevent the glass globe from cracking, and then she left it, hissing and bubbling, to be turned up by my Grandpa later on when he thought it safe. You can still see the same kind of light in places where gas is used. It had a little gauzy thimble of white stuff, very delicate, called a mantle, which glowed very bright on account of the gas burning inside it. I remember that sometimes the mantle got damaged or broken by a knock, and then Grandpa took a new one out of a little cardboard box. The rim of the thimble was fixed to a little white porcelain ring with three arms sticking out. Grandpa took off the porcelain ring of the old mantle and fixed the new mantle in place. Then he set fire to the mantle to burn the protective gummy stuff that kept it stiff

OIL

CANDLE

EARLY
GAS

INCANDESCENT
GAS

GAS-FILLED LAMP

ARC

VACUUM LAMP

CARBON LAMP

while it was still in its box.   Afterwards he lighted the lamp in the ordinary way.

"While we were having tea, Clara used to go round the house with her taper, lighting all the gas jets in the house. There were not any more lamps of the incandescent kind with mantles.   The early gas lamps had what was called a bat's-wing burner of the kind you can still see in an acetylene bicycle lamp. It made a flame something like Peter's oil lamp, only blue near the burner and hollow instead of rounded at the top.   The points at the sides gave it the appearance of a bat's wing.   The flame was shielded from draughts by a big glass globe, which was either plain or with a fancy pattern etched on the outside. Even so, it used to flicker and dance, rather like a candle.   I remember there was one of these lamps just by the foot of the stairs, another on the landing at the top, one in the bathroom (with the glass globe missing) one in the W.C., and two in each of the bedrooms.   If Clara lit the lamps before tea I used to go round with her.   I wished I was tall enough to do it myself.   She generally lifted me up to let me light one of them.

"I remember the first electric lamps.   On dull foggy days the shops were all lighted up.   Some of the shops had big lamps hanging out over the pavement.   I remember one shop with three great lanterns in a row over the pavement.   They had opal glass globes underneath—enormous they were—and over the outside was a tightly fitting wire net to catch the pieces if the globe got broken.   Inside each globe was an electric arc, which is the simplest sort of electric lamp, and the brightest.   It consists of two sticks of graphite, like you have in a pencil only thicker, and when electric current is made to pass from one to the other across a small gap between them there is a splendidly bright flame called an arc. The lanterns outside this shop made the pavement brighter than the winter sun could ever do—bright with a sort of lilac-coloured light which often flickered. Arc lamps are still used for special purposes, but you never see them now in the streets. One place where they are used is in the cinematograph projector."

Here Peter interrupted his father.

"Weren't there any little glass bulbs like we have now," he said, "with fila—fila——?"

"Filaments?" suggested Father.

"Yes—with filaments inside?" concluded Peter.

"Yes," Father answered, "there was the carbon lamp, so called because it had a filament of carbon. You can still get carbon-filament lamps, and you can tell them from the others because the filament is in the form of a single unsupported loop. They give rather a dim orange-coloured light, and, compared with modern lamps, they are wasteful of current. But they stand a lot of knocking about and they last almost for ever. I remember seeing them in shops and in tram-cars. And I think that ends my story about old-fashioned lighting."

"Tell us about present-day lights, Daddy," urged Peter.

"Well," went on Father, "after the carbon-filament lamp there came the metal-filament lamp, using a thin wire which could be made to glow more brightly than the carbon filament, although passing less current. In the early metal-filament lamps the wire filament was wound zigzag fashion from top to bottom of the bulb, and the bulb was made a taper shape with a little pip or point at the bottom. All the air was sucked out of the bulb, making a vacuum inside. That was because the hot wire would burn up and become smoke if there were any air inside. Fire needs air, you know. The vacuum type of lamp was used for many years and some people use them still. The light they give is not so orange as that from the carbon lamp, but it is still rather yellowish.

"The next step was the present-day gas-filled lamp. In a vacuum the hot filament cannot burn, but it can turn slowly into a metal vapour, which blackens the inside of the glass bulb. This happens quite fast if the filament is made to glow too bright and, of course, very soon the filament is too thin to hold together any more, and it snaps. That is the end of the lamp. To stop the filament from vaporising, and so enable it to be made even hotter, the glass bulb nowadays is filled with some gas other than air which does not allow the filament to burn and which hinders the process of vaporisation. The filament of the gas-filled lamp glows with the whitest light of all, and it is arranged in the form of a horse-shoe. Because there is a lot of heat to be got rid of, the bulb is made with a longish neck. The gas goes up and down inside the bulb, being cooled in the neck part. The brass cap at the end is far enough away from the filament not to be damaged by the heat. You should avoid using gas-filled lamps in any position other than the hanging position, as they are designed to last longest when used in this way. You should also be careful not to wrap up a bulb in coloured paper or fabric to make pretty decorations. If you do, it will be unable to get rid of its heat, and it may get so hot as to start a fire. I once heard of someone who used a bulb to warm up a bed, and scorched great holes in her sheets and blankets. You see, it doesn't do to be too clever. If you invent anything, think of the possible snags, as well as of the advantages."

"Does the gas-filled lamp use less current than the vacuum lamp?" asked Peter.

"Yes, only about half as much for the same amount of light," answered Father. "But the modern mercury-vapour lamp and the sodium lamp use less current still. They are often used to light streets and factories. The mercury-vapour lamp is in the form of a tube with a drop of mercury or quicksilver in it. When this is turned into a vapour by heat, the electric current can be made to pass along the whole length of the tube, which thus emits a brilliant bluish-green light. It isn't a very nice light to see people under, as it makes their faces look rather ghastly. To remedy this, lamps are now being made with their tubes painted with a special paint which stops some of the blue light and makes it into red light instead. The paint that does this is called fluorescent paint, and anything which seems to shine brightly under the influence of a little blue or violet light is said to fluoresce. Anyway, the new fluorescent mercury-vapour lamps give a pleasant light, very like daylight. One place where you can see them is at Piccadilly Tube Railway Station in London.

"Sodium lamps give a yellow light, which makes people look even more terrible than they did under the original mercury-vapour lamps. And there is nothing anybody can do about it, as no paint will give back blue light for yellow and thus help to even things up. I expect sodium lamps will just be used for road lighting and, possibly, in an occasional factory."

Suddenly Mary cried out, "Oh look, Peter, your lamp is going out."

"Blow it out quickly," said Father; "it has run dry of oil, and the wick will burn."

Fluorescent lighting at Piccadilly Circus tube station, London.

"How do I do it?" asked Peter; "the chimney is too hot to take off."

"Just turn it low, and blow down the chimney from one side," answered Father. "And before you light it next time, trim the wick. You mustn't cut it. Just pat it into shape with a cloth and wipe away the char. If you keep your lamp clean and with no oil on the outside, it should never smell.

"Peter is quite right to want to know about oil lamps, as he is interested in trains. The head code lamps and the tail lamps of trains are still of the oil-burning kind even to-day. The beautiful up-to-date electric trains on the Southern Railway have big oil lamps fixed on, not electric ones. It seems odd, doesn't it? But you see, oil lamps are very reliable, and the men have a sort of drill or ritual to follow in moving them about. It would be silly to change them just for the sake of changing. The tail lamp is red and is very important. If a train goes by without a red lamp behind, the signalmen, stationmasters and other railway officials know that something has gone wrong. They conclude that the train must have broken in two and that some trucks or carriages have been left behind. They stop all the other trains coming along on the same line until they find out what has happened."

"Railway guards have oil lamps too," said Peter, "and they have green and red glass slides to put in front so that they can signal with them."

"Coal-miners have oil lamps as well," interposed Mary, "and they are called safety lamps, because they cannot set fire to gas in the air, even though they are surrounded by it. I don't understand how that is, but it is a fact."

"The flame is entirely enclosed in a wire-gauze cage," said

Father; " gas gets through the gauze and burns inside, but the flame cannot spread back through the gauze to the outside, because the wire absorbs all the heat and carries it away. If you try holding some wire gauze over a gas pipe an inch or two above the opening, then turn the gas on and light the gas over the gauze, you will find that the flame rests on the gauze and does not break through to burn underneath."

" I'll try to get a piece of gauze," said Mary, "and we will do the experiment some time in the kitchen."

" Well," said Peter, " I should think we know all there is to be known about lamps ancient and modern now, don't we, Dad? "

" Not all," said Father, " but quite a lot. Enough to be getting along with, anyway. Now you had getter go into the kitchen and have your supper: then off to bed. You can undress by the light of Peter's lamp if you like, but remember to fill it before you light it again. And don't get paraffin on your hands before you have your supper. It is hard to wash off, and it does not improve the taste of food. Run along, now."

CHAPTER THREE

PETER IN TROUBLE

MARY was sitting by the fire with her father after tea, and both were reading. Suddenly Father said, " Bother! I forgot to buy myself some envelopes, and now all the shops will be shut."

Mary looked at the clock. " A quarter to seven," she said; " yes, you are too late."

" Where's Peter? " Father asked, changing the subject.

" He's out somewhere," answered Mary.

" What does he want to go out for at this time, I wonder? " Father went on. " It's been dark the last half an hour or more."

Mary shrugged her shoulders as if to say Peter's doings were no concern of hers; then she went on with her reading.

At eight o'clock Father began to get restless. He was concerned at his son's absence. Mother knew no more about the matter than Mary, but remarked that he was probably at the house of some school friend.

At half-past eight there was a sudden very loud rat-a-tat-tat at the front door.

" Goodness! " cried Mother. " Whoever would knock like that at this time of night? It sounds like a telegram, or something urgent. You had better go, George."

Father went to the front door, and was surprised to find a burly policeman standing there. Peter was there too, and the policeman was holding him by the collar.

"Is this your son, sir?" asked the policeman.

"Yes," answered Father. "What has he been doing?"

"I found him loitering near Hawker's the jeweller's shop, playing an electric torch on the place. Very suspicious it looked to me, sir. I shouldn't wonder if he was trying to find a way in and commit a burglary. We've had a lot of trouble from boys lately."

"Can you explain the meaning of this, Peter?" said Father sternly, turning to the rather frightened little boy.

"Of course I can, Daddy," answered Peter. "I've been trying to tell the policeman what I was doing, but he doesn't seem to be interested in science, and he thinks I am just trying to make up an excuse. I was only doing an experiment. And anyway, it wasn't Hawker's shop I was interested in, but the big draper's next door. Hawker's has big wooden shutters up, but the draper's shop has got a large window that reflects my torch beautifully."

"Begin at the beginning, Peter, if you please," said Father.

"All right," said Peter, "I will. Do you remember, Dad, when we found that place near a chalk pit where, if we shouted, our voices were thrown back as an echo?"

"Yes, I remember it," answered Father.

"Well," went on Peter, "I knew that light got thrown back in the same way by mirrors and shop windows and other smooth shiny surfaces, and I wondered how much time it needed to come back again to where it was sent from. I went along with my flash lamp to the best shop window I could find, and I flashed a light at it from the opposite side of the road to see how long it was between when I flashed and when I saw the reflection of the flash in the window."

"And how long was it?" asked Father, laughing.

"I couldn't make it any time at all," said Peter. "The flash seemed to come back at the same time that I made it. I expect I couldn't get far enough away from the window. We were two hundred yards or more from that cliff, I remember, and the echo took about a second to come back."

"Well, Peter," said Father; "for your flash to take a second to come back you would need to stand just about ninety thousand miles away from the shop window, so it isn't surprising that you didn't notice any time lag with only the width of the road for your distance."

"Excuse me, sir," butted in the policeman, "but it looks as though the young gentleman had his reasons for being there after all, and so I think I can safely leave him in your hands. But if you'll take my advice, young man," he went on, turning to Peter, "you'll do your experiments in such a way in future as not to arouse the suspicions of other people. Good night to you all."

The policeman touched his helmet and went away.

Father shut the front door and led Peter to the sitting-room, where his mother and sister were anxiously waiting to learn what the trouble might be.

"Peter is a martyr to science, that's all," laughed Father. "He was doing Fizeau's experiment on the determination of the velocity of light in the main shopping street, and a policeman arrested him for loitering in a suspicious manner, as if intent on committing a felony."

"Oh, Father," cried Mary, "don't tease so! You can't expect us to know all those long words."

"People who do experiments are always liable to be thought mad or mischievous," went on Father; "old ladies who tried to find new cures for illnesses were often mistaken for witches and punished accordingly, and men like Galileo, who played in public with stones and bits of string, were solemnly tried by judges and asked to explain their conduct."

"Well, what WAS Peter doing?" persisted Mary.

"I've told you already," answered Father; "he was trying to find out how fast a flash of light travelled from his torch to a shop window and back again. He found that it didn't seem to take any time at all. Then the policeman came up and arrested him."

"Forget the policeman, Daddy," said Peter; "tell us about Fizeau, who tried to find out the same thing as I did, and tell us why I should need to stand ninety thousand miles away from the window to have the reflection taking one second to come back."

"I would remind you first of all that sound takes nearly five seconds to travel one mile," said Father; "Peter thought that light travelled at much about the same speed; but, as a matter of fact, light, like wireless waves, travels much faster. It goes at the rate of about one hundred and eighty thousand miles in a second. If you make a face at yourself in a mirror, you don't have to wait long to see your reflection making the same face. Even if the mirror was ninety thousand miles away you would only have to wait one second. Your grimace would take half a second to get to the mirror and half a second to come back again, ninety thousand miles being half of one hundred and eighty thousand miles."

" But I don't understand," said Mary. " If a mirror were put so far away you wouldn't be able to see anything at all. You wouldn't be able to see the biggest mirror in all the world, even at a hundredth of that distance. How could anybody do such an experiment? "

" Fizeau did it," said Father; " but he had a cleverer way of going to work. He put his mirror about five miles away and used a miniature searchlight to get his reflection. In front of the searchlight he put a revolving disc which had holes or slots cut in it. The disc let the light through in very short flashes. Supposing there were five hundred holes spaced equally round the disc, and suppose the disc went round fifty times a second, the time interval between flashes would be a fiftieth of a five-hundredth of a second, because there would be 50 by 500 or twenty-five thousand flashes a second. What Fizeau did was watch for the reflection of the flashes through the same disc in much the same way as I have shown in the sketch I am drawing on this old envelope. I cannot draw five hundred holes in the disc, so I have shown fewer. Also my envelope is not long enough to show five miles, so I have put the mirror much closer. But you can imagine what the arrangement would have to be like to work properly. The light shines out through the bottom of the disc and is reflected back to the observer through the top of the disc. The journey from searchlight to observer is ten miles. When the disc is at rest the light just streams out through the bottom hole of the disc and comes back through the top hole, which is diametrically opposite to the bottom one.

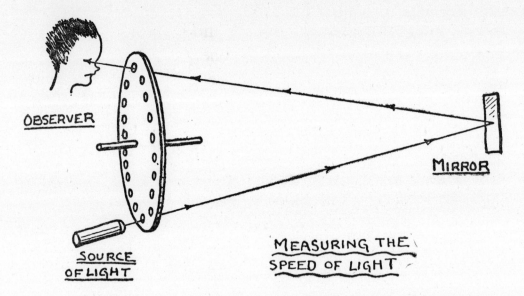

OBSERVER

MIRROR

SOURCE
OF LIGHT

MEASURING THE
SPEED OF LIGHT

Now, when the disc is rotated, short flashes of light are sent out from the bottom of the disc and, if the disc is not going too fast, each flash just manages to get back in time to go through the hole opposite to that from which it was sent out, and the observer sees the distant mirror brightly lighted. But when the disc goes faster, the reflected flash is too late to get through the hole in the disc; instead it hits the disc where there isn't a hole, and, of course, the observer doesn't see anything. In fact, the distant mirror looks dark to him. If the disc is made to go faster yet, the flash gets through a hole, but not the one opposite to that from which it was sent out. It gets through the next hole, which is a five-hundredth of a revolution behind the hole it used before. You can see now how Fizeau calculated the speed of light from his experiment. The flash of light travelled five miles out and five miles back—ten miles in all—while his disc revolved one five-hundredth of a revolution. The only question was, how fast did his disc rotate, and how long did it take to rotate through a five-hundredth part of one revolution? Well, in this particular experiment, the disc went round thirty-six times a second or two thousand one hundred and sixty times a minute. Consequently it did one revolution in one-thirty-sixth of a second and a five-hundredth of a revolution in

$$\frac{1}{36 \times 500}$$ second. In this very short time light travels ten miles, so in one second it will travel $10 \times 36 \times 500$ miles, which comes out to one hundred and eighty thousand miles."

"Oh, isn't that clever!" cried Mary; "I should never have thought of that."

"Of course you wouldn't," snorted Peter; "you aren't a great scientist."

Mary ignored Peter's remark because she was thinking of something else.

"Supposing the sun were to go out, Daddy," she said, "how long would it be before we knew anything about it?"

"You can easily work that out," replied Father. "The sun is ninety million miles away. Divide ninety million by one hundred and eighty thousand, and there's your answer in seconds. It comes to five hundred seconds, which is eight and one-third minutes. Next week the moon is going to get in the way of the sun and the sun will go gradually out of sight, but as the moon is only about two hundred and fifty thousand miles away, we shall be only a little more than a second behind in what we see of the occurrence. I am going to take a day off from work to watch it. It is called an eclipse of the sun, and eclipses do not happen very often, so I hope it will be a nice clear day with no clouds to hide everything.

"As you are asking questions about the speed of light, it may interest you to know that if one of the stars went out suddenly it would be years and years before we knew about it. The stars are so far away that the light coming from some of them takes hundreds and thousands of years to reach us, even though it is going at the rate of one hundred and eighty thousand miles a second. In fact, astronomers do not measure distances in miles at all, they measure them in light-years, one light-year being the distance travelled by light in a year. That comes to one hundred and eighty thousand miles multiplied by the number of seconds in a year."

"Wait," cried Mary, reaching for pencil and paper, "I can do it. There are three hundred and sixty-five days in a year, twenty-four hours in a day and three thousand six hundred seconds in an hour. That makes $365 \times 24 \times 3600$, or $31,536,000$ seconds in a year. Now I multiply this by one hundred and eighty thousand. It comes to $5,666,480,000,000$. So a light-year is more than five and a half million-million miles."

Peter waggled his head as if it had come loose and pretended to collapse.

"And I thought you marched us a good long way on our half-term holiday, Dad," he grumbled. "Ten miles, wasn't it?"

"Poof!" said Mary. "That's nothing. It wasn't a ten-thousandth part of a light-second. That would be eighteen miles, wouldn't it, Daddy? "

" Quite right, O brainy one! " laughed Father. " Well, that's enough about light. Mother, what's happened to the supper? "

" Oh dear," cried Mother, " I quite forgot. I was so interested in your talk that I never noticed the time. It's gone nine o'clock." So saying she ran out to prepare supper, and Mary went to help her.

CHAPTER FOUR

THE ECLIPSE OF THE SUN

PETER woke up early, and jumping out of bed he went to shake Mary, who was still sound asleep.

"I say, Mary," he cried, "it is a lovely morning, no clouds or anything like we were afraid there might be."

Mary said something that sounded like "Shut up and leave me alone," at the same time pulling the blankets over her head.

WAKE UP!

Then she remembered quite suddenly that, after breakfast, there was to be an eclipse of the sun, so she sat up, wide awake.

The two children dressed quickly and ran to the breakfast-room. They were all impatience until their father came downstairs. He had promised to tell them something about eclipses and also to blacken some clear pieces of glass with soot from a candle, so that everyone could watch the sun without fear of injuring the eyes.

"It's the eclipse to-day, Daddy," both children said in chorus

126

as their father appeared; "you promised to tell us when it would start."

"There's plenty of time," Father said, sitting down at the breakfast table; "nothing will happen until a quarter-past ten."

"So there's no need to bolt your food and gulp your tea," put in Mother, coming from the kitchen with a tray-load of good things.

"Yes," added Father, "eat your bacon while it is hot, and we will talk over the toast and marmalade."

The children found it hard to keep silent, but eventually Father saw they were ready, and he started to explain how an eclipse of the sun occurred.

"As you know, children," he began, "the moon is always circling slowly round the earth, and it appears to go right round it about once in twenty-five hours, allowing for the fact that the earth is spinning round too."

"The moon rises roughly an hour later each night," interrupted Peter, "but the sun rises much about the same time each morning, so a day measured by the moon is about an hour longer than the day measured by the sun."

"Yes," agreed Father, "the sun turns up once in every twenty-four hours, but the moon turns up roughly once in every twenty-five hours, so it gradually gets out of step with the sun. Sometimes it is on the same side of the earth as the sun, rising and setting with it. At such times we do not see it at all, because it is only up by day, and it is lighted by the sun on the far side that we cannot see, anyhow. Sometimes the moon is on the side of the earth opposite to the sun. Then it rises when the sun is setting, and it sets when the sun is rising. At such times it is brilliantly lighted by the sun on the side facing the earth, so that we can clearly see all of it. That is what we call full moon. In between times the moon is lighted partly on the side we can see and partly on the side we cannot see. You both know how it looks when it is 'new' and is just following the sun at sunset. As it gets more and more behind the sun, the crescent gets broader and broader until you have full moon, which rises as the sun sets. Then it gets so far behind the sun that it doesn't rise until long after you are in bed. You may find it shining high in the sky next morning, as the sun is rising, and the crescent gets thinner each morning as the moon gets later in rising, until at length, when moon and sun rise together, you cannot see any crescent at all.

"Generally the invisible moon comes up over the horizon at a different place from the sun, and it traces a different course through the sky. But this morning a very rare and unusual thing will happen. The path of the moon will cross the path of the sun; and moon and sun will get to the crossing place together, so that the moon, which is only two hundred and fifty thousand miles away, will come between the earth and the sun, which is ninety million miles away, and will hide the sun from us."

"Will it hide all of the sun, Daddy?" asked Mary, looking rather scared.

"Not this time, Mary," replied Father. "In some eclipses, called total eclipses, the whole of the sun is hidden, but this is a partial eclipse, and only part of the sun will be hidden. The disc of the moon will not accurately overlap the disc of the sun."

"If the moon is so much smaller than the sun, I do not see how it can ever hide the sun completely," said Peter.

"The moon is much nearer and, consequently, it appears to

be about the same size," explained Father. "You know very well that with your hand, which is a very tiny thing indeed, you can easily hide the sun, and indeed the whole of the heavens."

Mary fidgeted impatiently as she wanted to ask a question before Father had finished speaking. "If the sun and moon are sometimes on opposite sides of the earth," she said, "why is it that the earth's shadow never crosses the full moon?"

"But it does cross the full moon, Mary," answered Father; "that is when you get an eclipse of the moon."

"What is the time?" interposed Peter.

"Time to light a candle and smoke some pieces of glass," replied Father.

"Where are you going to get your glass?" asked Mother.

"We can borrow the glass out of some of our postcard frames," said Father. "We shall be careful not to crack the pieces or drop them, and we will wipe them clean before putting them back."

Father found a candle and lit it.

THE BEGINNING OF THE ECLIPSE

129

Then he held each piece of glass in turn over the candle, so that the tip of the flame just touched the surface and blackened it. By moving the glass about he covered nearly the whole surface with a black film of soot. He gave each child a piece of smoked glass and then he led the way into the garden. From the top of the lawn they could get a good view of the morning sun which, as yet, shone bright and clear.

THE BEGINNING

A LITTLE LATER

HALF TIME

LATER STILL

NEARLY OVER

HOW AN ECLIPSE PROGRESSES

"It is almost a quarter-past ten," said Father, looking at his watch; "the moon is close up against the sun, but you cannot see any sign of it yet."

From time to time the children looked at the sun through their smoked glasses. It looked a dull red colour through the soot. Suddenly Mary cried out with glee: "Someone's taken a nip out of the sun," she exclaimed. "Oh, Daddy, is that the disc of the moon just beginning to push in between us and our dear old sun?"

"Yes, that's it," replied Father, "and presently it will look as though someone has eaten up about three-quarters of the sun. In the olden days people believed that that is what happened and they became dreadfully afraid. They made sacrifices to their idols, and presently the sun got bigger again, so they gave thanks to their idols, thinking that

MOON
SETTING

SETTING
SUN

NORTH
POLE

SOUTH
POLE

MARY AND PETER
WATCH THE SUN
AND THE NEW MOON
SETTING TOGETHER

SETTING
SUN

MOON
RISING

NORTH
POLE

SOUTH
POLE

A FEW DAYS LATER

MARY AND PETER
WATCH AS THE SUN
SETS AND THE FULL
MOON RISES

their prayers had been heard and their sacrifices favourably received."

"It *is* getting rather dim," Peter said, shivering slightly. "What are all those birds doing?"

"I expect they are flying home to roost," answered Father; "they must think it is evening time already."

"Now the sun looks like a new moon," said Mary. "I hope it doesn't get any thinner."

Father looked at his watch. "The sun is at its thinnest now," he said; "by lunch-time the eclipse will be over."

Mary gazed around at the strangely dim countryside; then she looked at the tree shadows around her. The shadows on the wall caught her attention especially. The white blobs made by the sunlight shining through small gaps between the leaves were all crescent-shaped. "Look, oh look," Mary cried, "there are lots of little suns all over the wall."

"It is always like that," Father explained; "only when the sun is round the patches of light are round too, and nobody notices them, or thinks of them as images of the sun. Now that the sun is a funny shape the patches of light are something more than just blobs: they are the same funny shape as the sun, and you can see for yourself that they are images of the sun. As the crescent of the sun gets fatter, the crescent images on the wall and on the ground will get fatter too. You can watch them to see that they really and truly represent the course of the eclipse."

Mary and Peter compared the crescent images on the ground with what they could see of the sun through their pieces of smoked glass. "It is always the same," said Mary; "only the images on the ground are upside down. Why is that, Daddy?"

"You can get the same result with a pin-hole in a piece of thick black or brown paper," answered Father; "the light coming through the pin-hole makes a picture of whatever is in front of the paper. If you come indoors now we will talk about why that happens, and we will make a pin-hole camera. We have seen the best of the eclipse and there is no need to stay out here any longer."

CHAPTER FIVE

PIN-HOLE CAMERA

WHEN Father came home for lunch on the Saturday following the eclipse, the children were already waiting for him.

" Shall we be able to make a pin-hole camera this afternoon, Daddy? " asked Mary.

For answer, Father took a small packet out of his pocket and tossed it to his little daughter. " That is a box of photographic plates," he said. " If you can find a nice strong cardboard box with the end about as big as one of those plates, we can make your camera. You mustn't open the box of plates to measure them though. If the tiniest ray of light got into the packet for the tiniest fraction of a second, all the plates would be ruined. I will tell you the size of them. They are each four and a quarter inches long and three and a quarter inches wide. While I am having my lunch, you and Peter can be trying to find a box a little more than four and a quarter inches wide and a little more than three and a quarter inches deep. It should be five or six inches long, and the lid should be a good close fit. The best sort of box for our purpose is one with a lid that comes right down to the bottom. The more it overlaps, the less likelihood is there of stray light leaking into the box and spoiling the plate."

" Come on, Peter," cried Mary, " we will see if we can find the sort of box Daddy wants."

Both children went to the toy cupboard where, among other things, there were cardboard boxes of many different sizes, each containing odds and ends. The ones belonging to Peter were full of lead soldiers, "conkers," cigarette cards and old match-boxes. Mary had put old lengths of ribbon, cotton reels, picture

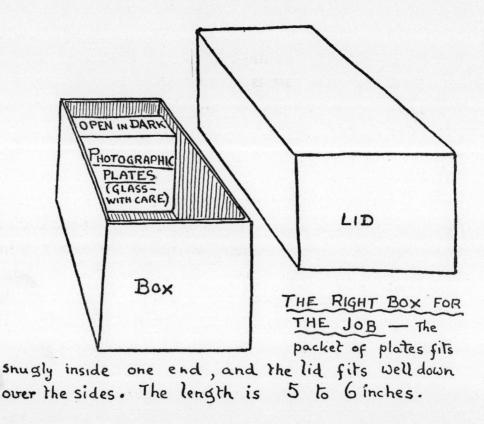

OPEN IN DARK

PHOTOGRAPHIC PLATES (GLASS—WITH CARE)

Box

LID

THE RIGHT BOX FOR THE JOB — The packet of plates fits snugly inside one end, and the lid fits well down over the sides. The length is 5 to 6 inches.

postcards and toffee papers into hers. Most of the boxes proved to be either much too large or much too small when Mary compared their ends with the packet of photographic plates her father had given to her. At last, however, they came to a box of Peter's that seemed to be just right. The packet of plates slipped down inside without leaving any room to spare either at the sides or the top, and the lid was nearly as deep as the box itself. Peter found room in another box for the soldiers it contained. Feeling very pleased with themselves, both children went to show the box to Father.

"Splendid!" he cried. "Now you can paint the whole of the inside with black paint, not forgetting to do the lid as well. You must use your powder paint, as that leaves a dull finish when it is dry. A shiny black finish wouldn't be satisfactory. If you do the painting in the garden, the wind and sun will dry the paint almost as fast as you can put it on."

When, half an hour later, the children brought the painted box to show Father, they found him busy with a ruler, a pair of scissors and some pieces of cardboard. Already he had carefully measured and cut out a piece of strong cardboard to serve as a dummy photographic plate. It was four and a quarter inches long, three and a quarter inches wide and about a tenth of an inch thick. Directly Father saw the box, he took it in his hands and tried the dummy plate inside, up against one end.

"We have to make something to hold it in position like this," he said. "It must slip in and out quite easily, but it must not be able to fall forward on its face."

"Why not paste in some strips of cardboard?" Mary suggested, "you only need one at each side."

Father handed her the ruler and the scissors, and very soon Mary had cut out two strips three and a quarter inches long and one inch wide. She ruled a line down each strip a quarter of an inch from one edge and three-quarters of an inch from the other. She then bent each strip along the ruler line so as to make the narrow part stand up at right angles to the wide part. She then put paste under the wide part and stuck it against the side of the box with the narrow part pressing against the dummy plate. When both strips were in position Mary looked at Father and said, "What next?"

"You now have to make a pin-hole in the centre of the opposite end of the box," answered Father. "To find the centre you must draw the diagonals, using ruler and pencil;

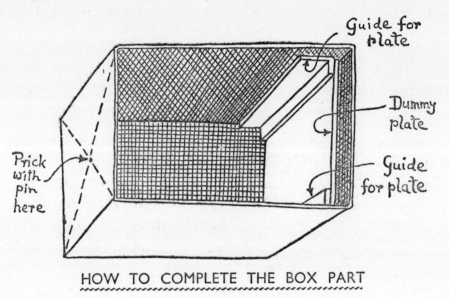

Guide for plate

Dummy plate

Guide for plate

Prick with pin here

HOW TO COMPLETE THE BOX PART

then prick through with a good fat pin where the two lines cross."

Mary had very soon carried out these instructions, but she noticed that when the lid was put on it covered the pin-hole completely. "Must I make another pin-hole in the lid, Daddy?" she asked.

"You would never get the two pin-holes to come opposite to one another," answered Father. "No, you must cut a big hole in the lid, one having a diameter of half an inch or more, and then the pin-hole in the end of the box is sure to be uncovered, even if the lid is put on a bit crooked."

Mary drew the diagonals on the end of the lid and marked

the place where they crossed. She put a farthing centrally over this point and drew round it. Then, with a sharp penknife, she cut along the circle, thus making a neat round hole as big as a farthing. She tried the lid on the box and saw to her satisfaction that the pin-hole in the box showed through the hole in the lid, being very nearly at the centre of this, as she had intended it to be.

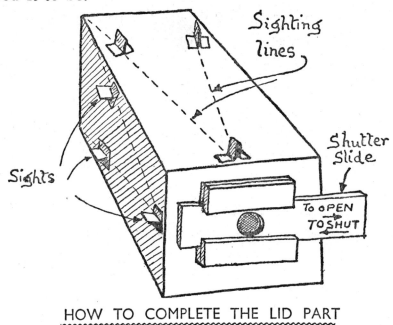

Sighting lines

Shutter Slide

Sights

To OPEN
TO SHUT

HOW TO COMPLETE THE LID PART

"The camera is practically finished now," said Father; "but it would be better if we had some kind of shutter so that we could keep the pin-hole covered up when we were not taking photographs. You see, the pin-hole does duty for the lens in an ordinary camera, and it must let light through only when a picture is being made. For a shutter I suggest a slide made of cardboard, about one inch wide and five inches long. About three inches from one end it can have a hole the size of a farthing. With the slide in one position the hole in it can

137

register with the hole Mary has just made. With the slide flicked over to the other position it will cover up the hole. The slide can be made to run between two strips of cardboard pasted on to the lid of the box, and on top of these guide strips two further strips can be pasted to overlap the slide a little and prevent it from falling forward."

Mary very quickly cut out the parts described by Father, and she pasted the guides to the lid of the box with the slide in position between them.

"Make sure the slide works freely," said Father, "and take it out while the paste is drying in case any gets on to it and makes it stick. We will leave the whole thing to dry while we have our tea, and afterwards we will load it."

"What does ' load it ' mean?" asked Peter.

"It means that we are going to put a real plate in it instead of a dummy one," answered Father.

USING THE CAMERA

After tea, Father inspected the pin-hole camera and complimented Mary on her work.

"The sun is still shining brightly," he said, "so we shall have time to try our camera. Instead of this white card I have used as a dummy plate I am going to put in a real plate. To do that I must go into a place that is perfectly dark. There mustn't be the least chink of light anywhere."

"How can you see to do anything then?" asked Peter.

"I can do everything by ' feel,' " answered Father; "but if I couldn't manage that I might safely use a very dim red light. I have used the back lamp of a bicycle on other occasions. It has to be an electric one with no ventilation holes to let out white light, and the red glass has to be real stained glass, not just white glass painted over. The paint gets scratched and the scratches let white light through. I once had a lamp with a painted glass, and I made it safe to use by putting two thicknesses of red cellophane behind the glass. Well, I'll shut myself in the coal cellar now. If you will stand outside, I will tell you what I am doing."

Father shut himself in the coal cellar and spoke to the children through the door.

" Now I am opening the box of plates," he said. " There are twelve plates in three packets of four. I have opened one packet by undoing the black paper round the plates. Now I can feel the four plates. One side of each plate is plain glass, the other side is coated with the photographic emulsion. The plates are packed in pairs, with emulsion side facing emulsion side. If I lift the top plate from the pile of four I know that the emulsion side is underneath. Now I am slipping the plate into the camera in place of the dummy, and I am putting it with the emulsion side facing towards the pin-hole. Now I am putting the lid on the camera. Now I am making sure that the shutter is shut."

" Hooray! " shouted Peter. " The camera is ready," and he put his hand on the door handle to open the cellar door.

" Wait a moment," shouted Father in great anxiety. " I haven't put away the other plates yet. I must wrap them in their paper again and put them safely away in their little dark box before you open that door."

At last Father emerged from the cellar. He was blinking a little at the brightness of the light, which seemed dazzling to him after the gloom of the cellar. "You nearly opened that door, didn't you, Peter?" he said. "Well, if you *had* opened it, the other three out of that packet of four plates would have been ruined, because the light would have got at them. The other eight might have been spoilt too."

"What picture shall we make with our camera, Daddy?" cried Mary.

"It must be something quite still," answered Father; "the pin-hole is very small, and it lets through very little light; consequently we must leave the shutter open for at least a minute. Shall we take a picture of our house?"

"Oh yes!" cried Mary.

"On second thoughts," said Father, "we won't. The wind is making the trees and bushes move about. We must do something indoors. We will make a picture of the opening horse-chestnut buds that Mother has put in the big flower vase. Perhaps we will take a picture of the house on another day when the air is calm."

Father led the way into the sitting-room. The sun was shining right across the floor, so he moved the vase to a suitable place on the carpet and put the camera on a low stool about three feet away.

"Without a view-finder this camera is rather awkward to aim," said Father; "but if you remember that a straight line drawn through the pin-hole from every point in the thing photographed must be able to reach the plate you ought to be able to place the camera correctly."

Saying these words, Father went behind the pot of buds and looked at the camera from above the buds, from below them and from each side. He imagined his line of sight to pass

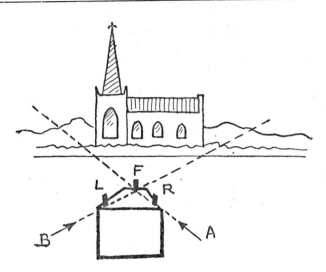

Sights L and F appear in line when viewed from B, and this line must run to the right of the subject. Sights R and F appear in line when viewed from A, and this line must run to the left of the subject.

The line through B and S must pass over the top of the subject; the line through T and S must pass under the subject

HOW TO USE THE SIGHTS

through the pin-hole, and gauged whether it would reach the end of the camera where the plate was fixed. It seemed to him at first that all these lines would miss the end and strike the sides of the camera or else the top or bottom, so he moved the camera farther back and took his sights again. This time he seemed satisfied.

"I think our picture will just about fill the plate," he said; "and to save ourselves the trouble of doing next time what I have done this time, we will rule some sighting lines on the outside of the camera and stick on some sights. But what we have to think about now is the length of exposure to give. If I were to use my best camera on this subject, I should give an exposure of a tenth of a second. I reckon this pin-hole camera is about one thousand six hundred times slower, so that we must give an exposure one thousand six hundred times as long. In other words, we must leave the slide open one hundred and sixty seconds."

"That comes to two minutes forty seconds," said Mary.

"You pull out the slide, then," said Father, "and you might as well sit between the camera and the window so that you screen the pin-hole from the direct light of the window. You have blackened the inside of the camera to prevent light from the side of the box being reflected on to the plate, but the extra precaution of shielding the pin-hole from one side is worth taking."

Mary took up her position and Father handed her his watch. She waited for the seconds hand to reach sixty, and then she pulled the shutter slide until the pin-hole became visible through it. Everyone sat very still for two minutes forty seconds, and then Mary pushed the shutter until the pin-hole was covered up again.

Chestnut buds.

A narrow bridge.
(Both pictures on this page were made with a pin-hole camera.)

"You have taken the picture now," said Father; "I will go into the cellar again and remove the plate. I will put it safely in another dark box until I am ready to develop it with some others that I want to do at the same time. Then I will give you back your camera and you can finish it by putting on sighting lines and sights, as I suggested just now."

So saying, Father retired into the cellar again and removed the plate from the camera, putting it into a light-tight box until he was ready to develop it. He then came out again and gave the camera back to Mary, who ruled sighting lines on the top and on one side, afterwards sticking on sights made of card.

HOW THE PIN-HOLE CAMERA WORKS

"Before I develop the plate," said Father, "I will explain how the camera makes a picture. To do so I will make a sketch of the camera and put a simple subject in front of it. The subject I am drawing is a T upside down, with a black triangle on the upstanding part. Now I have put letters against three points in the subject and I am going to talk about point A. Light from point A is scattered in every direction, as I have shown by little arrows, but just one ray, and only one, goes towards our pin-hole and through it to hit the point A' on the plate. You will notice that point A' on the plate cannot get light from anywhere else, because light can only travel in straight lines. Consequently if A is sending out red light, A' will show on the plate as a red dot. In the same way, points B' and C' on the plate can only receive light from points B and C on the subject. If C is green, C' will be green; if B is yellow, B' will be yellow, and so on. Every other point in the subject makes a corresponding point on the plate, and if we could see inside our box when the pin-hole was open, we should observe on our plate a faint picture of everything in front of the pin-hole. It would be a coloured picture and it would be upside down. The plate records this picture, but, of course, it cannot record colours except as different shades of grey between white and black.

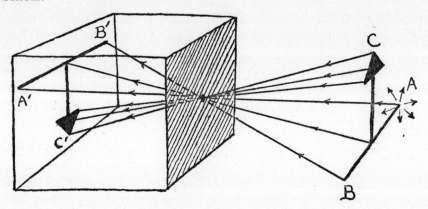

HOW IT WORKS

"As a matter of fact, if we put our dummy plate of white card in and point the camera, with its lid left off, towards an electric light, we shall see an image of the filament of the lamp on our 'plate.' I will do this now so that you can see for yourselves how it works."

Father opened the camera, inserted the dummy plate of white card, and then pointed the pin-hole towards a brightly shining electric lamp with a clear-glass bulb. The children saw the horseshoe shape of the filament faithfully reproduced on the card. The image was of the correct colour, but it was upside down.

"Now you can see how the tiny spaces between the leaves of

the trees caused crescent-shaped images of sun to appear on the ground during the eclipse," said Father. " They were not very clear images, and I am afraid the image of that lamp is not very clear either. Our picture will come out rather ' fuzzy,' and I tell you this now to prevent you from being disappointed. The smaller the pin-hole the sharper the picture, but, of course, a really tiny pin-hole makes it necessary to give a very long exposure. Our pin-hole is about a thirtieth of an inch in diameter. If we had one a sixtieth of an inch, it would let through only a quarter of the light, so that our exposure would have to be four times as long. Instead of giving two minutes forty seconds, which is what we did before, we should need to give ten minutes forty seconds.

" I have explained how the pin-hole camera works now," concluded Father, " and what do you think it teaches us? "

Mary looked at Peter and Peter looked at Mary, but neither knew what to answer. It did not seem possible to them to say in a few words all that they had learnt from making and using the camera.

" Well," went on Father, " since you do not seem able to decide for yourselves which is the most important thing you have learnt from the camera, I will tell you. I wanted you to realise that light travels in straight lines, and the pin-hole camera is about the best proof you could have that it does so."

THE RESULTS

Next day Mary and Peter tried loading the camera themselves, and in the evening they went out looking for a subject to photograph. Peter thought that a picture of the railway arch at the bottom of their road would look attractive, and so the children waited until there was a lull in the traffic and then made their photograph. They had to guess what exposure to give, but Mary had heard Father say that outdoor subjects needed only half the exposure of indoor subjects and far-away subjects only half the exposure of near subjects.

"The bridge is out of doors and much farther away than the buds we photographed yesterday, so I think we ought to give a quarter of the exposure we gave before. Yesterday we gave one hundred and sixty seconds, so to-day we will try forty seconds."

Later that evening Father went into the cellar and developed the plates. Both were quite good negatives, and when the time came to make prints from them they yielded recognisable likenesses of their subjects.

"Of course," said Father, "they are rather blurred on account of the large size of pin-hole we used. You will understand from what we have done that the pin-hole camera has drawbacks. This explains why nobody thinks of using them for serious photography. The same camera would take clearer pictures in much less time if it had a glass lens instead of a pin-hole. Some day I will tell you about lenses, and perhaps we will fit our camera with a lens so as to make it really useful."

CHAPTER SIX

THE MIRROR

THERE was a mirror over the dining-room mantelpiece, and Mary stood in front of it looking at her own reflection.

"Vain thing!" jeered Peter, when he saw what she was doing.

"No," said Mary thoughtfully, "I'm not being vain; I'm just wondering how the mirror manages to make another me."

"Well, if that's what you are wondering, Miss," laughed Mother, "you must be the first young lady in the world so to do, that's all I can say. Most girls are too pleased with what they can see in the mirror to start wondering how the glass does what it does."

"Leave her alone, Mother," said Father, looking up from his

THE OTHER MARY

newspaper; "lots of folk wonder how a mirror works the way it does, and I don't see why our Mary shouldn't be one of them. Not all girls are uninterested in science."

"Will you tell us how a mirror works, Daddy?" asked Mary.

"I won't *tell* you," answered Father, "but I will *show* you. The best sort of mirror to experiment with is a little one out of a lady's handbag. Let us have the one out of yours, Mother, please."

Mother sent Peter to fetch her handbag, and then she took the mirror from it and gave it to Father.

"Now we want the pastry board," said Father, "as I know Mother will let us stick pins into it. She might object if we stuck pins into the table."

"Indeed I should," cried Mother; "don't you dare try!"

Mary fetched the pastry board and gave it to Father.

"Cover it with a nice white sheet of drawing-paper," said Father, "and rule a line across the middle."

Mary fastened some paper on the board with drawing-pins, and then she ruled a line from side to side.

"Now," said Father, "we must make the mirror stand up on its edge along the line. How shall we do that?"

"I know," cried Mary. "We can stick two blobs of Plasticine on the line and press the mirror into them."

"A splendid idea!" said Father, and Peter went to fetch some Plasticine.

When the mirror was stuck to the board Father put a pin upright in front of it, and the children could see the reflection of this in the mirror.

"That pin in the mirror seems to be somewhere behind the mirror, doesn't it?" said Father. "We can find out exactly where it is by sticking another pin into the board behind the mirror and altering its position until it seems to be in the same place as the reflection or image of this pin in front."

"How can you tell when the pin behind the mirror is in the same spot as the image of the front pin?" asked Mary.

"That's easy," replied Father. "If you have two poles standing in line several feet apart and you are standing on that

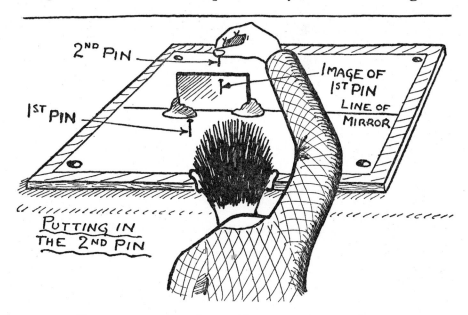

line some distance away, the poles appear to be one and the same pole, because the front one hides the back one. But if you move to one side or the other of the line, the back pole comes into sight. If the poles are moved quite close to one another you will not so easily get a view of the back one. In fact, you may have to walk a long way from the line in order to see it. If the back pole is actually touching the front one, you will not be able to see it from the front at all, as the two poles appear to move together when you go from side to side of the line."

If the poles are wide apart they look like one pole only when seen from some point on a line with them. From all other points they are seen well apart.

If the two poles are close together they are quite easily mistaken for one pole

PARALLAX — THE NAME GIVEN BY SCIENTISTS TO THE APPARENT CHANGE IN THE POSITION OF AN OBJECT CAUSED BY CHANGE OF POSITION OF OBSERVER.

"What has all this got to do with the mirror?" asked Peter.

"I'm coming to that," said Father. "I am now going to stick my second pin behind the mirror at the point where I think the image of the front pin is. At least I can put it in line with that image."

Father shut one eye and then put the second pin in the board behind the mirror on a line with the reflection of the first pin.

"Now," he went on, "if I have put that pin in the right place I shall be able to move my head from side to side and the pin I have just stuck in will appear to be followed by the reflection of the other pin."

Father moved his head from side to side, and the reflection always moved the same way as the pin at the back of the mirror, but this pin did not keep up with it.

"I have put the pin too far away," said Father, and he moved it closer to the mirror, still keeping it in line with the reflection of the other pin. This time the reflection seemed to move more slowly than the pin at the back when Father moved his head from side to side.

"Now I have put the pin too near," said Father, and he moved it back a little way. He kept trying different positions until it always appeared to be in line with the reflection of the front pin, no matter what point it was viewed from.

Having found the position of the image or reflection of the front pin, Father removed the mirror and the Plasticine lumps from the paper and drew a line joining the pricks made by the two pins.

"Why," cried Mary, "I do believe the image is as far behind the mirror as the real pin is in front!"

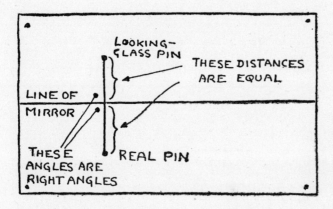

WHERE TO FIND "LOOKING-GLASS PIN"

"Measure it and see," suggested Father.

Mary measured the two distances with the ruler. "Yes," she said, "the distances are exactly the same."

"What is more," said Father, "the line between the object and its image is perpendicular to the mirror itself. In future you could tell without trial where a reflection must be. When you look into a mirror the image of your eye or of your nose is as far behind the mirror as the original is in front of the mirror, and it is on the continuation of a line drawn from the original perpendicular to the surface of the mirror. Perpendicular means so that you could fit a set-square between the mirror and the line on all sides of the line."

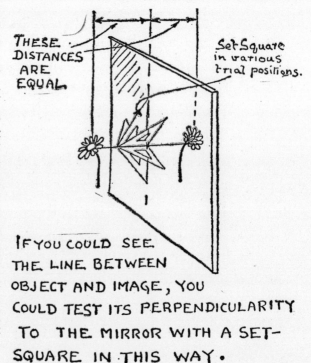

IF YOU COULD SEE THE LINE BETWEEN OBJECT AND IMAGE, YOU COULD TEST ITS PERPENDICULARITY TO THE MIRROR WITH A SET-SQUARE IN THIS WAY.

Mary frowned. "I still don't understand how the mirror makes a picture of what is in front of it, though," she said. "All you have told us is where the picture appears to be. It appears to be behind the mirror, and I knew that before, though I couldn't have said exactly where."

"Let us trace the path of the light, then," said Father. "Suppose my eye is at the point A (page 154), and suppose it is looking at the reflection I of the pin. The light appears to come from I straight to A. Actually of course it comes from the mirror at the point M, on the line IA. And the light from M comes originally from O along the line OM. So you see the light ray that enables me to see I is the bent line OMA. I said once that light always travelled in a straight line, but you can see now that a mirror causes it to bend.

"Now I will imagine that I am looking at I from point B. The light really comes from point N on the mirror, N being on the line IB; and the light from N comes originally from O, along the line ON. I will draw one more bent light ray showing how I can see the pin in the mirror from some point C, and then I will ask if you notice anything peculiar about the way these light rays are bent."

Father drew a third ray as he was speaking, and then the children gazed with puzzled frowns at the picture on the pastry board. It just looked a maze to them.

"Well," said Father, "the thing of interest is this. The part OM of the bent ray OMA makes the same angle with the mirror as the part MA. Similarly the part ON of the bent ray ONB makes the same angle with the mirror as the part NB. The angle made by the approaching light and the angle made by the reflected light appear to be always the same. Try it for yourselves by tracing the angles on one side and comparing them with the angles on the other."

Mary and Peter went hastily to search for tracing paper, and when they came back they soon found by trial that it was as

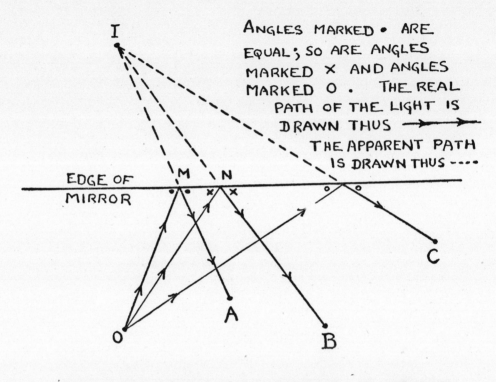

ANGLES MARKED • ARE EQUAL; SO ARE ANGLES MARKED X AND ANGLES MARKED O . THE REAL PATH OF THE LIGHT IS DRAWN THUS ⟶ THE APPARENT PATH IS DRAWN THUS ----

HOW LIGHT FROM AN OBJECT IN FRONT OF A MIRROR REACHES THE EYE

Father had said. The reflected light always made the same angle with the mirror as the approaching light.

"That is the all-important law of reflection," said Father. "Everything else follows from that. The light coming from *O*, on striking the mirror at different angles, is reflected at equal angles, and it is this that makes it seem to come from another point *I* behind the mirror. Light appears to come from a point

Reflection of Wells Cathedral in rippled water.

I in just the same way that it comes from *O*, and that is why you see a picture of *O* at *I*. Have I made the working of a mirror clear to you now, Mary? "

" Yes, I think you have, Daddy," answered Mary. " But can I ask just one more question? Is the reflection made by smooth water of houses and trees on the far side the same as the reflection from a mirror? I mean, is the reflected light thrown up at the same angle as the approaching light? "

" Yes," answered Father, " smooth water reflects light in exactly the same way as a mirror; so does any other smooth or highly polished surface."

CHAPTER SEVEN

SOME OPTICAL ILLUSIONS

MARY and Peter reached the pond at last. They had tramped three miles in the hope of being able to find some tadpoles and newts, and they had brought empty jam-jars with them; also Peter's home-made fishing rod.

It was rather early in the year to find tadpoles, but they found some frog spawn: great clusters of jelly-like substance with little black dots inside. Peter poked about with his rod at the bottom of the pond in the hope of finding something else, and he was just beginning to get tired of this occupation when Mary

PETER'S ROD APPEARED TO BE BROKEN

suddenly called out, " Oh, Peter! You have broken your rod."

" No, I haven't," contradicted Peter, and he pulled his rod out of the water to show Mary that it was still unbroken.

" Well! " exclaimed Mary, " that's funny. I was sure you had broken it. In the water it looked bent in the middle. Put it in again and let me see."

Peter put his rod back into the water, and from where Mary was standing the stick appeared to be broken, or at least badly bent.

"There it is again," said Mary. "Look, you give me the rod, and I'll hold it while you stand here; then you can see for yourself."

Mary changed places with Peter and held the rod in the water for Peter to observe.

"Yes," said Peter, "it does look broken. I wonder why?"

"We will ask Daddy when we get home," answered Mary.

At that moment Mary knocked over one of the jam-jars, and it rolled into the pond. It fell in the water on its side, filled up and sank instantly. "Bother!" exclaimed Mary.

"Never mind," cried Peter, "I'll get it. The water is quite shallow."

Peter started rolling up his knickers, then he sat on the bank of the pond with his feet in the water.

PETER'S LEGS APPEARED TO BE VERY SHORT

A moment later he slipped in. To his great surprise the water came up nearly to his middle, and, of course, his knickers were wetted almost to his waist.

"What *are* you doing?" cried Mary in alarm; "come out this minute!"

"I didn't think the water was so deep as this," said Peter. "It looked quite shallow."

Suddenly Mary began to laugh. "Your legs look ever so funny," she cried; "they've gone all short like a dwarf's legs."

"You *would* laugh," grumbled Peter; "but I can tell you it's jolly cold and uncomfortable for me. And I don't see how I am to get the jam-jar out even now. Even if I roll my sleeve up to my shoulder my arm is still too short."

"Put your foot inside it before you pull yourself out of the pond," suggested Mary.

Peter carried out Mary's instructions, and soon he was safe and sound on the bank again, with the rescued jam-jar by his side.

"Fortunately, it is sunny and there is no cold wind," he said, "my knickers will soon be dry, but, all the same, I think we'd better be walking home now. There's nothing else to be caught in this pond and we've been out two hours or more already. It will be dinner-time when we get home, even if we start at once. The walk back will take us at least an hour."

The two children arrived home just as Mother was dishing up the dinner.

"My shorts are wet," said Peter.

"Then run along and get into dry ones," said Mother; "but hurry, because your dinner will get cold if you don't."

At that moment Father appeared. "Wet shorts?" he queried. "I know how that happened. You dropped something into the pond, thought you could get it out, stepped into the water and found it deeper than you had supposed it to be merely from looking."

"Well," gasped Peter, "you must be a magician. That is exactly what did happen, but however did you guess?"

"Oh, everybody has made that mistake at some time or another," answered Father; "and many is the boy that has had a whipping from his mother for coming home wet and giving the excuse, ' I didn't think the water was so deep.' You see,

Graduations under the water
appear to be closer together.

The saucer appears to be shallower when it contains water.

When in water, the ruler appears to be bent.

it isn't many mothers who realise that there really is a deceptive appearance about water. It sounds like a weak excuse for naughtiness, but it isn't a weak excuse at all: it is a perfectly genuine excuse."

"We noticed other funny things about the water too, Daddy," said Mary. "Peter's rod seemed to be broken when he put it in; also, while he was paddling" (here she giggled mischievously), "his legs looked short, like a dwarf's."

"I will tell you the reason for all these optical illusions," said Father; "but first of all I will show you one more illusion."

"First of all you will do no such thing," interrupted Mother, bustling up crossly. "Dinner is spoiling and Peter will get rheumatism or a chill if you keep him standing about in damp clothes. You can talk about water, if you want to, after you have had dinner."

Half an hour later, Father sent Mary to fetch a saucer. The family was still sitting round the dinner-table.

"If this is some more science I will clear the table and do the washing up," said Mother.

"This is a lesson specially for mothers," teased Father; "I am going to show why it is wrong and unfair to smack little boys who, after getting their clothes wet, say, 'I didn't mean to, only the water was deeper than I thought it was.'"

"But I didn't smack Peter, and therefore I don't need the lesson," said Mother. "My Peter is a truthful boy, and I should always believe him if he said he had had an accident."

"Oh, well," laughed Father, "you can stay and watch, just for interest's sake."

So saying, he put a penny in the saucer. "Now, then," he went on, "from where you are sitting at the other side of the table I do not suppose you are able to see that penny. It lies below the rim of the saucer, out of sight. I am now going to bring the penny into view by pouring water into the saucer."

Father tipped some water from the water jug into the saucer, and Mary cried out in delight:

" I can see the penny now, Daddy."

" So can I," said Peter and his mother in chorus.

" You see," explained Father, " the presence of the water has made the saucer appear shallower than it really is, almost like a flat plate. It has lifted the bottom and brought it nearer to the surface, or at least it has produced the optical illusion of a raised bottom.

" You will understand now what happened to Peter's rod. The part he was holding was pointing towards where the point of it really was, on the bottom of the pond. But this point, together with the whole of the bottom of the pond, was, in appearance, lifted up, and so were those portions of the rod below the surface of the water, and therefore the dry part of the rod seemed to point to a deeper place than the submerged part; in other words, the stick appeared to be badly bent at the point where it entered the water.

" It is easy to see why Peter's legs were dwarfed, Mary. You could see Peter's waist where it really was, but his feet and his knees being below the water, had the appearance of being much higher than their real positions. Therefore, all those parts of Peter between his feet and his waist seemed to have been shortened or dwarfed.

" You get the same thing happening with glass. A sheet of glass never looks as thick as it really is. Any marks or spots on the far side seem closer to the near side than they really are."

THE EXPLANATION

" Why does water or glass have this curious effect? " asked Mary.

" The reason is very simple," answered Father; "and it is this. Whereas in air light travels at a speed of one hundred and eighty thousand miles a second, in water and in glass it travels rather more slowly. The denser medium seems to delay it, just as muddy ground slows up your speed when you are walking. In water the speed of light is one hundred and thirty-five thousand miles a second, and in glass the speed of light varies between one hundred and eighteen thousand miles a second and one hundred and ten thousand miles a second, depending on the kind of glass. A diamond slows up light more than any other transparent substance: the speed of light through a diamond is less than half its speed in air, being only seventy thousand miles a second. When light passes from one substance to another in a direction perpendicular to the surface at which both substances meet, you do not notice anything peculiar; but when the light takes a slanting direction, the rays become bent, and it is this bending, or refraction as the scientists call it, that causes the illusions you have noticed. The bending is rather like what would happen if a column of soldiers marched off their smooth hard parade ground, at an angle, into a ploughed field and tried to maintain their formation in a straight line."

At this point Father began to draw on the back of an old letter.

" Here," he said, " at A_1B_1 I have drawn a line of soldiers, calling the two end ones A and B. They march towards the ploughed field and presently, when the line has reached the position A_2B_2, B walks into it. Then the man next to him walks into it; then the man next to him again, and so on. Once in the ploughed field these men walk more slowly so

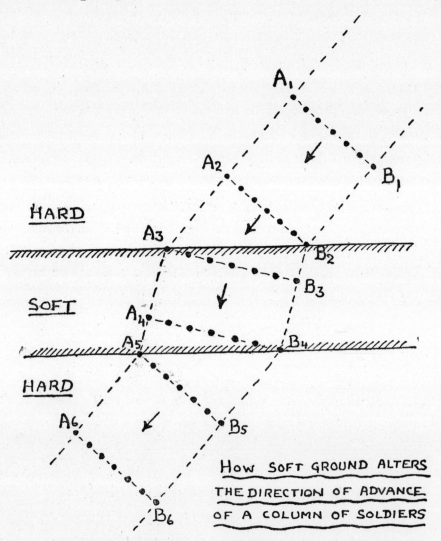

HOW SOFT GROUND ALTERS THE DIRECTION OF ADVANCE OF A COLUMN OF SOLDIERS

that the whole column begins to wheel round, the men still on the parade ground overtaking the ones in the ploughed field. By the time all the men are in the ploughed field the column of soldiers will make the line A_3B_3, and, as you can see, the direction of marching will have changed. They keep on through the ploughed field in the new direction, eventually reaching hard ground again at A_4B_4; B again being the first to experience the change. B speeds up; so does the man next to him; and then the man next to him again, and so on. Gradually the column wheels round until, at A_5B_5, when all the men are on hard ground once more, it is marching in its old direction again. That is exactly what happens when a ray of light passes through a slab of glass. It does not have to be a broad beam. Even the narrowest gleam of light, such as I could draw by a single line, is bent first one way then

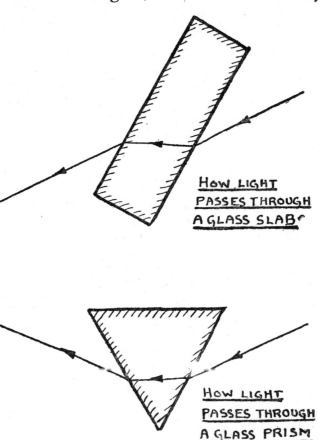

HOW LIGHT PASSES THROUGH A GLASS SLAB

HOW LIGHT PASSES THROUGH A GLASS PRISM

back again the other way to emerge in a direction parallel to the old direction. Of course, if the glass is shaped like a wedge, or a piece of cheese, to form what is called a prism, the second bending will not bring the light back to its old direction. The effect of such a prism is definitely to turn the light round a corner.

"Now I will explain why you get funny things happening to the appearance of things in water. When Peter's rod was in the water, the light from its tip did not reach Mary's eye in a

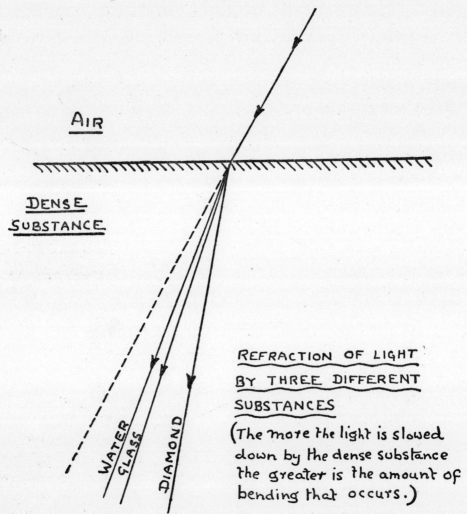

AIR

DENSE
SUBSTANCE

WATER
GLASS
DIAMOND

REFRACTION OF LIGHT
BY THREE DIFFERENT
SUBSTANCES
(The more the light is slowed
down by the dense substance
the greater is the amount of
bending that occurs.)

straight line—it came along a bent line, so that to see it she had to look in a direction that passed over its real position. To see his feet when he was wading in the pond she had to do the same thing—look much higher than they really were. And to see the penny in the saucer of water we looked along a line that passed over its real position. The light from the penny could not reach our eye when there was no water in the saucer, because then it would have had to go straight in order to do so, and the rim of the saucer was in the way. With water in the saucer, causing the light ray to bend up in the middle, the light was able to dodge round the rim of the saucer and make the penny visible to us."

" Well," said Mother, " if you have quite finished discussing the funny things that water can do to light, I will now ask someone to come and see what it will do to dirty plates and dishes. I am sure that with all your knowledge you will find it interesting and instructive to help me wash up the dinner things."

So saying, Mother got up from her place at table and started clearing away the remains of the meal.

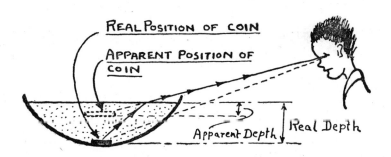

HOW THE INVISIBLE COIN IS MADE VISIBLE

CHAPTER EIGHT

A REAL CAMERA

"DADDY, when are we going to fix a lens to our pin-hole camera and make it better, like you promised we would?"

Father, hidden behind his newspaper, mumbled something, so Mary tried again: "Would an old magnifying glass do, Daddy?" she persisted.

Father realised that he would get no peace until he answered Mary's questions, so he put down his newspaper and said, "No; it would very probably have too short a focal length."

Mary's jaw dropped in mock bewilderment and her eyes rolled until only the whites showed. It was the way the girls at her school looked when pretending to be stunned by the wise remark of somebody else.

"Oh, dear!" exclaimed Father; "have I got to go into all that? I forgot that we had never talked about lenses. You and Peter had better collect all the magnifying glasses and lenses you've got and bring them here. We will talk about them, and if suitable, we could use one in our camera."

"There's the little stamp magnifier Auntie gave you, Peter," said Mary, turning to her brother, "and the glass out of your magic-lantern."

"Yes," agreed Peter, "and you can take the lenses out of your toy telescope."

"Run along and get all the lenses you are talking about,"

said Father, "and I will get our big reading-glass too. I will meet you in the summer-house at the end of the lawn."

A few minutes later the children joined their father at the appointed place. They brought various loose magnifying glasses and some optical toys with lenses in them; also the pin-hole camera they had made some days before. Father had brought the big family reading-glass, which was six inches in diameter and had a long black handle.

"A lens is made of glass, which, as you know, has the ability to bend light rays," began Father, "and its two sides are curved so that the light coming from it, like the light coming from a prism, usually takes a new direction altogether. Light approaching from a distance and passing through this reading-glass here is all brought to a single point called the focal point. I will show you."

Father held the reading-glass with one side facing the sun, and he moved it towards a piece of paper, which was also facing the sun, until the light coming through the glass was concentrated into a dazzlingly bright spot on the paper.

"The paper is now at what is called the focal point of the lens," said Father; "all the light and all the heat passing through the glass is concentrated at that spot. If you were to put your finger there you would feel the heat. In fact, the paper is feeling it already and is beginning to burn—look!"

As Father spoke, the paper began to smoke and then, quite suddenly, it caught fire and flared up.

"That bright spot on the paper was really an image of the sun," said Father, "for the lens acts like a pin-hole and makes an image of everything in front of it. One difference is that the image is a much brighter one because the lens passes so much more light than a pin-hole, being of much bigger aperture; another difference is that the image is made at a definite place and is of a definite size. You cannot get a larger and larger image by putting the paper farther and farther away, as you can with a pin-hole. To get an image of distant objects you must put the paper at or near the focal point, which is why

FINDING THE FOCAL LENGTH OF A LENS

the focal length of a lens matters. The focal length is the distance from the lens to the focal point, and for our purpose we want a lens with a focal length equal to the length of your camera box, a little more or a little less. You can now try out all the lenses you've got, focusing the sun on a sheet of paper and measuring the distance of the image from the lens with a ruler. When you have done them all come and tell me the results. I am going indoors to see what the postman has brought this morning."

Mary was a methodical little person, and she was not satisfied to rely on memory for a record of the measurements. She went to fetch a pencil and paper, and then she made out a table, putting the description of the lens on one side and a space for its measured focal length on the other. When the table was completed it looked like this:

DESCRIPTION OF LENS	FOCAL LENGTH
Peter's stamp magnifier	3½ inches
Daddy's big reading-glass	8 inches
The lens from Peter's lantern	4½ inches
The big lens from the toy telescope	6 inches
The small lens from the toy telescope	Could not make any image of the sun with this

When Mary showed the table to Father he was still reading his letters.

"That's fine," he said; "I am glad you wrote it all down. People who are lazy and trust too much to memory are always making mistakes. And if anything goes wrong with them in the middle of doing a job of work, nobody can tell how far the work has proceeded, so it all has to be done again from the very beginning by somebody else."

"Well," said Mary, "will any of those lenses do for our camera?"

"What do you think?" countered Father.

"I think the one out of the toy telescope might suit," answered Mary; "our box is five and a half inches long from the pin-hole to the plate inside, but we could stick the lens on the front somehow I should think."

" Do you want to take scenes of distant subjects, like hills and trees and houses, or do you want to take portraits? " asked Father. " If you want to take distant subjects, the lens can be put a distance equal to the focal length from the plate; but if you want to take near things, the lens must be put a little farther away. You see, the nearer the subject, the farther back must the plate be in relation to the lens."

" I would like to take portraits," said Mary.

" I would like to take aeroplanes and engines," said Peter.

" You will have to compromise, then," said Father. " I suggest that you fix the lens so that everything ten feet in front of the camera is sharply in focus on the plate. Then, if you want to take things farther away, you will have to stop the lens down. By that I mean you will have to use only a tiny round bit in the centre, making it more like the pin-hole again. You will have to use only a small bit, anyway, because, if you used all of it, it would let through too much light. Your photo would be made in about a fiftieth of a second, and you could not work your home-made shutter fast enough. If I were you I should open out your pin-hole to a diameter equal to about one-twenty-fourth of the focal length of your lens—say to a quarter of an inch. You will then have to give an exposure of half a second or more, which you could do nicely with your shutter. But if this works stiffly so that you are in danger of shaking the camera when taking a photo, you could use a cap over the lens instead like studio photographers do. Your shutter would then be used as a safety device: opened before and after you make the exposure with the cap, but securely closed at all other times. The cap would have to be a loose fit so as to come off easily and without shaking the camera. You could not rely on it to keep on when you were carrying the camera about, and therefore you had better have it tied to the camera by a tape or string to prevent it from getting lost."

"Just a minute, Daddy," cried Mary. "We haven't made the cap yet, or even fixed the lens in our camera! Where shall we begin?"

"The first thing to do," answered Father, "is to go into the dining-room and stand ten feet back from the window. From there you must focus the image of its bars on to a piece of paper, and find how far the paper must be put from the lens. When you have done that, come and let me know the result."

Mary and Peter ran off to do as they were told. They measured out a distance of ten feet from the window back into the room. Then Peter held up the lens at this distance so that it faced the window, while Mary moved a stiff piece of white card to and fro behind it until she could see a clear little picture of the window frame and window bars on its surface. Holding the card quite still in the correct position, she measured its distance from the lens. "Six and a quarter inches," she said, and she made a note of it underneath the table she had already written out.

When the children told Father of this result, he explained to them that they would need to fix the lens in front of the shutter because the shutter was less than six inches from the plate.

"You will have to make a lens mount and stick it on to the two shutter guides," he said; "I suggest something like this," and he drew a sketch of a tube, big enough to admit the lens

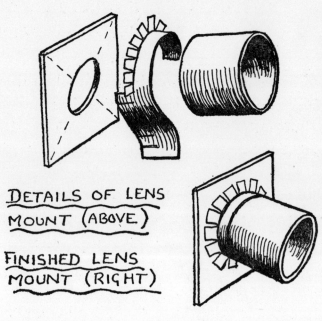

DETAILS OF LENS
MOUNT (ABOVE.)

FINISHED LENS
MOUNT (RIGHT)

inside it, stuck on to a square piece of cardboard over a hole nearly as big as the lens itself.

"You can make the tube out of brown paper tape that has gum on one side of it. A piece about twelve times as long as the lens is across will do. You wet the gum and roll up the tape round the edge of the lens, taking the lens out again while the gum dries.

"To stick the tube on the square card you will need another length of tape with cuts running to the middle from one edge. The length of this piece of tape should be just over three times the outside diameter of the tube.

"When the tube has been fixed to the cardboard, you can stick the cardboard on to the shutter guides, being

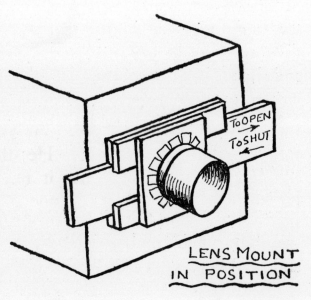

TO OPEN
TO SHUT

LENS MOUNT
IN POSITION

careful to keep its centre in line with the centre of the enlarged pin-hole."

" That's enough to be going on with, Daddy," said Mary. " We will do all that you suggest and then come back for more instructions when we have finished."

Mary found the roll of gummed brown-paper tape which Father kept for sealing large envelopes and parcels. It was an inch wide.

" To save making the lens sticky, I shall draw round it on a piece of card and cut out a disc of cardboard, using that to roll the tape round," she said.

Mary carried out her plan with great success; and very soon the lens mount was finished and stuck to the shutter guides of the camera. Father was very pleased with her work, which was clean and neat.

" To fix the lens in exactly the right position, six and a quarter inches from the plate, you had better make a stick of that length," he said. " You can be doing that, Peter, while Mary cuts out a number of cardboard rings of the same diameter outside as the lens and with round central holes half an inch or more in diameter."

When the stick and the rings were brought to Father, he put the dummy plate in the camera, put on the lid, opened the shutter, and stood the camera on end with the lens mount pointing upwards. He then dropped the stick through the shutter so that it rested on the plate at the bottom end. The top end came about half-way up the tube that was to contain the lens. Father dropped into this tube some of the cardboard rings Mary had made. He dropped them in one at a time until the topmost ring came level with the top of the stick. "Five rings," he said; "make a note of it!"

Mary jotted down the number "five," and Father turned the camera over to tip out the rings and the stick.

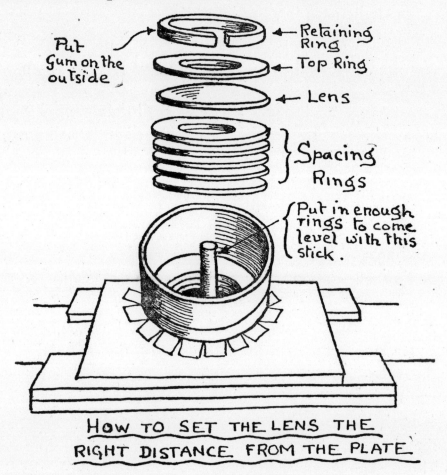

Put Gum on the outside

← Retaining Ring

← Top Ring

← Lens

} Spacing Rings

{ Put in enough rings to come level with this stick.

HOW TO SET THE LENS THE
RIGHT DISTANCE FROM THE PLATE

"Now we are ready to put the lens in," he said, and with these words he stood the camera on its back end again, with the lens tube pointing upwards. Then he put back the five rings and after this he put in the lens, which, of course, rested at a point exactly six and a quarter inches above the dummy plate.

"If we stick one more of your rings in position over the lens,

Dolores.
(A portrait made with the camera shown below.)

A home-made camera.

we shall secure it," he said. " I suggest gumming a strip of cardboard round the inside of the tube just above the topmost ring. That ought to hold everything inside the tube in its proper place."

Mary cut out a strip of the required width and, after trying it in position, she cut it to the proper length.

" We had better clean the lens before we finally fix it, hadn't we, Daddy? " suggested Peter.

" Good idea! " exclaimed Father; " it is a bit smeary-looking."

The lens was tipped out and carefully wiped with a linen handkerchief.

" You used to be able to buy quite good little lenses for about sixpence," said Father, " and if they were wiped with a clean handkerchief or a piece of chamois leather, they lasted quite well. More expensive lenses shouldn't be handled or touched at all except at the edges, and if they do have to be cleaned they should only be wiped very lightly with chamois leather. A wide-aperture lens for a first-rate camera may cost one hundred pounds or more, so it wouldn't do to scratch it. The lenses of binoculars and telescopes are expensive too, so they ought to be kept covered up when not in use and never be touched except for an occasional cleaning."

Father put the lens back in the lens mount and dropped a cardboard ring on top of it. Then Mary pasted the strip of cardboard round the inside of the tube and pushed it down firmly on the ring over the lens.

" While that is drying you can make a cap to go over the lens tube," said Father. " It must fit over the tube loosely but not shakily, and it must be light-tight. The part that goes over the tube can be made of gummed paper tape, like the tube itself, but it should be lined with ordinary paper so that there is no chance of the gum causing the cap to stick to the lens mount at any time. At the end of the cap you must fix a cardboard disc between two narrow strips of cardboard pasted round the inside of the cap tube. Make the disc a good tight fit, and don't let the joins in the two strips come opposite to one another. That way you should be able to prevent light from getting in. When the cap is made you must paint the inside with your black poster paint. And don't forget to tie it to the camera with a length of tape or string to prevent it from getting lost."

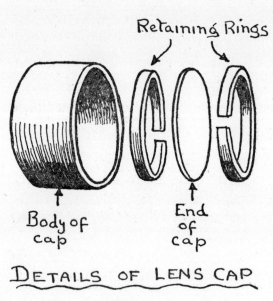

DETAILS OF LENS CAP

Retaining Rings

Body of cap

End of cap

Mary and Peter ran off to finish the last of the work needed to complete their camera. When everything was done, Father said that the camera was ready for use. He loaded it with a plate and then explained how it was to be used.

"Your subject must be a still one," he said, "because you will not be able to take the cap off and put it on again in under about half a second. If you take a photo of a friend, make sure that that friend sits still for a second or so. You must rest the camera on something firm and hold it still while you take off the cap. Don't forget to open the safety shutter before you make your exposure, and don't forget to shut it again when you have finished."

Mary and Peter set out with their camera to look for a suitable subject to photograph. Suddenly Mary said, " There's Dolores, let's take her."

Peter said he would prefer to photograph an engine, but Mary said he could do that another time.

Mary showed the camera to Dolores and asked her if she would sit for her portrait. Dolores consented, and she sat on the ground in front of a bush while Mary looked round for something on which to rest the camera. There was a seat nearby, so she asked Peter to help her move that into position. Eventually the camera was set up in front of Dolores, about eight feet away and about two feet from the ground. Mary pulled out the shutter, rested her left hand on the camera to hold it steady and took hold of the lens cap with her right hand. " Smile, please," she said to Dolores in a professional manner, and Dolores smiled. Instantly Mary lifted off the cap and, with hardly a pause, put it on again.

" Thank you," she said, closing the shutter and picking the camera up, " I will give you a print of the photo when it is developed."

That evening Father developed the photo of Dolores. It was completely successful, the only fault being that the lower half was a little fainter than the top half.

" That is because, when you lifted off the cap, you let light in at the bottom of the lens before you did at the top," said Father, " and when you put the cap on again the bottom part of the lens was the last to be covered. Altogether, then, the bottom of the lens was uncovered longer than the top, so that the plate taking light from this part of the lens was exposed longer than the other part. The negative is darker where it shows the lower parts of Dolores for this reason, and hence the print is lighter in the corresponding place. But it is a nice picture of a nice young friend. I am glad you chose to photograph Dolores; she is old enough to sit still."

"She will be fourteen in another three months' time," said Mary.

"You can give her a copy of the picture when you see her," said Father, "and if she is pleased with it, we will give her an enlargement of it in a frame for her fourteenth birthday. Now, cherubs, are you pleased with your new camera?"

"Oh yes, Daddy," cried both children in chorus, "it's lovely."

"You can take lots of pictures with it this summer," said Father. "There are nine more plates in the packet I bought for use in the pin-hole camera, but I can get some more when they are all used up."

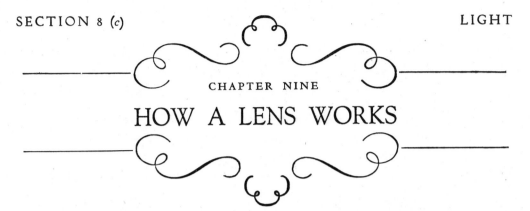

CHAPTER NINE

HOW A LENS WORKS

MARY was turning out one of her many cardboard boxes full of treasures on a wet Sunday morning. It amused her to read old letters and gaze at old Christmas cards. After delving into her store for an hour or so, she came across the table she had written out some weeks before, giving the focal lengths of the family collection of lenses and magnifying glasses. There was one lens mentioned in the table for which no measurement had been made. Mary and Peter had not found it possible to cast an image of the sun on their white sheet of cardboard with the small eye-piece lens of their toy telescope. It was a funny sort of lens, anyway: it diminished things instead of magnifying them.

Mary held the table of figures up in the air for Peter to see. "Do you remember this?" she said; "I wrote it out when we were making our camera. I meant to ask Daddy to explain lenses to us, but he kept us so busy making our camera that I forgot about it. He told us how a pin-hole made images of things—I want to know why a lens does it. Let us get all the lenses together again and go and ask him."

The two children gathered up the toys of which lenses formed a part—the telescope, the magic-lantern, the stamp magnifier and so on—and then they went to look for their father. They found him hunting for a book.

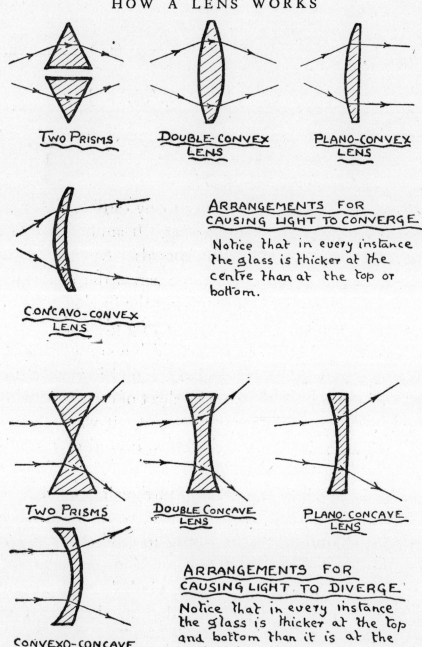

TWO PRISMS

DOUBLE-CONVEX LENS

PLANO-CONVEX LENS

CONCAVO-CONVEX LENS

ARRANGEMENTS FOR CAUSING LIGHT TO CONVERGE

Notice that in every instance the glass is thicker at the centre than at the top or bottom.

TWO PRISMS

DOUBLE CONCAVE LENS

PLANO-CONCAVE LENS

CONVEXO-CONCAVE LENS

ARRANGEMENTS FOR CAUSING LIGHT TO DIVERGE

Notice that in every instance the glass is thicker at the top and bottom than it is at the centre.

"We want you to tell us some more about lenses," said Mary, waving an arm towards Peter and his burden of optical toys. "How is it that a lens acts like a pin-hole and makes an image, and why couldn't we get an image with the smallest lens of our telescope?"

"Put all those toys on the dining-room table and then go and get some white drawing-paper," Father answered.

"Now," said Father, a few minutes later, as he took a seat at the table between Mary and Peter, "there are really only two kinds of lenses, though each kind is made in a variety of different ways. The most interesting kind gathers in light that is scattering or spreading in all directions and brings it back to a point or focus again. You might call this kind of lens a converging lens, because it causes light beams to converge, which means to become narrower. You can always tell this kind of lens from any other kind because it acts as a magnifying glass. Generally, both sides bulge outwards, but sometimes only one side bulges; the other side may be flat or even slightly hollow. With a lens of this kind you can always make an image of distant objects on a sheet of paper—of a window on the opposite wall, for instance. I will show you how it does this by drawing a side view of a lens that bulges on both sides —what opticians call a double-convex lens—and I will put a little figure in front (page 182). Now, light spreads from point A of this little figure in all directions, and some of the rays go towards the lens. I can tell you at once what happens to three of them. The one that goes through the nearest focal point (F_1) is bent by the lens at point (1) and emerges in a direction parallel to the axis of the lens. The ray that travels parallel to the lens axis in the first instance is bent by the lens at point (2), so that it goes through the more distant focal point F_2. The ray that strikes the lens at the centre, at point (3), goes practically straight on, because, at the centre, the two faces of the lens are parallel to one another and the lens behaves like an ordinary sheet of glass. All these rays start from *A*, and when bent they meet a point *A'* on the far side of the lens. If you put a piece of paper at *A'* you would see on it a picture of *A* and it would be upside down. In fact, you would see an image of the whole of the little figure. You could see this image without using a piece of paper, merely by going to some point *B* and looking towards the lens. You could prove that the inverted

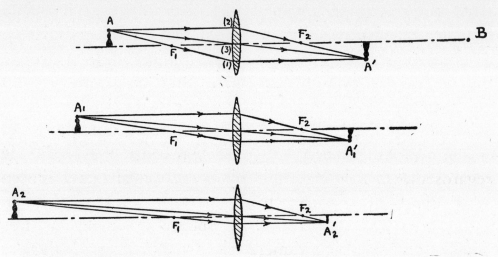

MAGNIFYING GLASS   A real, inverted image is formed of an object put beyond the focal point; it is nearer to the lens, and smaller, when the object is put further away.

image of the figure was at *A'* by holding a pin up in front of you at the same place *A'* and moving your head from side to side to prove that the image and the pin kept together. To view the image at *A'* comfortably your eye at *B* needs to be at least six inches and preferably ten inches from *A'*. If you approach too closely, the image at *A'* gets out of focus, just as a book held too close to the eye gets out of focus, and you find yourself squinting at it in an endeavour to see it. The image is a real one, because you can receive it on a piece of paper. Some images made by lenses, like those made by ordinary mirrors, are virtual images, because they lie behind the glass and have no real existence. They cannot be received on a sheet of paper.

"If you try the effect of moving the little figure A nearer to the lens or farther away, you will see that different things happen. You can predict what will happen by drawing sketches like I have drawn, following three of the rays starting from A towards the lens, and then you can verify the results by actual experiment with one of your magnifying glasses.

"First of all I will draw the figure farther away, at A_1, and then at A_2. You will see that the image at A_1' is nearer to the lens than the image at A'. The image at A_2' is nearer still. If we could move the figure an infinite distance away the image would eventually appear at F_2 the focal point of the lens. As regards the size of the image, this gets smaller and smaller when the object from which it is derived is removed farther and farther away. All this corresponds with what you find happens with a folding camera. The image made by the lens is always upside down and always smaller when the object photographed is farther away. To get the object in focus you must move the camera bellows in or out. The farther away the object, the less you need to extend the bellows. To photograph very near objects you have to pull the bellows out to the limit.

"Now I will try the effect of putting the figure or object A closer to the lens, at A_3 and A_4 (see page 184). You can see that the image at A_3' is bigger than that at A' and also farther away from the lens, while that at A_4' is bigger and farther away still. If I put the figure at the focal point F_1, the image becomes

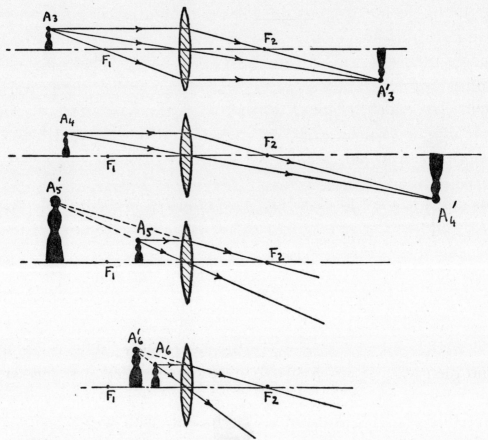

MAGNIFYING GLASS A real, inverted image is formed of an object put beyond the focal point; it is further from the lens and larger when the object is put closer to the lens. When the object is put inside the focal distance an upright, enlarged virtual image is formed on the same side of the lens as the object. This becomes smaller if the object is put closer to the lens.

infinitely large and infinitely far away. I cannot show this in a sketch.

"What happens if I put the figure so close to the lens that it lies inside the focal distance? Well, the image now turns into a virtual one, and it appears on the same side of the lens as the figure itself. At first, when the figure is at A_5, near to F_1, the virtual image, at A_5', is very large; then, as the figure is moved nearer to the lens, to A_6, for example, it gets smaller, as you can see, at A_6'; but always it is bigger than the object from which it is derived, and always it is upright. When you use a lens as a magnifying glass, it is the virtual image you try to get. If you like to find out where this image is, you can do it by putting a pin or a pencil where you think it is, just as you did to find the image made by a mirror, and wagging your head from side to side, shifting the pin or pencil until the image keeps level with it as you move your head."

Mary and Peter did some simple experiments with their magnifying glasses to satisfy themselves that object and image were related to one another, in the way Father had described, and then Mary held up the small lens from the eye-piece of the toy telescope.

" When we were measuring the focal lengths of our lenses, I was never able to make an image of the sun with this one," she said.

" No," answered Father, " you wouldn't ever make a real image of anything with that kind of lens. It is made hollow, or concave, on both sides, and it is called a double-concave lens. Being thicker towards the edges than at the middle, it is of the light-diverging kind. All light rays scatter or spread apart more rapidly after passing through the lens than they did when approaching it. It does make an image of the sun at its focal point, but the image is a virtual one. If you look at the sun through such a lens you see it as a very tiny bright spot behind the lens. It would be very dangerous to look at the sun through a magnifying glass, but it is fairly safe to do so through a lens of this kind.

" To measure the focal length of a diminishing glass you have to resort to the pin method to find the place where the sun's image is formed. You look at the sun, or any other very distant object through your lens, and you put a pin behind the lens where you think the image should be. You watch the pin over

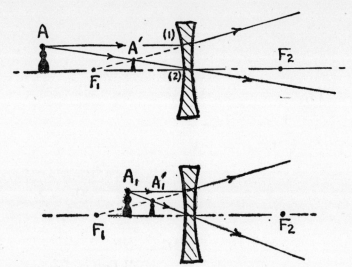

DIMINISHING GLASS — The image formed by a real object is always upright and diminished.

the top of the lens, and also the image of the distant object through the lens, and then you move your head from side to side to see if there is any parallax effect. If the pin and the image seem to move together, then the pin is at the correct distance from the lens, and you can measure the focal length straightway. If the pin and the image seem to separate, then you must move the pin nearer to the lens or farther away until you get the two keeping together, however much you move your head about. Having found the focal point, you can make drawings to find the relation between image and object for a diminishing glass just as you can for a magnifying glass. I will draw a sketch of such a lens as it would appear if cut in half along a diameter and viewed on the cut face, and I will put a figure in front of it at A and draw two light rays from A to the lens. The one that goes parallel to the axis and strikes the lens at (1) is bent outwards, so that it seems to come from the direction of the focus F_1. The one that goes to the centre of the lens at (2) passes practically straight on, the lens being like a flat piece of glass here. The image of A is at A', where the two refracted light rays seem to come from. The image of the whole figure is nearer to the lens than the object figure itself, but it is on the same side of the lens, and therefore it is a virtual image; also it is smaller and it is upright. Wherever I care to put the object figure, whether I put it outside the focal distance, as at A, or close up to the lens inside the focal distance as at A_1, I get an upright diminished and virtual image. By looking at the object through the lens you can see its image, and you can very easily tell that it is near the lens, because if you come too close to the lens you find yourself straining your eye to keep the image clear. Although the tiny picture of the object *seems* far away, it is really getting as near as a page of print held uncomfortably close, say four or five inches away. You can, of course, check the truth of this by using the pin method to discover the exact position of the image."

When Father stopped talking the children played with the diminishing lens for a little while and then Mary began to start asking questions again.

" How can a telescope magnify things, Daddy," she asked,

"when it uses a magnifying glass at one end and a diminishing glass at the other? Don't the two lenses neutralise each other? It seems silly to me."

"Not all telescopes use a magnifying glass at one end and a diminishing glass at the other. Some telescopes use two magnifying glasses, a weak one with a long focal length at the big end and a strong one with a short focal length at the eye end. The glass with the long focal length makes a real image

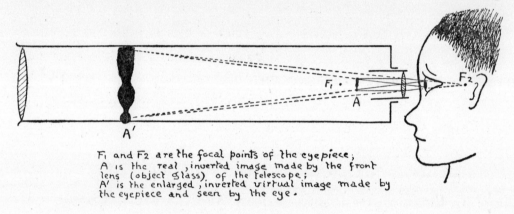

Fᵢ and F₂ are the focal points of the eyepiece;
A is the real, inverted image made by the front
lens (object glass) of the telescope;
A′ is the enlarged, inverted virtual image made by
the eyepiece and seen by the eye.

KEPLER'S TELESCOPE

of the distant object, and because the focal length is so great the image is a comparatively large one—much larger than the image made by a glass of short focal length would be. The lens near the eye is used as a magnifying glass with which to look at this image. It is moved in and out when you focus the telescope and when the focus is right, the image made by the front glass is brought just inside the focus of the eye-piece, so that you get an enlarged virtual image of it. You are really looking at the image of an image. Unhappily, the front glass makes its image upside down, and as the eye-piece does not turn it up the right way again you see things upside down when using this simple telescope. Such a telescope can be used for studying the stars, and it was invented for this purpose by an astronomer called Kepler more than three hundred years ago, but it is not of much use for everyday purposes. It is what you might call an ' astronomical ' telescope. A ' terrestrial ' telescope has a compound eye-piece, by which I mean an eye-piece made of several lenses to form a microscope. This microscope can be much more powerful than a simple magnifying glass, and it is made so as to turn the inverted image of the front glass the right way up. The drawback to telescopes of this kind is their great length. They use a front glass with a focal length of a foot or more, and an eye-piece with a focal length of something less than an inch, and the combination needs a tube at least a foot long. A compound eye-piece may add another six or eight inches to the length.

" The modern way of overcoming these difficulties is to go back to the simple magnifying-glass eye-piece and use an arrangement of prisms in between the two magnifying glasses. The prisms serve two purposes: they turn the inverted image of the front glass up the right way and they also ' fold up ' the light rays between the two glasses so as to make them occupy a much shorter tube. The light from the front glass is sent back and forth in the tube by the prisms, so that it traverses the whole length of the tube three times before reaching the eye-piece. The prism-binocular is really a couple of Kepler's telescopes made compact and serviceable in this way. If you look at one of these binoculars you will notice that the eye-pieces are not in line with the front or object glasses as they are in the ordinary type of opera glass. That is because the internal prisms displace the light rays sideways as well as to and fro between the lenses."

"You haven't said one single word about how our toy telescope works yet," protested Mary; "that has only two glasses, and one of them is a diminishing glass."

"I am coming to that now," said Father. "Cheap

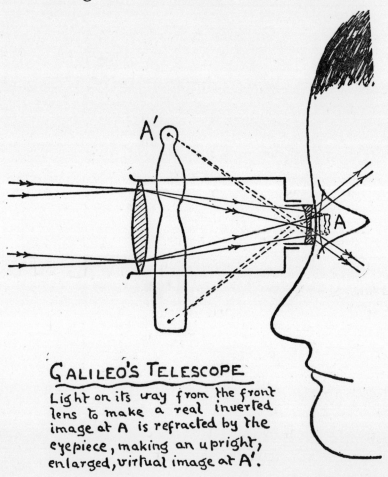

GALILEO'S TELESCOPE

Light on its way from the front lens to make a real inverted image at A is refracted by the eyepiece, making an upright, enlarged, virtual image at A'.

binoculars, or opera glasses as they are often called, work on the same principle as your toy telescope. The combination of a magnifying glass and a diminishing glass is due to an astronomer called Galileo, who lived in Italy about three hundred years ago. The diminishing glass is put near enough to the magnifying one to prevent the formation of a real image by the magnifying one. The light which is converging to a focus is refracted and caused to diverge by the diminishing eye-piece, and it appears to come from a point in front of this eye-piece, from a very large virtual image. In my sketch of the arrangement I have shown where the real image would be by the letter *A*. This inverted image is prevented from forming by the eye-piece, and a virtual upright image is created at *A'* instead. So you see, a diminishing glass *can* magnify— it turns a relatively small *real* image into a much larger *virtual* image. An advantage of Galileo's telescope is that it can be made short, because the magnifying glass at the front is not required to make a real image. The eye-piece can be put closer to the front glass than is permissible in the astronomical type of telescope, because it does not have to be behind where the real image would be but in front of it. Another advantage is that it shows things as they really are, that is, upright."

"How does a microscope work?" asked Peter.

"Just like an astronomical telescope," answered Father, "only

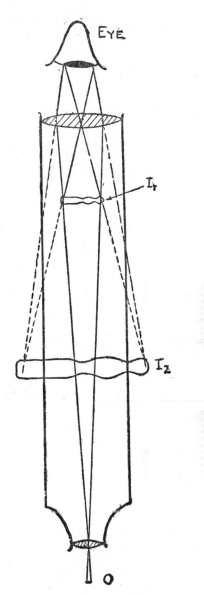

MICROSCOPE

O is the object being viewed; I_1 is the real image made by the bottom lens; I_2 is the virtual image made by the top lens.

the front or object glass is a short-focus magnifying glass which is brought quite close to the object being magnified. In fact, this is at a distance only a little more than the focal length away. The real inverted image of the object is some distance up the tube of the microscope, and it is an enlarged image. This enlarged image is viewed through another magnifying glass so that it is magnified still more. The image of the front glass is brought inside the focal length of the eye-piece so that the eye-piece creates an enlarged virtual image of it. A microscope gives you an upside-down picture of your object, but this does not matter, as you can easily put your object upside down to begin with and thus get an upright view of it. You cannot alter the position of things viewed with a telescope as they are so far away, and they could not be interfered with anyhow; that is why it is preferable to have a telescope which shows everything the right way up."

CHAPTER TEN

COLOUR

THE summer was over, but the warm sunny weather had continued into late September.

"I wonder if it will keep like this for the last week of Daddy's holiday?" said Mary one fine evening as she and Peter put away the garden tools after a hard day's work in the open air; "it starts next Saturday."

On Friday night Mary woke up to hear the sound of torrential rain, and then she knew that the weather had changed for the worse. "What a shame!" she thought; "I wish the fine weather could have lasted a few days longer."

It was still raining when she fell asleep again, but she was awakened by the sun which shone through the window, as it had done every morning for many weeks past. "Hooray!" she cried, "it is fine after all."

She woke Peter and, after dressing quickly, the two children ran out into the garden to see if the rain clouds had quite gone away. They soon saw that, although the sky overhead was clear and blue, many patches of black cloud lay all around low down on the horizon. As often happens in spring or autumn, heavy showers were chasing each other from West to East, and, by the time one ceased, giving way to clear sunshine, another threatening-looking bank of cloud could already be seen racing up. In the garden glittering raindrops were hanging from every leaf and twig and from every blade of grass. Mary had seen raindrops in the sunshine before, but she had not taken particular notice of them. This morning she was more observant, possibly because there had not been any raindrops to see in all the long fine summer days that had gone before.

"Why, Peter," she cried, "the raindrops are all different colours; and when you move your head you get all sorts of pretty coloured lights from each single drop."

"I can't see anything special," said Peter, "except a lot of wetness we didn't want."

"You have to shut one eye," said Mary, "and then you have to look for one specially bright drop that shines red or yellow or violet in your other eye. The least movement of your head up or down changes the colour that you can see. I am looking at a drop that is shining bright red just now. If I lift up my head, or go a little nearer, the colour turns to orange, then yellow, then green, then blue and then violet. After violet there isn't anything; the drop goes dark."

"Oh, I can see one now," cried Peter; "the colours are just like those you can see sometimes when Daddy's cut-glass paper weight is standing in the sunshine."

"Or Mummy's little hand mirror with the bevelled edge," added Mary.

"They are like the colours of the rainbow," Peter went on.

Just then the children heard Mother calling them. "It's breakfast-time," she cried; "wipe your feet as you come in."

When Father appeared at the breakfast table the children looked glum.

Sunshine after rain.

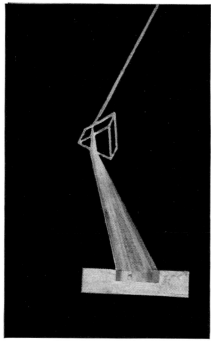

Light passing through a prism.

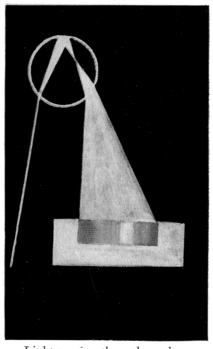

Light passing through a sphere.

"The fine weather has finished, Daddy," Mary said.

"Look, it is raining again already," Peter added, glancing out of the window.

"It is only showers," said Father; "we must enjoy the sunshine in between."

"We saw something ever so pretty this morning," Mary said, and then she described to her Father how they had seen brightly coloured light coming from the raindrops.

"So you have discovered one of Nature's best-kept secrets at last!" exclaimed Father. "I suppose now you want me to tell you all about it."

"Oh yes, Daddy," cried Mary, "I love secrets. What is this one you say we have discovered?"

"The secret you have discovered is that the white light from the sun is really made up of light of different colours all mixed together. Sometimes something happens to separate out the different kinds of light, but not everybody notices when it happens. The only time that everyone notices is when the sun shines before a shower is over and causes a rainbow. That is a beautiful sight which nobody could miss. We may see one to-day, but you can only see a rainbow in the early morning or in the evening. If the sun is high in the sky, it cannot make a rainbow; it must be low down, like it is shortly after sunrise, or an hour or two before sunset. To be precise, the sun must be less than forty-one degrees above the horizon if it is to form a rainbow.

"The raindrops you saw were splitting the light of the sun up into its different coloured components. A rainbow occurs when there are millions and millions of raindrops falling through the air in bright sunshine. Some of these drops are momentarily in a position to send you red light, and these lie on the surface of a big imaginary cone in the sky. When they drop out of position others fall into their place so that there will always be raindrops to send you red light provided the shower lasts. On a smaller cone there will be drops that can send you yellow light; on smaller cones still, drops that can send green light, blue light and violet light."

"How can drops of water make white light into coloured light, Daddy?" Mary asked. "The water itself is quite clear, not like the coloured water in those great bottles chemists put in their shop windows."

"I will explain," answered Father. "Already I have told you that light travels more slowly in a dense medium than in empty space or in air. If a ray of light enters glass at an angle it becomes bent as a direct consequence of the retarding action of the glass. What I did not tell you was that light of different colours is slowed down by different amounts, violet light being slowed down most and red light least. When a narrow ray of sunlight falls on a prism of glass, it is not only bent but dispersed. It becomes broadened out, the red light being bent least and the violet light most. On leaving the prism the different-coloured lights take different directions, and if a piece of white paper is put in their way you will see a lovely rainbow-coloured patch appear on it. The dispersion is very slight when light enters glass at the angles which are usual, and you do not notice it when you are looking through a window, or playing with lenses; but a prism is a device made purposely to exaggerate the dispersion effect, and a raindrop or a dewdrop serves even better than a prism. Light entering a round drop is sent back again at an angle of about forty-one degrees with its original direction, but being resolved into its component colours the returning ray is a divergent one instead of a parallel one. If you are some distance from the drop, only part of the divergent ray enters your eye: it may be the red part or the violet part or some in-between part. If several people looked at the same drop, they might see different colours, being in positions to receive different parts of the dispersed light ray. When you look at a rainbow your back is to the sun, and the drops that provide the pretty sight lie on lines making an angle of forty-one degrees, a little more or a little less, with the imaginary line going from the sun through the back of your

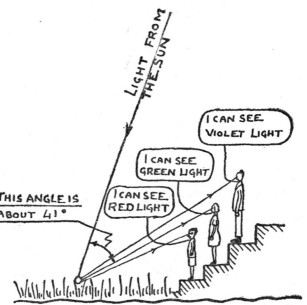

A DEWDROP IN THE GRASS SPARKLES WITH BRIGHT COLOURS, THE COLOUR SEEN DEPENDING ON THE POSITION OF THE OBSERVER

head and out at the front. Along some of these lines there may be more drops than along others, and the bow appears brightest where there are most drops. Lines below the horizontal end in the ground, and are therefore very short. You do not see the bottom part of the complete rainbow circle for this reason. Lines going up into the sky continue a long way, and in these directions there may be thousands of drops to send you their little gleams of coloured light. Lines ending in trees or in the sides of distant hills or houses are often long enough to thread their way through very many raindrops, and so you can often see trees or hills or houses through part of a rainbow. A complete bow makes a circle, so that there is not really any such thing as the 'end' of a rainbow. And even if you think of

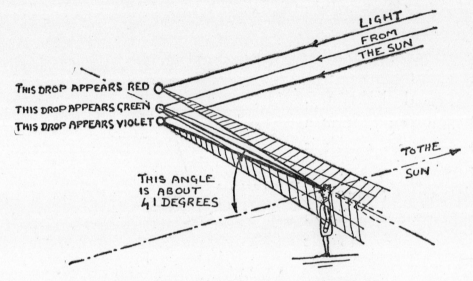

THIS DROP APPEARS RED

THIS DROP APPEARS GREEN

THIS DROP APPEARS VIOLET

LIGHT FROM THE SUN

TO THE SUN

THIS ANGLE IS ABOUT 41 DEGREES

WHEN THEY ARE IN THE RIGHT ANGULAR POSITIONS, FALLING RAINDROPS APPEAR TO BE BRIGHTLY COLOURED

the bow as stopping where it appears to go into the ground, the end would be a long line stretching from close in front of you to perhaps two or three miles away.

"A friend standing near you does not see the same rainbow as you do. For him the bow is made by an altogether different set of drops lying on lines at forty-one degrees or so with the line joining *his* head to the sun. All the little diagrams I am drawing while I am talking to you should help you to understand these mysteries.

" You can make your own rainbow any evening you like by going out into the garden near sunset with a pail of water and a water sprayer or squirt. If you stand with your back to the sun and send up a good shower of tiny droplets, you will see a beautiful ' rainbow ' for a second or two. You can often see a

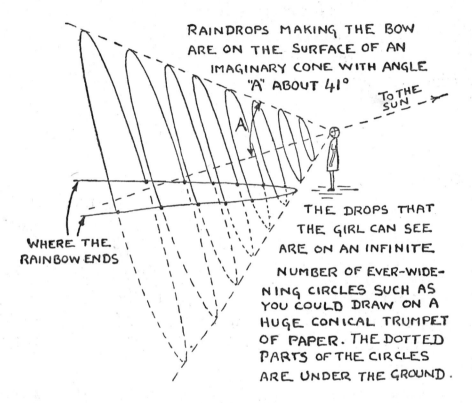

RAINDROPS MAKING THE BOW ARE ON THE SURFACE OF AN IMAGINARY CONE WITH ANGLE "A" ABOUT 41°

TO THE SUN

WHERE THE RAINBOW ENDS

THE DROPS THAT THE GIRL CAN SEE ARE ON AN INFINITE NUMBER OF EVER-WIDE-NING CIRCLES SUCH AS YOU COULD DRAW ON A HUGE CONICAL TRUMPET OF PAPER. THE DOTTED PARTS OF THE CIRCLES ARE UNDER THE GROUND.

rainbow when you are watching someone who is using a hose-pipe, but the best artificial rainbows are to be seen near a fountain or a waterfall. I have even seen one at the seaside and on board ship when a big wave has thrown up a shower of spray."

At this moment Mother interrupted by saying that she wanted to clear the breakfast table.

" We will go for a walk," said Father, " and we will take

sandwiches with us. Perhaps we shall see a rainbow some time to-day."

Very soon Mary and Peter were tramping over the hills with their father. They had their oilskins over their arms, ready for the heavy showers that fell about once in every hour, and Peter carried sandwiches for everybody in his school satchel. Several times the sun came out before the rain had stopped falling, and the children turned their backs to it hopefully, expecting to see a rainbow. But, as Father pointed out, the sun was now well up in the sky, its elevation being more than forty-one degrees above the horizon, so that they could not really expect to see any rainbow. Later in the afternoon, however, the sun began to sink in the west and then Father said, " We might see a rainbow after the next shower has passed. You will see the bow in an easterly direction, opposite to the sun."

When the next shower came, Father and the two children were climbing up the last hill before reaching home. They ran to some sheltering trees as the rainfall reached its climax. On the opposite side of the road was a wooden fence, over which they could see miles of wooded country and distant hills lying to the east.

" If the sun shines after this shower we ought to see a lovely rainbow," said Father.

Ten minutes later the rainfall slackened and the sun began to shine with a pale light. A very faint bow appeared in the sky.

" The sunshine has not yet penetrated much farther east than the place where we are standing," said Father. " When it is shining out over those woods, you will see the rainbow much more clearly."

Every instant the colours of the rainbow became brighter and brighter. Presently the rain stopped completely, and Mary was surprised to see a little friend of hers run out from underneath another tree farther up the road and go to look over the fence.

"It is Jill," cried Mary; "she has her best green coat and red beret on. Fancy going out like that on such a showery day!"

Jill did not hear her friend's remark, but stood gazing in rapturous delight at the gorgeous rainbow. It shone vividly against the dark sky and the still darker background of the distant hill. It even covered up a part of wooded landscape, and it seemed to end in a green clearing about half a mile away.

"Sometimes you can see a larger and fainter bow outside the main bow," said Father. "Raindrops make that one too, but the light is reflected twice before it comes out of the drops, and the colours of the bow are reversed, red being on the inside and violet on the outside."

Jill made the most of the sunny interval, and ran home without ever noticing Mary in her shelter under the trees. Mary followed with Peter and Father a few minutes later. The rainbow faded slowly from the sky as they walked along and, eventually, only a short length of it remained. This glowed for a few minutes longer and then that disappeared too.

The sun went down quickly, and from the top of the hill Father and the children watched it setting.

"Do you remember that glorious sunset we saw when we went to that cottage with the oil lamp?" Mary said. "What happened then to make the sun so red looking?"

"When sunlight has to thread its way through tiny particles of dust and mist, the violet and blue and green light get scattered and do not come through," said Father; "only the red and orange light manage to penetrate, and that is why the sun goes orange or red in colour. The scattered light comes to us from the tiny particles of dust or moisture in the air, and it comes to us from all directions, which is why the whole dome of the sky is blue looking on a fine day. When we get home I will make a home-made sunset for you. I will make a bright white circle of light on the wall with my big electric torch by shining it through a flask of freshly made photographic 'hypo,' which looks like plain, clear water. Then I will add some drops of hydrochloric acid, which your mother keeps for some cleaning job or other, and you will see the white patch on the wall go gradually yellow, then orange, then red and then dark. The hypo, at first quite clear, will go a smoky blue colour, because it is stopping and scattering the blue light from the torch and only letting the red and yellow go through. What happens is that the mixture of the two chemicals causes a very fine powder to form in the liquid—sulphur to be exact—and the tiny particles of the powder behave like the tiny particles in the atmosphere. They stop the blue and violet light from going on with the red and yellow light, causing it to scatter in all directions.

"Some sunsets give you all the colours of the spectrum. The sun itself is red, the glow just round it is orange, fading to pale yellow. You get green bits of clear sky peeping through the clouds, which may glow crimson and violet. Farther away from the sun you may see clear blue sky. And all this wondrous spectacle is provided in the first instance by a blaze of white light."

"Do you think it is nice to know how lovely things like sunsets and rainbows are caused, Daddy?" Mary asked thoughtfully. "Isn't it best just to let them please you, and not try to find out how to imitate them?"

"Not at all," answered Father. "It may seem unromantic of me if I tell you that to anyone five miles up in the air there wouldn't be any rainbow or any sunset to see—that these beautiful sights only come to us because we are tiny and can see only a tiny part of the universe from where we stand; but if you will stop to think, you must agree with me when I say that really and truly I have hardly explained anything. I have told you that a rainbow is caused by so dull a thing as drops of water, and a sunset by common dust, but I haven't attempted to tell you what light itself is. That is a real mystery. The great English scientist, Sir Isaac Newton, thought light to be a stream of tiny particles, and he wrote about what is called the 'corpuscular' theory of light. Later on another English scientist called Young suggested that light was really a sort of wave or ripple in space. The biggest waves he thought were red and the smallest violet, waves for the other colours being in between. This wave idea helps to explain why violet and blue light are more easily scattered or refracted than red and orange light. In a pond, the tiny ripples are much more easily reflected and broken up by obstacles in the water than the big waves. The big waves just lift up anything floating in their way and pass on. Red light is supposed to do much the same thing to particles of dust in the air, though these are large enough to deflect the violet and blue light.

"But the farther you delve into things like this the more you get puzzled, because you never really get to the bottom of the mystery. You can still feel romantic if you like about rainbows and sunsets, because there is a great deal about these things that still remains to be explained. I could not explain everything to you, and neither could anybody else. Knowledge should serve to increase our wonder and perplexity rather than to diminish it, because the higher we climb in our search for truth the greater becomes the view around us of unexplored realms. A hundred years ago scientists thought they knew nearly everything there was to be known. Now, although they know ten times as much as they did then, they realise that what they do know is only a very small beginning to what they hope to find out in the distant future."

CHAPTER ONE

FIRE

FATHER woke up suddenly, thinking it must be late. But Mother was still asleep, and the bedside clock said only six o'clock. What had awakened Father was a strange noise downstairs—a furtive rustling of paper, and stealthy footsteps.

"Burglars!" exclaimed Father to himself, and he leapt lightly out of bed. He put on his dressing-gown and then his slippers. He selected the poker as being the most useful weapon in the bedroom, and then he crept silently out on to the landing and down the stairs.

FATHER GOES TO LOOK FOR BURGLARS

The curious noises came from the breakfast-room, so Father softly pushed open the door and peeped in.

What he saw then was not burglars at all, but Mary, who was on her knees in front of the fireplace, trying to light the fire. "Gracious me!" exclaimed Father, "what on earth are you doing?"

Mary gave a start on hearing her father behind her. She turned round and showed a very black and unhappy face. "Oh,

THE NOISE WAS CAUSED BY
MARY TRYING TO LIGHT THE FIRE

Daddy," she cried, nearly in tears, "I cannot get it to go, and this is the third time I've laid the sticks and paper and everything."

"But it isn't your job to light the fire, Mary," protested Father; "whatever made you try?"

"Mummy said she felt ill yesterday, so I wanted to help," Mary replied; "I wanted to give her a nice surprise, and have everything ready for breakfast before she came down."

"Oh, I see," Father said, dropping his voice to a whisper. "Can I help, now that I am in the secret too?"

"If you could get the fire to start I could do all the rest," Mary answered.

"You are laying that wrongly," Father said. "It will never go if you lay it like that. Lots of people do not know how to lay a fire. They do not realise that every part of a fire needs air to keep it going. A fire does not burn only the fuel you put on —it burns air as well. Air is a mixture of two invisible gases called oxygen and nitrogen, and you must make sure that your fire has a chance of getting plenty of atmospheric oxygen, or it will just be smothered and go out. The way you have laid your fire will cause the flames to be smothered. Directly the paper at the bottom burns and takes up less space, the sticks will fall down and fill up the gap. If ever any of the sticks start to burn and collapse, the coal will fall into the gap. All the time your bed of fuel will just be one tight mass of paper and wood and coal, with no space ever open for air to enter."

Father started to pick out the coal from the fireplace. When he had done this he pulled out the sticks. What was left of the paper he unscrewed, for Mary had twisted it up into tight rolls.

"Now we are ready to begin at the beginning," Father said. "First of all you must put in the paper loosely. Do not screw

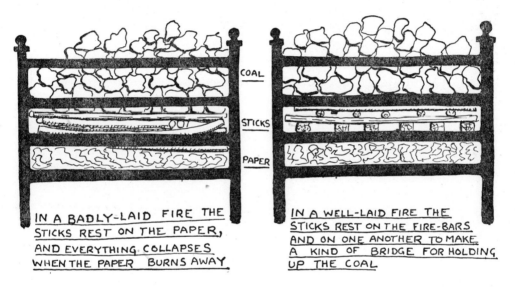

COAL

STICKS

PAPER

IN A BADLY-LAID FIRE THE STICKS REST ON THE PAPER, AND EVERYTHING COLLAPSES WHEN THE PAPER BURNS AWAY

IN A WELL-LAID FIRE THE STICKS REST ON THE FIRE-BARS AND ON ONE ANOTHER TO MAKE A KIND OF BRIDGE FOR HOLDING UP THE COAL

it up hard and tight. Then you must use your sticks to build a sort of bridge that will not fall down directly the support of the paper underneath is burnt away. If sticks and coal all fall down directly the paper starts to burn, the flames will just be put out by a want of air."

Father laid the biggest and strongest sticks across the grate like another set of firebars, leaving a big space underneath for the paper. On top of the big sticks Father laid the smaller sticks criss-cross fashion. They did not fill up the gaps between the big sticks, but made the big gaps into smaller ones, so that the lumps of coal could not fall through. When he had made a good strong wooden platform to support the coal, he replaced the knobs one by one, being careful not to use very small ones that would fit and stop up all the holes in the wooden platform, nor yet very large ones that would be slow to catch fire.

"Now we can light it," Father said at last. "If the paper burns away before the wood takes fire, it will not matter, as we shall be able to push in some more, and keep on pushing it in until the wood is well alight."

Mary touched the paper with a lighted match, and it blazed up at once. When the flames began to die down she pushed some more paper between the bars, a little at a time. At last the wood started to blaze. It had been a little damp, but by the use of plenty of paper it was soon dried out and made fit for burning.

"Can I leave it now that the wood is burning?" Mary asked her father.

"Yes, it should go all right now," Father answered. "If you think there is any danger of the wooden bridge collapsing before the coal has started to burn, you can put in a poker to hold it up. And if, despite all your care, the whole thing falls into a solid mass at the bottom of the grate, you can often save it from going out by making a stronger draught. To do that you hold an old tin tray up over the front of the grate so that any air passing up the chimney has to go in at the bottom of the grate and through the fire-bed. Some people hold up a sheet of newspaper instead of an old tray, but if you do that you must be very careful, as it is easy for the newspaper to catch fire and burn you."

While Father was speaking, the fire blazed up nicely, and

Mary could see that the coal was well alight by the time the wood platform was nearly burnt through. " I shall not need to use either poker or old tray," she said.

" That was easy, then, wasn't it? " Father exclaimed. " People are often quite stupid about lighting fires, but really it is easy if you remember not to make one tight mass out of your paper and wood and sticks. You *must* make sure that air can easily get in, not only at the start but all the time."

Mary ran off to prepare the breakfast-table, and by the time Mother came downstairs everything was ready. She was delighted to find that there was no work to do.

" You are a dear, good girl to help me," she said. " I feel better already."

After breakfast, Mary went off as usual to school. It was rather a cold day, and Mary found that one of the teachers was missing.

" I do not know what to do with the little ones," the head-mistress said. " Miss Parkin hasn't turned up, so somebody will have to play with them."

" Could I play with them? " Mary asked.

" I would be glad if you would," the headmistress said. " Keep them out of doors, as it is healthier, and not so noisy for the rest of us."

Mary took the little ones to the wood at the bottom of the school garden, and here they played hide-and-seek and touch-wood for a little while. Then one child said, " Let's pretend to be elves."

" Couldn't we dress up for that? " another one suggested.

Mary went indoors and fetched the box of dressing-up clothes, and the children all made themselves into elves.

"Elves have a fire," one little boy suggested.

"Do they know how to make one?" Mary asked.

"Oh yes," answered the little boy. "You use paper and sticks and things."

"Go ahead, then," said Mary, laughing to herself.

The children gathered some sticks and made a sort of heap out of them.

"That won't do," Mary said; "you must make it so that it stands up strongly even when it is alight, and then the air can get in among the burning sticks. A fire must have air, or it is smothered and goes out."

Mary showed the children how to lay their sticks, and soon they were making a criss-cross arrangement with plenty of space between the sticks for air to get in between.

"That is worth a photograph," Mary said when it was nearly done; "wait here while I get my camera. I brought it to school last week to show my teacher, and I forgot to take it home. It is in my locker."

Mary fetched her camera, and she made a picture with it just as the last sticks were being put into place.

"May we light our fire?" one of the children asked.

"I asked the headmistress when I went to get my camera," Mary replied, "and she said you could. Here are the matches. Don't get too near, and don't leave the little sacks for the wood lying where sparks can jump on to them and burn holes in them."

Very soon the children had a big fire blazing away merrily. Some of them danced round it, while others went away to collect more sticks to keep it going.

At the end of the morning the headmistress praised Mary.

By permission of Miss Yelf, Wychcrest School

Sticks laid to make a fire.

"A chemical extinguisher." The special liquid used is converted into a heavy fire-killing vapour upon meeting the flames.

Inverting the extinguisher mixes gas-generating chemical, and a strong jet of water issues under gas pressure.

Four jets of chemical foam being projected through four "Pyrene" foam-making branch-pipes.

"You have kept them amused very nicely," she said; "I am not sure that they have learnt much, but that cannot be helped."

"I showed them the proper way to lay the sticks for a fire," Mary said.

"Well, that's something, to be sure," the headmistress replied; "I never was much good myself at making fires."

"Oh, it is quite easy really," Mary said. "May I show you?"

"You can show us all," the headmistress answered, looking rather stern; "this afternoon you can have my blackboard and chalk, and you can draw a picture for the whole school, showing how a fire should be laid. It would do us all good, I am sure."

The headmistress expected Mary to look awkward and rather scared; but, instead, she looked rather pleased. That afternoon she gave a little talk to the whole school about making and lighting fires. Everyone thought it was very good, especially the headmistress.

When Father heard of all that Mary had done that day he was very pleased with her.

"What a pity I did not know that you were to become a school lecturer so soon," he said. "I could have shown you a good experiment to do in front of a class. Fetch me a saucer of water, a glass tumbler and a candle, please."

Mary fetched all these things, and Father stood the candle up in the middle of the saucer of water. Then he lighted it and put the tumbler upside down over the lighted candle, allowing the edge of the tumbler to rest on the saucer beneath the level of the water. "That candle will soon go out," Father said; "it needs oxygen to keep it going, and it will soon use up the oxygen that is imprisoned in the tumbler." As Father spoke, the water in the saucer crept up inside the tumbler until it was higher inside than outside.

"The oxygen in the air is being used up," Father said, "and more air is trying to get in to take the place of the oxygen. To do that it must first of all push the water into the tumbler."

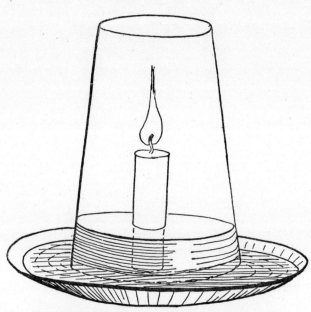

AS THE CANDLE BURNS, THE WATER IN THE SAUCER CLIMBS UP INSIDE THE TUMBLER. THEN THE CANDLE GOES OUT FOR WANT OF OXYGEN.

Just when it seemed likely that the water would all pass up into the tumbler, the candle went out.

"There!" exclaimed Father. "Now there isn't any more oxygen left."

"What has happened to it?" Mary asked.

"The tallow of the candle and the oxygen have joined together to make something different from either of them," Father answered. "Burning always means the same thing—the combining of atmospheric oxygen with the thing being burned. Most things you burn for fuel are made of two substances: one is a black substance called carbon, very much like coke, and the other is an invisible gas called hydrogen, which is even lighter than air, and which people use for filling balloons. Even paraffin oil and petrol consist of these two very dissimilar substances. In chemical combination the black solid, called carbon, and the invisible gas, called hydrogen, can make a transparent liquid. Chemistry is full of surprises like that.

"When carbon burns, it combines with oxygen to form another invisible gas—rather a heavy one—called carbon dioxide. Like oxygen and hydrogen, this is without smell. It is to us a useless gas, because we cannot breathe it, and it will not help a fire to go. It is, however, useful to plants, for these know how to get the carbon out of it again and release the oxygen. With the help of sunlight, plants and trees are always breathing in carbon dioxide and giving out oxygen. Plants do us the service of making the air fresh again after it has been robbed of its oxygen.

"Not only fires rob air of oxygen, but animals and humans do so too. When you breathe air into your lungs, you do it because your blood needs the oxygen. The lungs are a place where air and blood come very close together, so that an exchange of gases can take place. Your blood takes the oxygen, and in exchange it gives up carbon dioxide. Every time you breathe out you send carbon dioxide into the air, and the plants know how to turn this back into pure oxygen and carbon again. The carbon they make into wood, and wood may in turn become coal or petrol, as I will explain another time perhaps."

"What happens to the hydrogen of the candle when this burns?" Mary asked.

"That combines with oxygen too, and the result is plain water. You do not see water coming from a flame, because everything is so hot that the water can exist only as steam, and real steam is invisible. However, you can easily prove that fire makes water if you will hold a glass carafe or flask of cold water over a gas ring for a moment. The outside instantly becomes clouded with beads of water formed by the combining of the hydrogen in the coal gas with the oxygen in the air. The purpose of the cold flask is to condense the steam, as this would otherwise remain invisible.

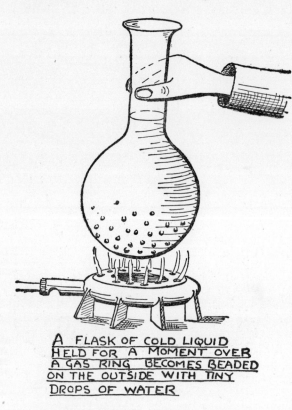

A FLASK OF COLD LIQUID HELD FOR A MOMENT OVER A GAS RING BECOMES BEADED ON THE OUTSIDE WITH TINY DROPS OF WATER

"When the candle burns inside a tumbler, oxygen is used up, and instead of this you get carbon dioxide. You get steam too, but as this quickly turns to water, it does not take up any appreciable space. The carbon dioxide takes up the same space as the oxygen helping to form it, but there is only a drop or so of water to replace the oxygen that combined with the hydrogen. This means that an empty space is left inside the tumbler when the candle burns. It is to fill up this empty space that the water rises inside the tumbler."

While Father spoke, Peter drew near. He had done some chemistry at his school, so that not everything Father said was strange to him. He recognised the experiment with the candle, and knew that Father had been telling Mary how hungry a fire was for air with oxygen in it.

"I have been reading about engines," Peter said; "do you know that an express engine has a fire-grate that may be six feet square, or even more, and that on every little square measuring one foot each way as much as a hundred pounds of coal may be burned in an hour; that means about a ton and a half an hour for the whole grate. Teacher says that each pound of coal needs at least eight pounds of air to make it burn properly, so the fire of an engine must use up twelve tons of air an hour. How many tumblerfuls is that, do you think?"

"Don't be silly, Peter," said Mary; "you don't measure air in tumblerfuls."

"Peter is only being funny," Father said; "but he is right to ask what volume of air a fire uses. Twelve tons of air would fill a space seventy feet long by seventy feet wide by seventy feet high. It is rather a lot of air, but then, all engines

A MOTOR ENGINE RUNNING IN A GARAGE WITH THE DOOR SHUT WILL SOON SEND YOU TO SLEEP — AND YOU MAY NEVER WAKE UP ANY MORE.

and all fires are greedy things, taking a great deal of air. It doesn't do to shut yourself up with a motor engine while it is burning petrol in a garage, as it soon changes the oxygen in any confined space into carbon dioxide, which you cannot breathe. Sometimes you hear of people dying as the result of trying out their car engines in their garages. They are suffocated by the lack of unused oxygen.

"A fire is supposed to ventilate a room by using up the air

in it and causing fresh air to come in and take the place of what has gone. This is true, so long as the fire has a chimney to carry away the carbon dioxide resulting from combustion. A fire or stove without a chimney, however, just takes the life out of the air. Oil stoves are not very healthy for this reason, nor are gas rings. You need to have a window open if you use these

STOVE WITH CHIMNEY.
RESULT: EVERYONE COMFORTABLE
AND HAPPY

STOVE WITHOUT CHIMNEY.
RESULT: EVERYONE VERY ILL FOR
WANT OF AIR

things. Electric fires and hot-water radiators do not use up oxygen, but they can be unhealthy too because, if they do not keep the room very warm, people are apt to keep the windows shut, and then they themselves quickly cause the air to become stuffy with carbon dioxide. The best way of warming a room is to use a fire with a chimney. This ventilates the room even if the windows and doors are shut. Enough air gets in through chinks, as you can easily feel by the draughts coming under the door and through the floorboards."

"What are the best ways of putting out a fire if it is dangerous?" Mary asked.

"There are two ways," Father answered. "One way is to use up all the heat it makes faster than more can be produced. You do that by squirting water on it. The heat is used to turn the water into steam, and if you put on enough water you will give the fire too much to do, so that it will go out. The other way of putting out a fire is to prevent air from reaching it. You can put out a fire in the chimney by stuffing an old blanket or sack up the chimney opening. You can prevent any fire from becoming really fierce if you can shut doors, windows or dampers that let in the air it wants.

"You can get chemical fire extinguishers that are used to put a special liquid on fires. This liquid turns into carbon dioxide when it is heated, and so the space round the fire becomes filled with this gas, which, as I told you just now, will not keep a fire going. It is a heavy gas, which settles down like a blanket over the spot where it is made, just smothering the fire that formed it."

"A fire is the better for being blown," Peter said; "yet how can this be if we only breathe out carbon dioxide and air that has been robbed of its oxygen?"

"Our breathing does not take all the oxygen out of the air," Father answered. "We normally breathe in more air than we really need to use; the fire gets the benefit of what is left over. As a matter of fact, it is usual to supply even an engine with more air than it really wants. An engine might manage on twelve tons of air an hour, but it is usually allowed to take fifteen tons or more, just to make certain that all the fuel is properly burnt.

" Fuel that is not properly burnt turns into black smoke and also a highly poisonous and highly dangerous gas called carbon monoxide. This is particularly dangerous, because you cannot see it or smell it. It just makes you feel drowsy and silly, and it can send you to sleep, so that you never wake up. There is some of this gas in the exhaust of many a motor-car, which is another reason why engines should not be run indoors without a long pipe to lead out the exhaust gases. There is plenty of carbon monoxide in the coal gas supplied to our homes, and that is why gas leaks are bad. Fortunately, the other ingredients in coal gas have a strong smell, so that you are not likely to have a gas leak without noticing it."

"What is an explosion, Daddy? " Mary asked.

" An explosion is when something burns very quickly, that is all," Father answered. " If you mix gas and air in exactly the right proportions, and then strike a light, or make a spark, you will get a terrific explosion. You shouldn't look for gas leaks with a match!

"Gunpowder, and other so-called explosives, will give you the same result as a mixture of gas and air, but they do not need any air. The oxygen needed by the explosives used in warfare is contained in the explosive itself. That is why it can be used in a confined space, or under water. You may not know it, but the heat energy contained in a pound of harmless coal is far greater than that in a pound of T.N.T. or nitro-glycerine or any other dangerous explosive, the reason being that the coal is all combustible fuel, whereas the explosive is fuel only in part, the rest being oxygen. If coal could be made to release all its energy in a split second, it too would be dangerous and destructive. As a matter of fact, if it is powdered or ' pulverised,' coal can

be mixed with air and exploded just like gas. Even ordinary baking flour, or dust from a room, can be exploded if blown up in a cloud with the right amount of air.

" The destructive effect of an explosion is caused by the action of great heat on the gases resulting from combustion. Heat expands things, forcing them to become far bigger than their normal size. If the air in a house is suddenly made ten or more times bigger than its normal volume (and that is what an explosion does to it) it will push down the walls and lift up the roof. But the expansive effect of heat is another story, and I will tell you about it some other time."

CHAPTER TWO

THE EXPANSION OF AIR BY HEAT

FATHER kept a glass tumbler in the bathroom with which to
"hone" or sharpen the blade of his safety razor when this
became blunt. He would fill the tumbler with hot water and

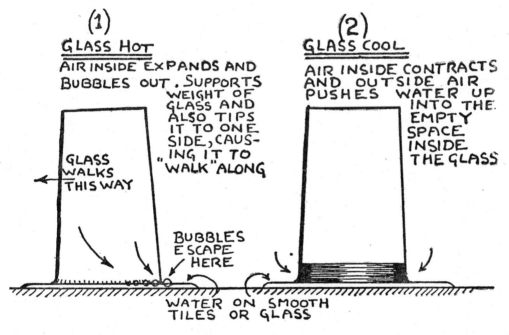

(1)

GLASS HOT

AIR INSIDE EXPANDS AND
BUBBLES OUT. SUPPORTS
WEIGHT OF
GLASS AND
ALSO TIPS
IT TO ONE
SIDE, CAUS-
ING IT TO
"WALK" ALONG

GLASS
WALKS
THIS WAY

BUBBLES
ESCAPE
HERE

(2)

GLASS COOL

AIR INSIDE CONTRACTS
AND OUTSIDE AIR
PUSHES WATER UP
INTO THE
EMPTY
SPACE
INSIDE
THE GLASS

WATER ON SMOOTH
TILES OR GLASS

HOW HEAT AFFECTS AIR
(EXPERIMENT WITH TUMBLER)

then rub the blade to and fro on the inside surface of the glass
underneath the hot water. One morning, after he had finished
using the glass, he noticed a funny thing happening, so he
called the two children to see it.

" There," he said, " I have just emptied hot water out of that tumbler and put it upside down on those shiny white tiles. Now look at it! "

The tumbler, which had drained out some water, was making a bubbling sound and slowly " walking " along.

Mary and Peter looked mystified.

" The explanation is quite simple," said Father. " The air imprisoned in that tumbler has become heated because the glass was hot after having hot water in it. When air is heated it expands, and consequently the air in that tumbler is now trying to make more room for itself and get out. This it is doing by lifting the glass up off the tiles. When it lifts, air is able to bubble out through the wetness on the tiles, but, of course, the tumbler is not any longer resting firmly on the tiles; it is practically floating and free to move anywhere at the least impulse. It is tipping over a little on one side to let the bubbles of air escape, and so it goes sliding along in tiny steps. Each time a bubble lifts it on the right it skids a little more to the left, and altogether it skids quite a long way.

" Now the bubbling and skidding have stopped. The air in the glass is about to cool down and shrink. Air will try to pass back into the glass again, and to do that it will have to bubble inwards, pushing the wetness inwards too. I will hurry it up by squeezing a cold wet flannel over the tumbler."

As Father spoke he let cold water trickle on to the upstanding bottom of the glass and down the sides. In this way he kept the tiles wet round the rim of the tumbler. As the air shrank inside the glass, water leaked in under the rim to fill up the emptiness until, at last, it filled the tumbler up to a level of nearly half an inch above the tiles.

" There are many other experiments you can do to show that heat makes air expand," went on Father, " but they are not so amusing as this easy one you have just seen. "

" How much does it expand, Daddy? " Mary asked.

" It all depends on how hot you make it," Father answered;

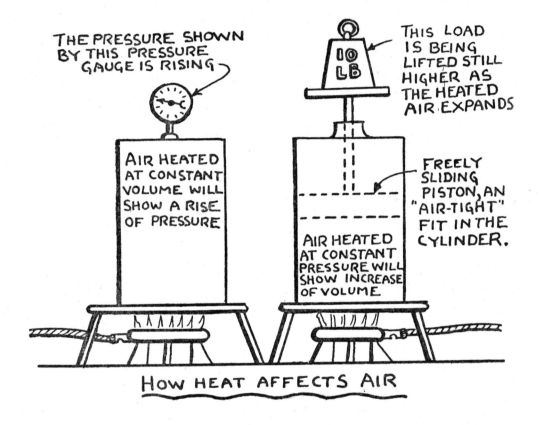

THE PRESSURE SHOWN BY THIS PRESSURE GAUGE IS RISING

THIS LOAD IS BEING LIFTED STILL HIGHER AS THE HEATED AIR EXPANDS

AIR HEATED AT CONSTANT VOLUME WILL SHOW A RISE OF PRESSURE

FREELY SLIDING PISTON, AN "AIR-TIGHT" FIT IN THE CYLINDER.

AIR HEATED AT CONSTANT PRESSURE WILL SHOW INCREASE OF VOLUME.

HOW HEAT AFFECTS AIR

" but supposing you started with three cubic feet of air that was freezing cold, and then made it as hot as boiling water, you would find that its volume had grown to more than four cubic feet. If you were to imprison the air so that it could not grow in volume, but had to stay in a space that remained three cubic feet, then its pressure would increase. If it were at the pressure of the atmosphere (15 pounds to the square inch) when you shut it up at freezing-point, then at boiling-point it would have a pressure about a third greater. What would that be, Peter? "

" Oh," exclaimed Peter, taken by surprise; " a third greater, let me see. A third of fifteen is five and five added to fifteen is twenty. The pressure would increase to twenty pounds on the square inch; is that right? "

" That is quite correct, Peter," Father answered; " you understand now how a motor-car engine works. This has a piston in a cylinder which draws in air and squeezes it up into a small space so that its pressure is made greater. In the air there is a little petrol vapour, and this is set on fire by an electric spark at the right moment. The heat which is developed makes the pressure of the air increase a great deal, and consequently the air is able to drive the piston down with great force. In a petrol engine the air is compressed first of all to a pressure of about ninety pounds to the square inch, but after the petrol has been burnt, the pressure is five hundred or more pounds to the square inch. The burning is so rapid that people call it an explosion, and petrol engines used to be called explosion engines.

" In some engines the air is squeezed up so small by the piston that its pressure reaches five hundred pounds to the square inch before any fuel is burnt in it. The squeezing makes it very hot, and if there were any petrol or other oil mixed in with it, this would catch fire before the squeezing was complete. In these engines therefore the fuel oil is not mixed with the air at the beginning, but squirted into the air after this has been squeezed up or compressed. It catches fire as it goes in, the heat in the cylinder already being enough to ignite it. These engines in which the heat of compression is used to ignite the fuel are called compression-ignition engines. They burn a coarser and cheaper kind of oil than petrol, and they use it very economically, so that many buses and lorries nowadays are fitted with compression-ignition engines. Sometimes these engines are called Diesel engines, because one of the first of the kind was built by a German inventor of that name. Yet another name for them is 'oil engines' or 'heavy-oil

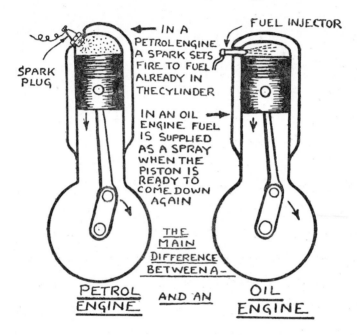

FUEL INJECTOR

SPARK PLUG

IN A PETROL ENGINE A SPARK SETS FIRE TO FUEL ALREADY IN THE CYLINDER

IN AN OIL ENGINE FUEL IS SUPPLIED AS A SPRAY WHEN THE PISTON IS READY TO COME DOWN AGAIN

THE MAIN DIFFERENCE BETWEEN A -

PETROL ENGINE   AND AN   OIL ENGINE

engines,' the term heavy-oil being used to distinguish Diesel fuel from petrol, which evaporates very easily and is therefore spoken of as a 'light' fuel.

"Well, all that I have said has to do with the effect of heat on air. Heat makes air bigger in volume or else greater in pressure, and the easiest way for you to prove this is to do the tumbler experiment I have just shown you. Now I must hurry up and have my shave or I shall be late for work."

NOTE.—In Vol. II on page 373 you will find a more complete description of the motor-car engine.

CHAPTER THREE

TEMPERATURE AND THERMOMETERS

FROM the last story you learnt that heat has the effect of expanding air. The hotter you make the air the greater the space it tries to occupy. Liquids expand with heat too, but not so much. You can measure the "hotness" of anything by the extent to which it causes air or some liquid to expand. The degree of "hotness" of anything is called its "temperature," and instruments for measuring temperature are called "thermometers."

Most thermometers show variations in temperature by the varying volume of a small quantity of liquid in a glass tube. Liquids are better thermometric substances than gases, because they expand more forcibly than gases. You can prevent air from expanding quite easily by enclosing it in a space that cannot alter. The effect of heat will then be only to make its pressure rise. If you try to confine a liquid you will need an immensely strong container for it, as it will easily burst anything of ordinary strength, such as a glass jar or bottle. This means that the volume of the liquid is a good measure of its temperature, regardless of the pressure acting on it. If you used air for a thermometric substance, you would have to be sure that you were keeping it always at the same pressure, and this would not be easy because, as you already know, even the pressure of the atmosphere varies from day to day. With a liquid these small

226

pressure variations do not matter in the least. A further advantage of liquids is that they are visible and can give their own indications. A gas would have to be used with some movable index or pointer, as you cannot see the gas itself.

THE MERCURY THERMOMETER

The commonest kind of thermometer is a glass tube containing mercury or quicksilver. The tube has a very tiny bore, so that you could only just pass a hair down it. The glass is thick, however, and this acts as a magnifier, so that the bore looks quite big. At one end of the tube a bulb is made. This holds quite a lot of mercury. A large quantity of mercury expands with heat more than a small quantity, and that is why a fairly big bulb is used. The only way the mercury can find more room for itself when it expands is by running up the glass tube. Because the bore is so tiny it has to run far in order to find enough extra space.

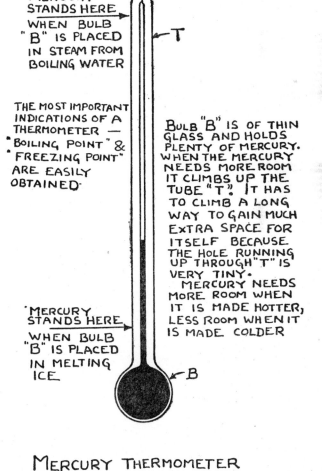

MERCURY STANDS HERE WHEN BULB "B" IS PLACED IN STEAM FROM BOILING WATER

T

THE MOST IMPORTANT INDICATIONS OF A THERMOMETER — "BOILING POINT" & "FREEZING POINT" ARE EASILY OBTAINED.

BULB "B" IS OF THIN GLASS AND HOLDS PLENTY OF MERCURY. WHEN THE MERCURY NEEDS MORE ROOM IT CLIMBS UP THE TUBE "T". IT HAS TO CLIMB A LONG WAY TO GAIN MUCH EXTRA SPACE FOR ITSELF BECAUSE THE HOLE RUNNING UP THROUGH "T" IS VERY TINY. MERCURY NEEDS MORE ROOM WHEN IT IS MADE HOTTER, LESS ROOM WHEN IT IS MADE COLDER

MERCURY STANDS HERE WHEN BULB "B" IS PLACED IN MELTING ICE

B

MERCURY THERMOMETER

Good thermometers have very long tubes, and they will show very small changes of temperature by quite big movements of the mercury column. An instrument which behaves in this way, giving a clear indication of some very small alteration in the quantity being measured, is said to be " sensitive."

When you have your mercury in its glass tube, you have a sensitive appliance for measuring variations of temperature, but it will not be of much use to you unless you fasten it to a board which has been marked so that you can gauge whether the column is moving much or little. The most important marks are those showing the positions of the mercury column when the bulb is put in wet snow or ice, and when it is put in boiling water. The first point is called " freezing-point " and the second is called " boiling-point." In most English thermometers the figure 32 is put against the freezing-point and 212 is put against the boiling-point. In between there are 180 equal divisions, each counting as one degree of temperature rise. This thermometric scale is called the Fahrenheit scale, after the name of the man who first used it. According to this scale, water freezes at 32 degrees Fahrenheit (32° F.) and boils at 212 degrees Fahrenheit (212° F.). The temperature of an ordinary sitting-room varies between 50° F. and 75° F., the most comfortable temperature being from 60 to 65° F. Fahrenheit was able to obtain temperatures lower than freezing-point, and his experiments led him to believe that the lowest obtainable temperature was 32 of his degrees below freezing. That is why he started his scale at 32 and not at 0. Actually, the lowest obtainable temperature is nearly 500 degrees Fahrenheit below freezing, but nobody has troubled to alter the Fahrenheit scale, and this continues to be the one in commonest use.

A more convenient scale is the " Centigrade " scale, much used in European countries. According to this scale, freezing-point is marked zero or 0, and boiling-point is marked 100. Between these two points there are 100 equal divisions each counting as one degree of temperature rise, the degree now being the Centigrade degree and not the Fahrenheit degree.

Some thermometers (the one shown on Mary's barometer, for instance, see page 286) have both scales marked on them. You can then compare them easily. But in any case it is easy to go from one measurement of temperature to the other. Suppose, for instance, the temperature of a room is 59° F. and you want to find out how much it is in degrees Centigrade. First of all you subtract 32 from 59, obtaining 27. This tells you that your room is 27° F. above freezing-point. Now 180° F. are equivalent to 100° C., the difference being that between freezing and boiling in each instance. This means that 18° F. are the same as 10° C. or 9° F. the same as 5° C. To find out what 27° F. measures in degrees Centigrade, all we have to ask ourselves is how many 9's the number 27 contains, and then multiply the answer by 5. Well, 9 is contained by 27 three times, and three multiplied by five is fifteen, so there is your final result:

$$59° \text{ F.} = 15° \text{ C.}$$

The rule for converting from degrees F. to degrees C. is as follows: *Subtract 32 and multiply the remainder by 5/9.*

To change a temperature measured in degrees Centigrade to one measured in degrees Fahrenheit, you work the other way. Suppose your temperature is 30° C. What is this in degrees Fahrenheit? Well, 100° C. are the same as 180° F., so that 10° C. are the same as 18° F., or 5° C. the same as 9° F. To

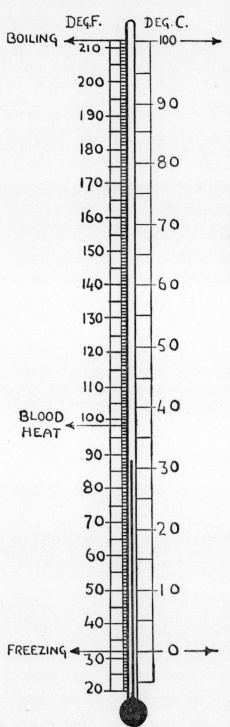

convert 30° C. to degrees F., we must find out how many times 30 contains 5, and multiply the answer by 9. You can easily do this in your head, for 30 divided by 5 is 6, and $6 \times 9 = 54$. Thus 30° C. is 54° F. above freezing-point. Freezing-point on the Fahrenheit scale is 32, and so we must now add on 32, obtaining $54 + 32 = 86$. Finally, then, we have: $30° \text{ C.} = 86° \text{ F.}$

The rule for converting from degrees C. to degrees F. is as follows: *Multiply by 9/5 and add 32.*

The scales are compared for you on Mary's barometer, but the drawing is too small for you to see properly, and so I have prepared a larger one, which you will find on this page.

OTHER THERMOMETERS

You can often see thermometers containing a red liquid instead of the familiar silver one. This red liquid is coloured alcohol. An advantage is that it is easier to see from a distance.

A drawback is that it does not become hot so quickly as mercury. Mercury is a metal, and heat passes to the inside of the bulb more quickly when this is full of mercury than when it is full of alcohol, mercury being what is called a good conductor of heat and alcohol a poor one.

Sometimes it is desirable to have a dial and pointer to tell you what the temperature is. You can read a dial from afar, just as you can a clock, and this is useful. Dial thermometers work in much the same way as an aneroid barometer (see page 294); but the capsule, instead of being empty, is full of the thermometric liquid. Barometric pressure variations no longer affect it, but the swelling or shrinking of the liquid inside makes a difference to the position of the top disc on which the little knob rests.

When you want your dial to be a long way from the place where the temperature is taken, you can use a very big bulb connected to a Bourdon pressure gauge (see page 319) by a long pipe.

Thermometers for measuring very high temperatures depend on the fact that electricity is generated when you heat a joint made between two dissimilar metals. This very tiny amount of electricity is used to work a sensitive dial instrument graduated in degrees C. or F. Thermometers for measuring high temperatures, as in a furnace, for instance, are called " Pyrometers."

WHEN THE DOCTOR COMES

When people are in good health their bodies are always at the same temperature—about 98½° F.—and this is often marked " Blood Heat " on thermometers. When they are ill their temperature generally becomes higher, often more than 100° F. A high temperature is such a sure sign of illness that doctors always carry a pocket thermometer with them, and the first thing they do when they come to see you is pop this thermo-

THE DOCTOR'S
THERMOMETER

meter in your mouth to find out how hot you are inside. The doctor's thermometer is called a clinical thermometer, and it is specially made so that once the mercury has gone up the tube it will not come down again unless the thermometer is vigorously shaken. The doctor or nurse has plenty of time in which to read a clinical thermometer because of this convenient habit the mercury has of sticking.

CHAPTER FOUR

WHAT A THERMOMETER TELLS US

MARY and Peter had had their Uncle George staying with them for a whole week. When he went away he gave them two half-crowns each.

"What will you spend yours on?" Peter asked Mary.

"I don't know," answered Mary; "what will you do with yours?"

The heat needed to increase the temperature of anything by 10, 20, 30 or more degrees is 10, 20, 30 or more times as much as the heat needed to increase its temperature by 1 degree

It follows that

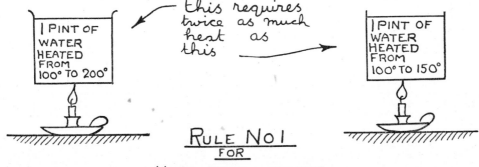

this requires twice as much heat as this

| 1 PINT OF WATER HEATED FROM 100° TO 200° |

| 1 PINT OF WATER HEATED FROM 100° TO 150° |

RULE No 1
FOR
HEAT CALCULATIONS

Peter shrugged his shoulders and made a face, for he did not know what he was going to buy either. In the end both children decided to spend Saturday morning in town, just looking into shop windows for ideas.

Mary soon spent her five shillings on books, but Peter was still undecided about what to buy; then Mary noticed that the Town Hall clock showed dinner-time. "You will have to come home without buying anything," she said; "we can come again another day."

"No," Peter argued, "I must buy something to-day. I am going back to the ironmonger's shop to buy a thermometer. I saw some for five shillings each when we were there a little while ago, and I haven't seen anything I like better."

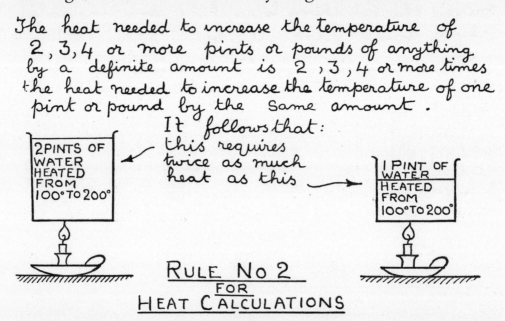

The heat needed to increase the temperature of 2, 3, 4 or more pints or pounds of anything by a definite amount is 2, 3, 4 or more times the heat needed to increase the temperature of one pint or pound by the same amount.
It follows that:
this requires twice as much heat as this

2 PINTS OF WATER HEATED FROM 100° TO 200°

1 PINT OF WATER HEATED FROM 100° TO 200°

RULE No 2
FOR
HEAT CALCULATIONS

"Well, hurry up, then," grumbled Mary; "I will go to the bus stop and wait for you there."

Peter ran off to buy his thermometer, and then he rejoined Mary. A few minutes later they were on their way home in the bus.

Mother could not understand what Peter wanted with a thermometer. "You have wasted your money," she said.

Father disagreed, however, and he promised to show the

children a few experiments that could be done with the aid of a thermometer. "You can keep track of heat with a thermometer," he said; "for although heat is invisible, a thermometer almost helps you to see it."

"What do you mean by that?" Peter asked.

"Well," said Father, "do you know what happens when you mix hot and cold water together on bath night?"

When things at different temperatures are mixed the hot thing loses heat and the cold thing gains heat, the gain of the one being exactly equal to the loss of the other.

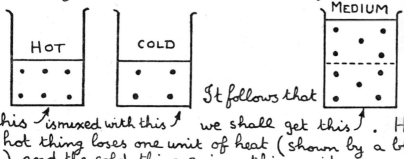

if this ↗ is mixed with this ↗ we shall get this ↗. Here the hot thing loses one unit of heat (shown by a black dot) and the cold thing gains this unit.

RULE No 3
FOR
HEAT CALCULATIONS

Peter shook his head. "I've never thought about it," he said.

"I can tell you what happens," went on Father, "and your thermometer will show you that I am right. Some of the heat in the hot water passes into the cold water, so that all the water may share the heat equally. Of course, the mixture is neither so hot as the hot water was before, nor so cold as the cold water was before. Come, we will try an experiment."

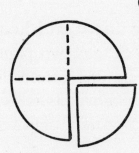

Could you divide a cake
so that Mary had 3 times as
much as Peter?
To do this, you must cut
it into 4 parts, giving
Mary 3 and Peter 1

Could you divide half-a-crown so that
Peter had twice as much as Mary?
To do this you must
cut it into 3 parts of 10^d
each, giving Mary one of
them and Peter $2 \times 10^d = 1s\ 8^d$

RULE FOR DIVIDING THINGS
You can see now
that when anything is to be divided it
must be cut up into the total number
of parts wanted. If somebody is to get
5 times as much as someone else, the total
number of parts wanted = 5 + 1 = 6.

ANOTHER EXAMPLE
Could you find
a temperature between 100° and
200° so that its difference below
200° is 3 times its excess
above 100°? To do this you
must divide 200 - 100 by 4,
which gives 25. The temperature you
want to find is 125°.

WATER MIXING

If one pint of water at 200°
is mixed with 3 pints at 100°
what will be the final temperature?
Dividing 200° - 100° by 4 gives us 25°.
The pint of hot gives up $3 \times 25 = 75°$,
so that each of the 3 pints of cold can
gain 25°. Thus, the temperature of
the mixture will be 125°.

236

Father put a pint of water in a saucepan and started heating it on the gas-ring in the kitchen. Then he put two pints of water in another and much larger saucepan, and placed it on one side. "Take the temperature of the two pints of water in this large saucepan," he said to Peter; "but wait until I give you the word."

When the water in the small saucepan was getting really

| 1 PINT AT 100° | mixed with | 1 PINT AT 200° | makes | 2 PINTS AT 150° |

EXPLANATION Hot and cold water being equal in amount the temperature fall of the hot (50°) equals the temperature rise of the cold (50°)

| 1 PINT AT 180° | mixed with | 2 PINTS AT 90° | makes | 3 PINTS AT 120° |

EXPLANATION The hot water being half the cold in amount, its temperature fall (60°) is twice the temperature rise of the cold (30°)

| 2 PINTS AT 200° | mixed with | 1 PINT AT 110° | makes | 3 PINTS AT 170° |

EXPLANATION. The hot water being twice the cold in amount, its temperature fall (30°) is half the temperature rise of the cold (60°)

When hot and cold liquids are mixed, the temperature of the mixture comes between the original hot and cold temperatures, and can easily be calculated in such simple examples as those given above. The example Father worked out for Mary and Peter was only a little more difficult.

hot, Father told Peter to make a note of the temperature of the cold water in the large saucepan.

"Fifty-five degrees Fahrenheit," said Peter.

Father then took the saucepan off the gas-ring and told Peter to make a note of the temperature of the heated water inside.

"A hundred and eighty degrees Fahrenheit," said Peter.

Father quickly tipped the pint of hot water into the two pints of cold water and stirred them together with a long pencil from his pocket. " Take the temperature of the mixture," he said, " quickly! "

Peter was about to tell Father the temperature of the mixture, but Father held up his hand. " Stop! " he said, " I will work out what the temperature ought to be, and then you can tell me if I am right. Listen!

" The pint of hot water has given some of its heat to the cold water, and so it has fallen in temperature by some

A substance needing only one tenth of the heat that water needs in order to change its temperature from one figure to another is said to have a "Specific Heat" of one tenth.

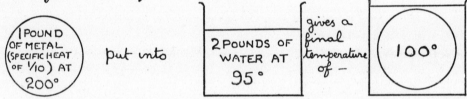

EXPLANATION One pound of metal (specific Heat ¹⁄₁₀) being equivalent to only a twentieth of 2 pounds of water, its temperature fall (100°) is 20 times the temperature rise of the water (5°).

unknown number of degrees—say x degrees. The cold water has gained the heat lost by the hot water, so that it has risen in temperature; and because there was twice as much cold water as hot, the rise in temperature of the cold water must be only half as much as the fall in temperature of the hot. Therefore the cold water has risen in temperature by $\frac{1}{2} x$ degrees. However, the final temperature of the cold water is equal to the final temperature of the hot water."

Here Father paused to take an old envelope out of his

pocket. "I will write down the final temperature of the hot water," he said. "It is 180 degrees less x degrees," and he wrote:

$$180 - x.$$

"Now I will write down the final temperature of the cold water," he went on, and he wrote:

$$55 + \tfrac{1}{2}x.$$

"These two temperatures must be equal," Father explained, so he wrote:

$$180 - x = 55 + \tfrac{1}{2}x.$$

"The puzzle is to find how much x is," he said. "What number, taken from 180, leaves a remainder equal to 55 and half that number?"

Mary scratched her head and frowned; so did Peter.

"Any ideas on how to do the puzzle?" Father asked.

Both children shook their heads.

"It is an easy one really," Father said; "but to do puzzles of this kind you need to remember certain rules. If you have two things that are equal, you can always add equal amounts to both or take equal amounts from both without affecting their equality. If, for instance, you and Mary each had ten cakes and then Mother gave you both five cakes more, you would both still have the same number of cakes. And if someone then robbed you both of seven cakes each, you would both still have eight cakes each. Very well, then, I am going to do some adding and subtracting so as to make my puzzle look easier. First of all I am going to add x degrees to both temperatures, like this":

$$180 - x \qquad\qquad 55 + \tfrac{1}{2}x$$
$$\underline{x} \qquad\qquad \underline{x}$$
$$180 \qquad\qquad 55 + 1\tfrac{1}{2}x$$

"Oh, what a wangle!" exclaimed Peter. "Why do you get only one hundred and eighty on the left-hand side?"

"The left-hand side said one hundred and eighty less x to begin with," explained Father; "if, besides taking away x from 180 I add x to 180, it comes to the same thing as leaving 180 alone, does it not? That is why I finish up with only 180 on the left. On the right I have to add $\tfrac{1}{2}x$ to 55 and then another x as well, so I finish up with $55 + 1\tfrac{1}{2}x$. But I have added the same thing, namely, x, to amounts that were equal before; consequently the amended amounts are also equal and therefore I can write:

$$180 = 55 + 1\tfrac{1}{2}x.$$

Does this make the puzzle any easier?"

"No," exclaimed both children together, "we still cannot see what x is."

"Very well, then," said Father; "I must simplify it some more. I will now take 55 from both sides like this:

$$180 \qquad\qquad 55 + 1\tfrac{1}{2}x$$
$$\underline{55} \qquad\qquad \underline{55}$$
$$125 \qquad\qquad 1\tfrac{1}{2}x$$

and because I have taken the same quantity from two amounts that were equal before, I have equal remainders. Consequently, I can write:

$$125 = 1\tfrac{1}{2}x.$$

Now can you see the answer?"

"No," said Peter, "I can't."

Mary looked thoughtful, but eventually she shook her head.

"I will make it easier for you by doubling both sides," said Father; and he wrote:

$$\begin{array}{ccc} 125 & & 1\frac{1}{2}\,x \\ \times\,2 & & \times\,2 \\ \hline 250 & = & 3\,x \end{array}$$

"Now," he concluded, "I will divide both sides by three, and this will give us x." So saying he wrote:

$$250 \div 3 = 3\,x \div 3$$

$$\text{or } 83\tfrac{1}{3} = x$$

"The puzzle is solved," said Father; "x is $83\frac{1}{3}$ degrees. Now I must find out the temperature of the mixed hot and cold water. The hot water lost $83\frac{1}{3}$ degrees of temperature, and the cold water gained half the same. The final temperature of the hot water was:

$$\begin{array}{r} 180 \\ -\ 83\frac{1}{3} \\ \hline 96\frac{2}{3} \end{array}$$

and the final temperature of the cold water was 55 plus half of $83\frac{1}{3}$:

$$\begin{array}{r} 55 \\ +\,41\frac{2}{3} \\ \hline 96\frac{2}{3} \end{array}$$

—both the same, you see, just as I said.

"Now, then, Peter's thermometer should have given $96\frac{2}{3}$ degrees Fahrenheit as the temperature of the mixture, but the experiment was not quite so simple as I have made it appear here. When the hot water went into the cold water it heated up the cold water, but it also heated up the cold saucepan and the pencil I used to stir hot and cold water together. I should think that Peter's thermometer gave ninety degrees Fahrenheit as the temperature of the mixture."

"It gave ninety-one degrees," grinned Peter, "so you are one degree wrong."

"Not a bad guess!" said Father.

Mary was frowning horribly, so Father asked her what was wrong.

"That puzzle you did to find x," she said; "it wouldn't be called algebra by any chance, would it?"

Father looked guilty. "Some people give the solving of jolly puzzles that name," he admitted.

"Oh!" gasped Mary, grabbing up the empty saucepan that had held the hot water; "run for your life. I *hate* algebra!"

Father dashed out of the kitchen in great haste, chased by Mary, who threatened to hit him with the saucepan. "You deceiver!" Mary cried; "you artful old humbug; making us do algebra on a Saturday afternoon and calling it 'jolly puzzles.' Oh!!!"

LATER

"Am I forgiven now, Mary?" Father said very meekly at tea-time; "will you let me do another experiment for you with Peter's thermometer?"

"Do you want us to solve another algebraic equation?" Mary asked.

"As you please," Father answered; "I thought I would show you that, pound for pound, there is much more heat in water than in anything else raised to the same temperature—in a lump of iron, for instance.

"A pint of water weighs a pound and a quarter, and you saw that when heated to 180 degrees it was able to raise the temperature of two pints of cold water from 55 degrees to $96\frac{2}{3}$ degrees, in theory at least. If I had used a pound and a quarter of iron heated to the same temperature of 180 degrees, it would not have heated up the cold water nearly so much. It would have lost many more degrees of temperature itself in order to give the cold water only a few degrees of temperature rise."

"Let us try it," said Mary.

Father tied up the pound weight of Mother's kitchen scales, together with the four-ounce weight, in a small piece of rag, and then he put them in a saucepan of water so that they could be heated up to 180 degrees.

"I put them in this rag so that they can be quickly lifted out together and be popped into the cold water," he said.

"Shall I get the two pints of cold water ready?" Peter asked.

"Yes, do," answered Father; "two pints at 55 degrees is what we want."

Peter measured out two pints of cold water and took the temperature. "It is only 54 degrees this time," he said.

"Never mind," said Father, "we cannot have everything our own way in this world. The sun has gone down, so I suppose our cold-water pipe is a bit cooler than it was after dinner."

Peter put his thermometer in the water on the gas-ring. "Your iron is up to 120 degrees now, Father," he said.

"Watch it, then," said Father, "and pick out the weights when the thermometer says 180 degrees. Pop them as quickly as you can out of one saucepan into the other."

A few minutes later, Peter carried out the important experiment of putting $1\frac{1}{4}$ pounds of iron at 180 degrees Fahrenheit into two pints of water at 54 degrees Fahrenheit. He moved the weights round in the water, holding on to a corner of the rag for this purpose, and he watched his thermometer which he held in the cold water with his other hand. The mercury kept on rising, but at last it reached 60 degrees and stayed there.

"A rise of only six degrees!" exclaimed Peter; "we had a rise of more than six times that amount when we used hot water instead of hot iron."

"Yes," said Father, "it is what I expected; the iron weighing $1\frac{1}{4}$ pounds has lost 120 degrees of temperature in heating up double its own weight of water by only six degrees. Although it was as hot as the pint of hot water we used before, it had not nearly so much heat to give up in the process of cooling down. All the metals are like iron in this; they show a thermal capacity greatly inferior to that of water. When they cool down you get from them only a fraction of the heat you would get from an equal amount of water cooling by the same number of degrees. That fraction is called the 'Specific Heat' of the material in question. If anything has a Specific Heat of, say, one-half, it means that you get only half the heat from it that you would from water."

"If you get less heat from it when it is cooling, does that

mean you can make it hot with less heat when you are warming it?" asked Peter.

"Certainly," answered Father; "you put less heat in and therefore you get less heat out."

"Can we work out the Specific Heat of iron from our experiment?" asked Mary.

"Yes," answered Father, "if you don't mind a bit more algebra."

"You have our permission to do a little algebra," said Mary; "hasn't he, Peter?"

Peter nodded assent, and so Father said, "Very well, I will call the Specific Heat of our iron S. By that I mean that one pound of iron counts as S pounds of water, where actually I expect S to be quite a small fraction of a pound. Now, then, our iron cooled from 180 degrees to 60 degrees, that is, 120 degrees, and it counted as $1\frac{1}{4}$ S pounds of water doing the same thing. You could say that it gave up to $1\frac{1}{4}$ S units of heat for each degree fall of temperature, or $120 \times 1\frac{1}{4}$ S units altogether. The cold water weighing $2\frac{1}{2}$ pounds gained $2\frac{1}{2}$ units of heat for each degree rise of temperature, or $6 \times 2\frac{1}{2}$ units altogether, its temperature rise being from 54 degrees to 60 degrees. Since the heat lost on the one hand was equal to the heat gained on the other, we have:

$$120 \times 1\frac{1}{4}\, S = 6 \times 2\frac{1}{2}.$$

There is your puzzle for you—a simple algebraic equation to find S. Can you do it?"

Mary looked at the figures and then at her father. "Shall I do the multiplications?" she asked.

"Need you?" countered Father; "if you can divide both sides by the same figure I should do it, because then you get rid of figures and save work. I can see that both sides can be divided by six, leaving you with:

$$20 \times 1\tfrac{1}{4} \, S = 2\tfrac{1}{2}.$$

Then again, $2\tfrac{1}{2}$ is twice $1\tfrac{1}{4}$, so both sides can be divided by $1\tfrac{1}{4}$, leaving you with:

$$20 \, S = 2.$$

Lastly, both sides can be divided by two, leaving you with:

$$10 \, S = 1;$$

which means that $S = \tfrac{1}{10}$.

"Thus our experiment shows that the Specific Heat of iron is a tenth. This is about right, though, if I remember correctly, the real value is a little more."

"Could we find out the real Specific Heats of things from your big encyclopædia?" asked Mary.

"Bright idea!" exclaimed Father; "I hadn't thought of that, but I am sure we can."

Mary and Peter hunted up the volume that went from GOU to HIP and looked up the article on "Heat." They found tables giving the thermal properties of solids and liquids.

"What solids are you interested in, Peter?" asked Mary.

"Iron, copper, glass and a few others," answered Peter.

"Any liquids?" asked Mary.

"Mercury and water," answered Peter.

"Oh, and here are gases," said Mary; "are we interested in any gases?"

"Yes, air," answered Peter.

"I shall make a table, then," said Mary; "I shall copy out the Specific Heats of all the things we are interested in."

Mary took some paper and a pencil, and she started to make out a table.

While she was doing it Father interrupted her to suggest that she should put in the values for the Specific Gravity as well as those for the Specific Heat.

" What is Specific Gravity? " asked Mary.

" A gallon of water weighs ten pounds," answered Father; " and a gallon of petrol weighs eight pounds, so that, compared with water, petrol weighs only eight-tenths as much. Eight-tenths is the Specific Gravity of petrol. It will be written 0·8 in the table."

" What does a gallon of iron weigh? " giggled Peter.

" Iron having the same volume as a gallon of water weighs seventy-five pounds," answered Father in a serious voice; " so iron has a specific gravity of 7·5. Now then, go to it, and complete your table."

Mary ruled another column in her table for the Specific Gravity figures, and then she started to fill in the two columns.

MARY'S TABLE

Substance	Specific Heat	Specific Gravity	Comparative Volumes
Water . .	1·00	1·0	1·000
Iron . .	0·1 1	7·5	0·1 34
Copper. .	0·09	8·9	0·112
Glass . .	0·15	2·6	0·385
Aluminium .	0·22	2·6	0·385
Lead . .	0·03	1 1·4	0·088
Mercury .	0·03	13·6	0·074
Air . .	0·24	0·0013	770·0
Hydrogen .	3·41	0·00009	11750·0

"Just one more thing," Father added; "I suggest that you leave a fourth column for the comparative volumes. Thus, if a given weight of water has a volume of one—one pint, one gallon, one cubic foot or anything else you like—iron of the same weight will have a volume of less than a seventh, because it weighs more than seven times as much as water. The comparative volumes will be the number one divided by the Specific Gravity."

"You can do the divisions," Mary said.

"All right," agreed Father; "and I suggest that we put hydrogen in our table. That is the stuff used to fill balloons. It is much lighter than air, so, for a given weight, it is tremendously bulky. It is really rather an interesting substance."

When the table was done, Mary and Peter gazed at it with interest.

"I would like you to notice that the heavy substances, having little volume for a given weight, are the ones with the lowest Specific Heats," said Father; "lead and mercury, which take up very little space, also absorb very little heat for their weight when their temperature is raised. On the other hand, hydrogen takes up a lot of space and also a lot of heat for its weight. In our great world of water, rocks, minerals and so on, the heat seems to be distributed more nearly according to volume than according to weight, so that in a given amount of space, whether it be filled with one substance or another, the amount of heat for a given temperature tends to be the same— only very roughly, mind. How rough this rule is you can see for yourselves if you will divide the Specific Heats by the Comparative Volumes. For water you get unit heat into unit space. With iron you do not get so much heat into your space, 0·11 being less than 0·134. As a matter of fact this division of 0·11 by 0·134 gives you 0·82. Aluminium is still less effective, the division giving you only 0·57; mercury, which is the heaviest metal, gives you 0·4. Not only by weight, then, but by bulk also water is the leading substance among solids and liquids for storing away a great deal of heat. It is more than twice as good as mercury.

"When space is filled with a gas at ordinary atmospheric pressure, the amount of heat in a given volume is very small. Dividing the figures for air (0·24 ÷ 770) you get 0·00031, or about three parts in ten thousand. You get almost the same when your space is filled with hydrogen, for 3·41 divided by 11,750, comes to 0·00029.

"All this has a great bearing on climate, as you will realise if you compare the heat in ocean, land and air. The land consists of materials, such as stones, earth, rocks, sand and so on, for which the division of specific heat by comparative volume would give you about 0·4, or less than half, showing you that land masses have not so great a store of heat as water masses. The air above both land and sea has a smaller store of heat still —bulk for bulk only about one three-thousandth part as much as the sea. You can get an idea from this why it is that land and sea temperatures affect the temperature of the wind rather than the other way round. And you can understand too why the sea controls the climate of Britain. It is a huge reservoir of heat compared with which our own hills and plains are like a pint pot—soon filled up and as soon emptied."

CHAPTER FIVE

THE EXPANSION OF SOLIDS

"IS there any easy way to show that a piece of metal **expands** when you heat it?" Mary asked her father one afternoon.

"Get three of your steel knitting needles and an ordinary

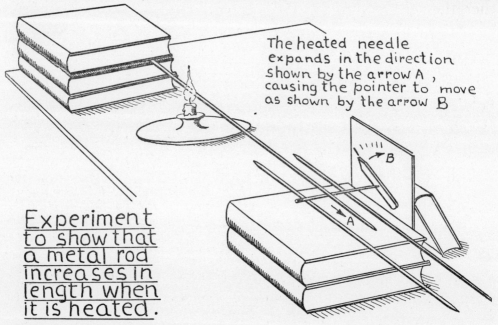

The heated needle expands in the direction shown by the arrow A, causing the pointer to move as shown by the arrow B

Experiment to show that a metal rod increases in length when it is heated.

sewing needle," replied Father, "and I will soon show you that heat causes a knitting needle to become longer."

While Mary was gone, Father took five volumes of the encyclopædia out of the bookcase and laid them on the table. Then he found a piece of white card and some scissors. Finally, he chose a small but fat book from the bookcase and laid that

on the table too. Peter looked mystified by all these preparations, but Father gave him something to do also. "Fetch a
short candle and a box of matches, Peter," he said.

When everything was ready to hand Father laid two encyclopædia volumes on top of one another on his right and two
more on his left. The distance between the two pairs was
about eight inches. Then he put two of Mary's knitting
needles side by side on the right-hand pair of books, with the
ordinary needle running across them. The third knitting
needle he put with one end resting on the sewing needle and
the other end resting on the left-hand pair of books. This end
he clamped down in position by putting the fifth volume of
the encyclopædia on top of it.

"Now," said Father, "if I make the knitting needle hot
between where it is fixed and where it rests on the sewing
needle, it will grow in length, and all its growth will have to
be to the right, because the left-hand end cannot move. Thus
it will roll the sewing needle along. To show you that the
sewing needle really turns, I am going to stick a piece of card
on its pointed end. That will serve as a pointer. Behind the
pointer I am going to stand my big white sheet of card. As it
will not stand by itself, I will put the small flat book behind it.
Now I will make a small mark on the sheet to show where the
pointer points when the needle is cold. Light the candle, Peter."

Peter lit the candle, and Father held it so that the knitting
needle was in the flame. He ran the candle up and down
between the two pairs of encyclopædias, so as to heat as much
as possible of the needle.

"Oh!" exclaimed Mary, "the pointer is moving."

"Yes," replied Father; "it is moving the same way round

as the hands of a clock. That shows us the knitting needle is increasing in length."

As Father continued to heat the needle, the pointer moved more and more, but eventually it seemed that the needle could not be made any hotter, so the pointer stopped. When Father took away the candle the needle started to cool down and the pointer gradually returned to its original position opposite the mark on the sheet.

"It is very important, in an experiment of this kind, to see if things go back to how they were in the beginning," said Father. "If my pointer refused to return, it would show that part of its movement had been caused by the pointer slipping on the sewing needle, or by someone jogging the books. The experiment would have been what scientists call 'inconclusive.' As it is, you see, the pointer has gone back to my mark exactly. It moved away because the knitting needle expanded, and it has gone back because the knitting needle contracted and regained its original length when I took away the candle."

Father repeated the experiment once more, and then left Mary and Peter to try it out as many times as they liked.

"How much does steel expand when heated?" Peter asked Father at last.

"For every degree increase of temperature a rod one mile long would grow nearly half an inch," replied Father; "a big bridge might have its temperature vary between freezing-point (or 32 degrees F.) and 150 degrees F., so that if it were made in one piece a mile long the engineers would have to leave a space at one end for expansion amounting to more than fifty inches. In laying railway lines or building steel bridges, the engineers must always allow for expansion due to varying temperature. If a bridge is fixed at one end, it is made to rest on rollers at the other. Between lengths of railway line a short gap is always left, as you can see for yourselves. The rods for operating railway points from a signal box are often very long, and if there were no way of allowing for thermal expansion, the coming-out or going-in of the sun might work the points and so cause a terrible accident to the trains. In the middle of a long point-operating rod there is a compensating arrangement which is very simple. The rod is divided at this point, and the two ends are pivoted to a lever which itself is pivoted to a fixed support at the centre. Both halves of the rod can grow from the ends towards the middle, and their growth just turns the lever round its pivot by a small amount. When the two halves shrink or contract, the lever goes back. The points can always be operated, whatever the position of the lever, yet variation in the total length of rod does not shift the points in the least."

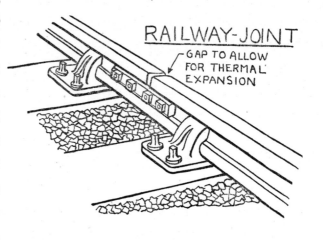

RAILWAY-JOINT

GAP TO ALLOW FOR THERMAL EXPANSION

TEMPERATURE COMPENSATOR FOR POINT-OPERATING ROD ON RAILWAY

Both halves of rod are free to expand as shown by arrows, the far ends remaining fixed in the meantime

"Expansion seems to be an inconvenience in every instance," said Peter.

"Yes," agreed Father; "the expansion of solids is nearly

always inconvenient. You see, a solid is meant to be solid, and when an engineer uses something solid, he wants it to be of constant size, not varying day by day. He can take advantage of expanding fluids, especially of expanding gases, but the expansion of solids and liquids is very small, too small to have any useful practical applications, and therefore, when it occurs, it is just a nuisance."

"Where else is the expansion of solids a nuisance?" asked Mary.

"In a clock or a watch," answered Father. "You see, the time of swing of a pendulum depends on its length, and if this length increases with heat, the clock begins to lose. Every good clock has some way of keeping the pendulum, in effect, of constant length. Advantage is taken of the fact that some materials expand more with heat than others. Aluminium expands about twice as much as steel. In one form of pendulum, called the 'grid-iron pendulum,' you might have the weight or bob supported by downgoing rods of steel and upgoing rods of aluminium, in the manner I am sketching for you now. The long steel rods let the weight down when they expand, but the shorter aluminium rods lift it up again; and if the lengths of steel and aluminium are rightly proportioned, the bob will neither rise nor fall when the temperature changes. The grid-iron pendulum is only one form of temperature-compensated pendulum. In French clocks you may see the pendulum made with a bob in the form of two glass tubes containing mercury. As the steel rod expands and lets down the bob, so the mercury expands and rises up the glass tubes. Thus the effective length of the pendulum remains the same, irrespective of the temperature change."

"A watch does not have a pendulum," said Peter; "it has a little wheel that turns to and fro."

"The effects of a rise in temperature are to make the little wheel bigger and the hairspring weaker," said Father; "both effects cause the little wheel to oscillate more slowly, and this

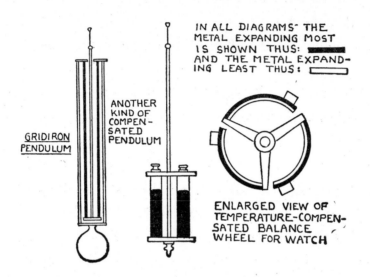

IN ALL DIAGRAMS THE METAL EXPANDING MOST IS SHOWN THUS:
AND THE METAL EXPANDING LEAST THUS:

GRIDIRON PENDULUM

ANOTHER KIND OF COMPEN-SATED PENDULUM

ENLARGED VIEW OF TEMPERATURE-COMPEN-SATED BALANCE WHEEL FOR WATCH

means that the watch loses. To compensate for temperature effects, the best watches have specially-made balance-wheels with rims made of two different metals, say steel inside and brass outside. The rim is cut in three places and it carries little weights near the cuts. Brass expands more than steel, so that when the temperature rises and the spokes of the wheel lengthen, the rim begins to curl inwards, like the cover of a book held too near the fire. The brass grows longer than the steel, and it makes more room for itself by bending the steel. Because this causes the little weights to move inwards, the effective size of the wheel is really smaller at high temperature than at low temperature. In this way you get compensation for the weakening of the hairspring.

"A strip made of two metals fastened face to face is called a 'bimetallic element,' and bimetallic elements have many uses. They can be used to close electric contacts and give an alarm in the event of a fire—or they can start and stop heating appliances in a room that has its temperature controlled automatically. In these applications the bimetallic element forms part of what is called a 'thermostat.'"

"The expansion of solids is not always useless, then," said Mary.

"In this case, no," agreed Father; "use is made of such expansion; but equally good thermostatic devices could be made (and indeed *are* made) to work by the expansion of liquids or gases. On the whole we should be glad if metals did not expand when heated. Scientists have tried to find a metal with no expansion, and there is one alloy of steel and nickel called 'Invar' that has practically no expansion. It is very useful for making parts of clocks, watches and scientific instruments."

CHAPTER SIX

HOW DOES HEAT JOURNEY FROM PLACE TO PLACE?

EVERYONE is familiar with the way in which heat creeps along to the handle of a poker that has been left sticking in the fire. The truth that heat can flow along a metal rod from a

This ice does not begin to melt until long after the water at the top has started to boil

E x P E R I M E N T T O S H O W T H A T
WATER IS A POOR CONDUCTOR OF HEAT

place of high temperature to a place of low temperature is brought home to us in our earliest infancy, when we touch things that, though they look black and cold, are really scalding hot. The process whereby heat flows from place to place through solid material is called "conduction." Metals are called good conductors of heat because if any part of a metal object be warmed, the whole will quickly rise in temperature, and even the part most remote from the source of heat will eventually become affected. Wood is a poor conductor, because we can safely hold one end of a wooden stick even though the other end be on fire.

Heat can flow from place to place by conduction through liquids and gases, though the more usual way for heat to pass from place to place in a fluid substance is by movements or currents in the substance itself. When there is an absence of any movement in a fluid, we generally find that very little heat can be persuaded to pass through it. Water, for example, is a very poor conductor, and air is even worse. A classic experiment to prove that water is a poor conductor is to heat the water at the top of a long inclined flask which has ice in the bottom. Long before the ice melts, the water at the top will be boiling.

The reluctance of heat to pass by conduction through water has some important results in Nature. Thus a cold wind is able to rob the surface layer of a pond of its heat and make the water freeze, but it may be many months before such a wind is able to reduce the rest of the pond to freezing-point. The water near the top is continually being made colder, and as it grows colder it shrinks in volume and becomes heavier in relation to its displacement, so sinking to the bottom and displacing warmer water upwards. The warmer water becomes chilled in its turn, and then that too sinks, sending up some more water to be chilled. Eventually the whole pond may have its temperature lowered to just under 40 degrees Fahrenheit. Water chilled below this temperature does not become more dense, it actually becomes less dense, so that it stays on the surface to become colder and colder, eventually freezing. Having frozen, it is indeed quite a lot lighter than the surrounding water, and this explains why ice floats. Under the ice covering a pond there is water at about 40 degrees Fahrenheit that no longer goes up and down under the action of the chilling wind over the surface. Any heat that is lost by the water at the bottom must now pass by conduction through the water above, and this process is so slow that you will rarely see water frozen into a solid block even in the coldest parts of the world. It is fortunate for the fishes that water stops getting heavier just short of freezing-point (32 degrees Fahrenheit) because if it were not for this useful peculiarity of water, they would find themselves entombed almost any winter in a solid lump of ice and, of course, they would then be killed.

When water is made by a chill wind to give up its heat, the process is fairly slow for another reason. Water contains far more heat, weight for weight, than any other substance at the same temperature (see page 247), and consequently when a cold wind blows over it the victory goes to the water and not to the wind. The chill wind is made warm before the warm water can be made cold. A country like Britain, that is everywhere near the sea, can never be very cold, because the cold winds approaching it are warmed by the ever-warm sea. Only when a wind blows from the East across Siberia does England feel really bitter. That is because the chilly East wind has only a short stretch of sea to cross—the North Sea—and it cannot pick up much heat on its way. A wind from any other quarter either comes across warm southerly places or else over thousands of miles of ocean. The ocean absorbs heat from the sun in

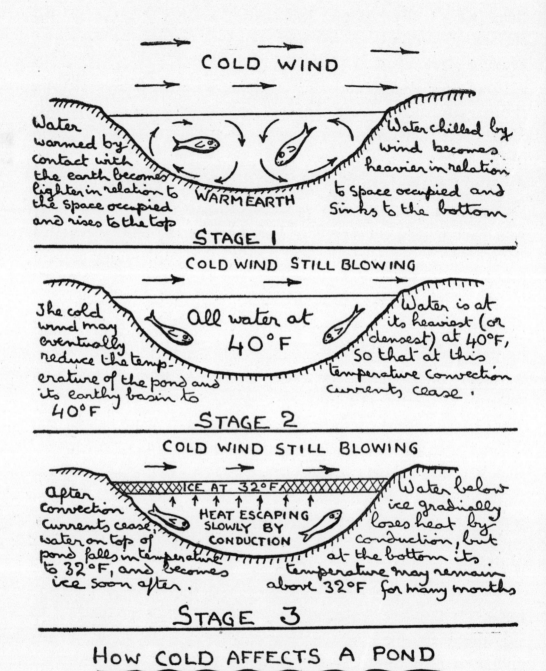

COLD WIND

Water warmed by contact with the earth becomes lighter in relation to the space occupied and rises to the top

WARM EARTH

Water chilled by wind becomes heavier in relation to space occupied and sinks to the bottom

STAGE 1

COLD WIND STILL BLOWING

The cold wind may eventually reduce the temperature of the pond and its earthly basin to 40°F

All water at 40°F

Water is at its heaviest (or densest) at 40°F, so that at this temperature convection currents cease.

STAGE 2

COLD WIND STILL BLOWING

After convection currents cease, water on top of pond falls in temperature to 32°F, and becomes ice soon after.

ICE AT 32°F
HEAT ESCAPING SLOWLY BY CONDUCTION

Water below ice gradually loses heat by conduction, but at the bottom its temperature may remain above 32°F for many months

STAGE 3

HOW COLD AFFECTS A POND

summer, and it is such a vast reservoir of heat that it never becomes reduced to freezing-point, even in the longest winter. In polar regions, where the sun is feeble in summer and invisible for six months during winter, the sea does indeed become frozen on the surface, forming ice many feet thick, but underneath it is still warm enough to keep fish and seals quite comfortable.

Places a long way from the sea may become terribly hot in summer, because earth and rocks cannot store the heat of the sun without rising in temperature a great deal. The sea could absorb more than twice as much and yet not be so hot at the finish. You hear of inland places being hotter than seaside ones, and this is the reason why.

But things that become hot easily also become cold easily. Earth and rocks, however hot they may be, soon cool down if a chill wind crosses them. In fact, they may cool down by themselves during the night by a process called radiation. You often hear that very hot inland places, such as Madrid in Spain, are surprisingly cold a few hours after nightfall. This is the reason why. A place by the sea cannot grow cold in a single night or indeed in a whole winter season, because neither winds nor radiation effects can rob the sea of its vast store of heat by enough to diminish its temperature to an uncomfortable extent.

People who study their own comfort choose to live near the sea rather than inland, because they know that the sea helps to even things out. In the summer, when the sun is very hot, the sea rises in temperature, but only very slowly, and consequently the place stays cool. In winter the chill winds blow, and they cool the sea, but only very slowly, and so the place may remain quite warm, even though the chill wind lasts for weeks.

Mention has already been made of the way a fluid, when chilled, becomes denser or heavier for a given bulk, so sinking to the bottom and sending up less chilly fluid. This movement of a fluid under the influence of heat is called "convection," and convection currents are important as a means of carrying heat from place to place. The water in your linen cupboard at home is warmed by convection. The boiler in the kitchen heats water and makes it expand, so that it becomes less dense than the cooler water in the tank above. The cold water in the tank above over-balances the hot water in the boiler, so that it comes down one pipe and drives the hot water up the other pipe. Becoming heated in its turn, it has to give way to the water in the tank when its temperature rises above the temperature of the latter. Between boiler and tank there is thus a continual circulation, and the water going round and round forms a convection current whereby heat from the boiler downstairs is conveyed to the tank upstairs (see Vol. II, page 309).

You get similar convection currents in the air too. Any very light piece of paper held over the chimney of a lamp will show great agitation, because the heat of the lamp is causing air to rise continually up through the chimney. A radiator near a wall sends up a current of air that is constantly sweeping the wall above. Air always being dust laden, it makes the wall and ceiling above a radiator quite black, and I am sure you have often observed the dirty marks near hot pipes and radiators.

The heat of the sun is always causing huge convection currents in our atmosphere. In a hot place the air in contact with the ground may become far warmer than the air high

1. Cloud formation two hours before tornado strikes.

2. Funnel begins to form.

3. Tornado draws water from a pond in its path.

4. Tornado strikes and wrecks a ranch.

Damage done in St. Louis, Missouri, September 30, 1927, by tornado lasting five minutes.

Straws driven into the bark of a tree by a wind of hurricane force occurring in Minnesota, U.S.A.

up. Being made less dense by the rise in temperature, it starts to climb up higher and higher, leaving a space which has to be filled by air coming in from the sides. Air rushing towards hot places away from cold ones forms what we call the wind. If the heated air chooses a particular place at which to rise, it may do so with great violence, forming a whirlwind or tornado.

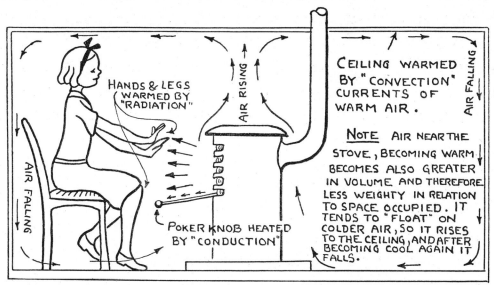

HEAT TRAVELS FROM PLACE TO PLACE IN 3 WAYS; BY CONDUCTION, CONVECTION & RADIATION.
NOTE FEET MAY BE CHILLED BY COLD CONVECTION CURRENT AND DRAUGHT FROM UNDER A DOOR

At the seaside you may notice that on a summer day the wind blows from the cool sea to the warm land. At evening the breeze drops, and later on it may blow from the cool land to the not-so-cool sea, the land having lost its heat by radiation in the night hours.

Radiation is the passage of heat through empty space. as a wave motion like wireless waves or light waves. Heat reaches us from the sun as radiant heat. When we walk *under* a hot steam-pipe, we feel its heat by radiation, for though convection currents can carry heat upwards, they cannot bring it downwards, and the conduction of air is too feeble to be of much help. The heat we enjoy from a coal fire on a winter's evening is mainly radiant heat.

Radiant heat can be reflected in the same way as light can be reflected. A bowl electric fire proves this, for if you get in the beam formed by the bowl, you feel much warmer than you do on either side. Radiant heat can also be refracted, which explains why a magnifying glass can cause a fire when it is used to make an image of the sun on wood or paper. Besides bringing the *light* of the sun to a focus, it brings the *heat* to a focus.

Clouds reflect the light of the sun, and glow white or orange or red according to the colour of the light they receive. Clouds can also reflect heat, and on a dull cloudy night the earth does not become nearly so cold as on a clear night, when the stars are visible. The sand and stones radiate away the heat of day at night, but if there are clouds to intercept this heat, much of it gets reflected back again, and thus the ground is prevented from becoming too cold. On clear nights this heat of the soil is radiated into fathomless space, never to return, and so the soil becomes colder and ever colder. During short summer nights the cooling process reaches the point where the soil becomes cold enough to chill the air above it to the dew point, so that it parts with some of the moisture it carries to form beads of dew. In process of separating out from the air, this moisture may cause ground mists. During long winter nights the process goes much farther. The soil cools down so far that it not only extracts moisture from the air but converts this moisture to ice. Instead of getting beads of water on everything, you get fringes and frills of ice, the result being what we call frost.

Frost is a great enemy of the fruit grower in spring-time—it nips the blossom or newly formed fruit in April and May. To combat frost at night the farmers may try to keep the air above the ground from becoming quite motionless as it normally does on windless nights, thus becoming colder and ever colder. Fires or stoves may be used in an orchard to keep the air in motion and supply a little radiant heat, but the best remedy against frost is to locate orchards on gently falling ground on the side of a hill. Air that is cooled by contact with sloping ground tends to slide to the bottom of the hill. Fresh air comes in from the summit and none of it stays in contact with the ground long enough to reach freezing-point. The worst place for an orchard is in a hollow that receives all the chilled air from the sloping ground around. The air in a hollow is bound to become progressively colder and colder, for it cannot move on and have its place taken by warmer air from above.

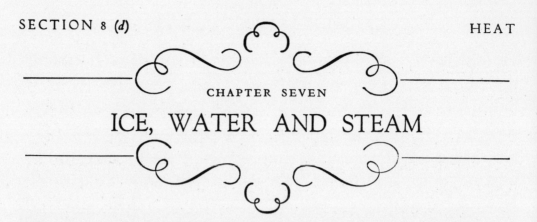

CHAPTER SEVEN

ICE, WATER AND STEAM

WE are accustomed to think of solids, liquids and gases as being quite distinct from one another, but in reality they may all three be the same thing in different guises. Water, for instance, is normally a liquid, but if it is made sufficiently cold it turns into the solid substance we call ice, and if made sufficiently hot it turns into the invisible gas we call steam. Other substances may only be in need of more or less heat to change their state, from solid to liquid, liquid to gas, or *vice versa.* Steel can be melted to a liquid and can even be turned into a gas, thus showing a general similarity to water; other metals are the same. A few substances may pass from one extreme condition to the other without appearing in the intermediate state. Carbon is like this; normally a black solid, it can be heated until it becomes gaseous, but it misses out the intermediate state of being a liquid.

Water is by far the most interesting and useful of the substances that are habitually altering from one state to another. Immense quantities of it exist in a state of Nature, and climatic changes alone are able to convert it into a solid or a gas.

Gases in contact with the liquid from which they come, and easily converted back into liquid, are often referred to as vapours, so that the gaseous water which is always mixed with our air is commonly spoken of as water vapour. The same vapour, with more heat added to it to make it hotter, behaves like the air itself or any other gas very far removed from the liquid state. It can be compressed and even cooled without showing any sign of becoming a liquid. There is, however, always a limit to the amount of cooling and compressing that a gas will stand. Even air, when cooled down sufficiently, can be squeezed up until it becomes a liquid, and if the cooling is carried to an extreme point, it will become liquid by itself and without any squeezing. You can obtain liquid air that appears just like water. It can be poured from a jug into a glass, and it will "keep" in an open vessel for an appreciable time. A puddle of it left in the open dries up more quickly than a puddle of water, but otherwise you could mistake it for water. If by any chance any of it fell on your hand, you would know the difference, because liquid air is exceedingly cold, and very cold things are as injurious to human flesh as scalding-hot ones. A flower dipped into liquid air becomes as brittle as thin glass and can be crumbled to an icy powder between finger and thumb.

ICE

If you are fortunate enough to have a refrigerator in your home, you can obtain ice at any time of the year, and with this you can do simple experiments. The following is a simple experiment to prove that ice can absorb heat and yet show no increase of temperature.

Crush up enough ice to cover the bottom of a jam-jar to a depth of about 2 inches. Now pour in cold water to give you a depth of about 4 inches. Stir well and note the temperature with a thermometer. You will see the temperature fall to 32 degrees Fahrenheit. Now put the jam-jar over a low gas and gently heat. While stirring continuously, observe the temperature. You will be interested to notice that, although you are all the time supplying heat to the contents of the jam-jar, no sign of a rise in temperature above 32 degrees Fahrenheit is apparent *until all the ice has melted*. After this, the temperature goes up quickly enough, proving that the heat from the gas ring certainly managed to reach the contents of the jam-jar, notwithstanding appearances to the contrary.

The following is another simple experiment, which shows that it needs a great deal of heat to melt quite a small quantity of ice.

Measure out a quart of cold water and put it in a jug that will hold 3 or 4 pints. Stir well for a few minutes, and then take its temperature. Now put in 4 ounces of dry crushed ice and stir again until it is all melted. Watch your thermometer while this is happening and notice the lowest temperature it reaches.

When Mary and Peter did this experiment the temperature of the water just before they put in the ice was 60 degrees Fahrenheit. After stirring the contents of the jug until the ice had all melted they found the temperature had fallen to 45 degrees Fahrenheit. Their father explained to them that if they had put in 4 ounces of *water* at the temperature of freezing (32 degrees Fahrenheit), the temperature in the jug would have dropped by only $2\frac{1}{2}$ degrees Fahrenheit to $57\frac{1}{2}$ degrees Fahrenheit. The ice, however, had absorbed a lot of heat merely to melt it and before it was ready to have its temperature raised above 32 degrees Fahrenheit. It was this extra absorption of heat by the melting ice that caused the temperature in the jug to fall the extra $12\frac{1}{2}$ degrees Fahrenheit.

From the figures obtained by Mary and Peter you can **work** out how much heat ice seems to need to melt it.

Directly after it was melted the 4 ounces of ice became 4 ounces of water at 32 degrees Fahrenheit. This water robbed the 40 ounces of water already in the jug of enough heat to bring its temperature up by 13 degrees from 32 degrees Fahrenheit to 45 degrees Fahrenheit. As there were 40 ounces in the jug (or ten times 4 ounces), the temperature of this larger quantity would be reduced by only a tenth part of 13 degrees, namely, 1·3 degree, as a result of this robbery. Actually the temperature was reduced not 1·3 degree but 15 degrees. To account for the extra 13·7 degrees, there was the heat robbed from the 40 ounces of water by the ice in process of melting and before it became water at 32 degrees. We see that the ice, in melting, was able to reduce by 13·7 degrees Fahrenheit the temperature of ten times as much water. In other words, as much heat is necessary to melt ice as would be needed to heat 137 times as much water through 1 degree. This heat, which is absorbed by ice to change its state without changing its tem-

By mixing ice and water you can show that a pound of ice needs 142 units of heat to melt it, a unit of heat being the amount needed to raise the temperature of a pound of water by 1°. Look at the experiments below

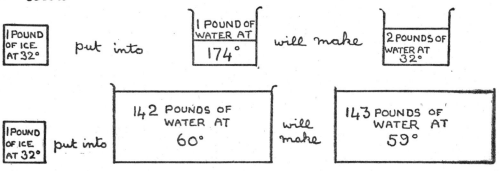

perature, is called the " latent heat of fusion of ice," and it is generally considered to be not 137 but 142 units. It is called latent heat because it can be absorbed without being revealed as a rise of temperature.

If you ever do an experiment to find out the value of the latent heat of fusion of ice, do not be disappointed if you do not get the figure quite right. The melting ice robs the jug as well as the water in it of heat, and you cannot take account of this. Also, when the jug and its contents become colder than the surrounding air, heat passes into the jug from this surrounding air to lessen the temperature fall. You cannot estimate how much heat goes into the jug while you are doing your experiment, and so you cannot see the whole effect of the melting ice when you look at your thermometer. Because of these happenings, which tend to spoil your experiment, you cannot be sure of getting an accurate value for the latent heat of fusion of ice—you will probably get a figure nearer to 130 than 140. The right figure can only be obtained with special apparatus and by taking great precautions in a scientific laboratory.

Snow is really ice in the form of feathery (and very pretty) crystals, loosely packed together, so this too needs a lot of heat to melt it. You will understand now why snow and ice may hang about for many days after the temperature of the air has become warmer. Melting snow and ice need so much heat to convert them from the solid state into water that the warm air has to blow over them for a long time before the change of state is completed.

The effect of ice and snow on a wind passing over it is to cool it down to freezing-point, and this cooling takes place very

By courtesy of Canadian Pacific Railway Co.

Where snow is expected for months on end every winter the people are prepared for it and they
have sledges on which to make their journeys and move their merchandise.

Canadian Pacific Photograph

A sledge is useful, but here you see one which is for joy-rides down a slippery slope.

Quebec, where even the grown-ups enjoy having a slide!

quickly, because whereas the snow and ice need much heat, the air has comparatively little to give away and is thus soon robbed of all. Winds blowing across Siberia or other snowy regions are always very cold when they reach us, because all the warmth has been taken out of them by the ice and snow covering these regions.

Icebergs are huge masses of ice that break away from glaciers in Polar regions and drift into more temperate seas. Because they need so much heat to melt them they may last for many months and appear in relatively warm seas. Icebergs from the North often drift quite far down in the Atlantic Ocean between Great Britain and America, and they make the crossing of this ocean dangerous for ships not fitted with suitable appliances for detecting their presence in the dark or during a fog. In 1912, before such appliances were invented, a beautiful new steamship of great size, called the *Titanic,* collided with an iceberg in the middle of the night and sank, so that many hundreds of people were drowned. (See also the article on Radar, page 412.)

STEAM

If you heat water in an open saucepan or kettle, you will find that its temperature gradually rises to 212 degrees Fahrenheit, but will not go any higher. At 212 degrees Fahrenheit the water becomes very agitated, owing to the formation of many bubbles which rise to the surface and burst, letting out steam. Continued heating of the water causes it to disappear gradually. It becomes converted into steam, which rises into the air and is lost. Water disappears in this way, though very slowly, even if we do not heat it at all. Puddles in the streets dry up because the water gets enough heat from the ground, or from the wind, or from direct sunlight to turn it into an invisible vapour. Our atmosphere is always getting new loads of water vapour to carry. A big railway engine may make ten or more tons of vapour for the air to carry in every hour that it is working, and, of course, the warm winds blowing over the sea evaporate and bear aloft vast quantities of water in the form of an invisible vapour. Even a tree may send up about half a ton of moisture into the air during a warm day of summer. When warm moisture-laden air rises to a great height (it may be forced to do this by mountains) it may encounter conditions that are much colder, and then the burden of moisture may become too much. The result is that the invisible vapour turns into water again, appearing first as countless billions of minute droplets widely spread through space and forming a mist or fog or cloud. The pretty fleecy-white shapes we see in the sky are really only patches of mist reflecting the white light of the sun. Sometimes these patches join together to cover the whole sky. Then we get a dull sun-less day. If clouds are very thick and large they may stop most of the light from the sun and appear terribly dark and threatening. In a very big cloud the tiny droplets tend to get together and form bigger droplets. Small droplets, like tiny dust particles, can float about in space indefinitely, but the bigger ones have to fall. In relation to their surface their weight becomes excessive; so, instead of sailing about like feathers or thistledown, they come tumbling down like so many little pebbles. That is when we get rain.

When steam (or water vapour) turns back into water it gives up a lot of heat to the surrounding air and this prevents the air from becoming any colder. It is never very cold when rain

Photograph by H. L. Butler

Clouds are just patches and wisps of mist high up in the air.

A Jump on Skis.

With long pieces of wood called skis on your feet, to prevent you from sinking into the soft snow, you can glide along at great speeds and even leap into the air.

threatens, because the condensing water vapour is giving up its heat. Even snow may bring with it an agreeable rise in atmospheric temperature. Before the fall of snow there may have been many degrees of frost (degrees below freezing-point), but with the gathering of the snow-clouds the temperature may rise to within a degree or two either way of 32 degrees Fahrenheit.

To show that a great deal of heat is absorbed by water when it becomes steam, we can turn steam back into water and measure the heat we get out of it. This experiment is a little more awkward to do than the ice experiments, because we shall need a piece of glass tubing we can bend and push through the cork of the bottle or flask in which we are to heat the water.

To bend a straight piece of glass tube you must make it red-hot at the point where the bend is to occur, holding it in a gas-flame for this purpose and twisting it round and round to make the heating quite even. Heated glass is as soft as chewing gum and therefore it is easily bent. Let your bent tube cool naturally; you will crack it if you are impatient and blow on it or dip it in water.

The bent tube is meant to carry off the steam generated in the heated flask and lead it into cold water in another vessel. Here the steam is turned back into water again. It gives up a great deal of heat to the cold water when it condenses, thus warming it up. After a very little while the cold water becomes quite hot, although it may have received steam equivalent to only a thimbleful or so of evaporated water.

When Mary and Peter did this experiment they dipped their glass tube into a vessel that held exactly 2 pints (40 ounces) of water at 60 degrees Fahrenheit, and they stopped the experi-

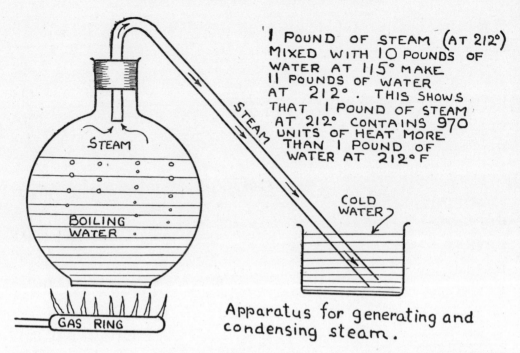

STEAM

BOILING
WATER

GAS RING

1 POUND OF STEAM (AT 212°)
MIXED WITH 10 POUNDS OF
WATER AT 115° MAKE
11 POUNDS OF WATER
AT 212°. THIS SHOWS
THAT 1 POUND OF STEAM
AT 212° CONTAINS 970
UNITS OF HEAT MORE
THAN 1 POUND OF
WATER AT 212° F

STEAM

COLD
WATER

Apparatus for generating and
condensing steam.

ment when the temperature reached 112 degrees Fahrenheit. They then measured out the water to find how much condensed steam had mixed with it, and they found that instead of being 40 ounces the water in the vessel was now 42 ounces, showing that 2 ounces of steam had been condensed. This 2 ounces of steam had formed water at 212 degrees Fahrenheit, and this water in cooling 100 degrees from 212 degrees to 112 degrees must have heated up the 40 ounces by a twentieth of this amount, or 5 degrees, because 2 is only a twentieth of 40. The rest of the temperature rise, namely, 112 degrees − 65 degrees or 47 degrees, must have been caused by the heat given up by the steam in changing to water. One ounce of steam in condensing would have affected 20 ounces of water in this way, consequently the heat given up by it in condensing must have been enough to heat no less than $20 \times 47 = 940$ ounces of water through 1 degree Fahrenheit.

This heat, which is put into water to convert it into steam and which does not show on the thermometer as a rise of temperature, is called the "latent heat of vaporisation of steam," and the figure for it is usually given in scientific books as 970. The figure found by Mary and Peter was a little low, and if you do this experiment yourself I daresay you will get a low figure too, but because it is *very difficult* with ordinary

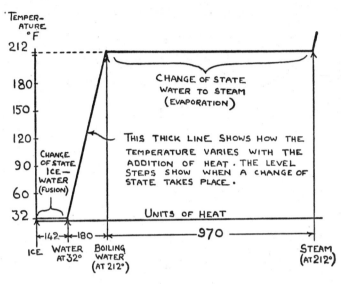

domestic appliances to measure accurately the small weight of steam condensed you must not expect your result to be very good. If you under-estimate the weight of steam condensed you may actually get a latent-heat figure of 1,000 or more.

EFFECTS OF PRESSURE ON ICE AND STEAM

If water is confined in a space where it cannot easily expand on becoming ice you will have to cool the water down well below 32 degrees Fahrenheit before it will freeze. When it eventually does freeze it may exert enough force to split the container. Ice already in existence will melt if it is subjected to enough pressure. When you stand on ice your weight may be enough to melt the small quantity immediately underfoot, meaning to say that when you try to stand on ice your weight will really be supported by a thin film of water. Perfectly dry ice would not be slippery, but when you stand on ice it ceases to be dry and so it becomes slippery. The purpose of skates is to concentrate your weight on a very small area of ice, so increasing the pressure and making sure that it is enough to melt some of the ice.

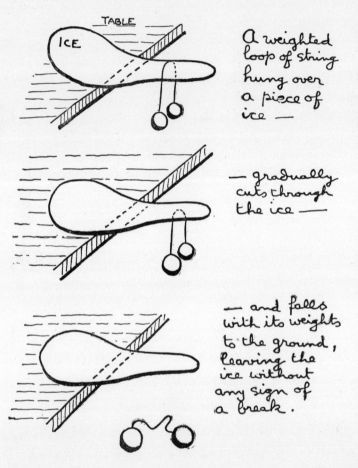

A weighted loop of string hung over a piece of ice —

— gradually cuts through the ice —

— and falls with its weights to the ground, leaving the ice without any sign of a break.

An interesting experiment showing the effect of pressure on ice is to loop a piece of string or wire over an ice block and hang heavy weights on both ends. The string melts the ice by pressure and slowly cuts right through it. The cut, or wound, behind the string heals up, however, for the water formed by the melting ice under the string passes round to the back of the string and freezes into ice again.

If water is enclosed in a boiler without any outlet it will not boil at 212 degrees Fahrenheit. It will have to be made much hotter. Once it starts boiling it will make steam at a much higher pressure than atmospheric pressure, and this steam can be conveyed by a pipe to an engine or turbine to make it work.

If a boiler is continually heated without there being any chance for the steam formed inside to get away, there may eventually be a terrific explosion. Every boiler used to make steam for an engine is fitted with a "safety valve," which begins to hiss and let steam escape if more steam is being made than the engine can use. This safety valve is a round disc that is held down on a round hole by a strong spring. The disc lifts to let out steam if the steam pushes up on its under side harder than the spring pushes down on its upper side.

The temperature at which water boils to make steam becomes progressively greater as the pressure increases, and

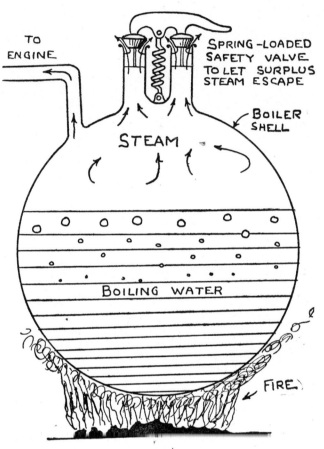

TO ENGINE

SPRING-LOADED SAFETY VALVE TO LET SURPLUS STEAM ESCAPE

BOILER SHELL

STEAM

BOILING WATER

FIRE

Steam must be given some way of escaping from a boiler or it will exert a great force and burst the boiler.

underneath you will see a table of figures to show what the boiling temperature is in boilers set to blow off at different pressures.

Pressure in Boiler Pounds per Square Inch	Temperature Degrees Fahrenheit
14·7 (atmospheric)	212
50	281
100	328
150	358
200	382
250	401
300	418
400	446
500	469

From this table you can see that steam will not form at high pressures until the temperature of the water is increased to well over 212 degrees Fahrenheit. You might now suppose that if the pressure on water could be reduced to below atmospheric it would boil *before* reaching 212 degrees Fahrenheit, and if you did suppose this you would be quite right. At a pressure of 12 pounds per square inch water will boil at 202 degrees Fahrenheit, and you could not possibly make it any hotter, for it would become steam if you tried. At 10 pounds per square inch water boils at 193 degrees Fahrenheit, and at

6 pounds per square inch it boils at 170 degrees Fahrenheit. This explains why you cannot make good tea or cook an egg satisfactorily when you are at the top of a high mountain: you cannot make the water hot enough. High up on a mountain the air is rarefield (see page 295), and exerts less than the normal atmospheric pressure of 14·7 pounds per square inch.

Two interesting experiments you can do are described below. Take an old empty tin of the flat-sided kind that is used to hold bicycle oil. Boil a little water in it until steam is issuing from the opening at the top. Now push a cork into this opening and take the tin away from the source of heat. If you quickly pour cold water over the outside of the tin or plunge it into a bowl of cold water, the flat sides will instantly collapse as though an enormously strong man squeezed them together with his hand. The explanation is that the steam inside the tin, having previously driven all the air out, is condensed by the cold douche applied to the outside of the tin, leaving a vacuum or total emptiness inside. The weight of the atmosphere pressing with a force of 14·7 pounds on every square inch of outside surface of the tin, is not opposed by any pressure of air inside the tin, and so it crushes the tin flat. At the same time, if you could see the water inside the tin, you would notice that it started boiling again when you cooled the outside. The loss of pressure on the surface of the water makes it possible for this water to boil, even though its temperature has dropped lower than 212 degrees Fahrenheit.

The second experiment is similar to the one described here, but you use a strong glass flask instead of a tin. This is not broken by the weight of the atmosphere when you cool the outside, and it allows you to watch the effect on the water inside. It seems strange that a stream of *cold* water on the flask should start a furious bubbling and boiling on the part of the water inside; nevertheless, it is so. Be careful to buy a good flask from a chemist for this last-mentioned experiment. A cheap flask might break and cause an accident.

HOW A REFRIGERATOR WORKS

When you put a little petrol or benzine or methylated spirit on your hand it feels very cold. All these liquids have low boiling temperatures, and even at ordinary temperatures they

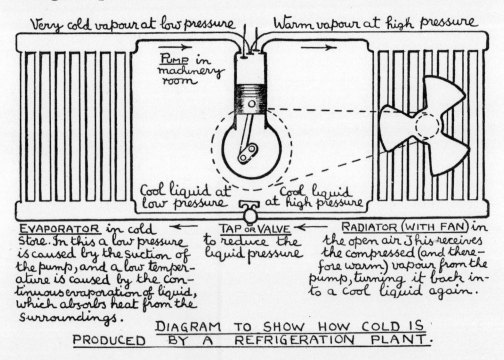

Very cold vapour at low pressure   Warm vapour at high pressure

PUMP in machinery room

Cool liquid at low pressure   Cool liquid at high pressure

EVAPORATOR in cold Store. In this a low pressure is caused by the suction of the pump, and a low temperature is caused by the continuous evaporation of liquid, which absorbs heat from the surroundings.

TAP or VALVE to reduce the liquid pressure

RADIATOR (WITH FAN) in the open air. This receives the compressed (and therefore warm) vapour from the pump, turning it back into a cool liquid again.

DIAGRAM TO SHOW HOW COLD IS PRODUCED BY A REFRIGERATION PLANT.

evaporate very fast. Like water they need a lot of heat to convert them into vapours, and to get this heat they rob your hand, making it colder.

The cold produced by a refrigerating machine is caused in the same way by the rapid evaporation of a liquid, the liquid in this instance being ammonia, carbon dioxide or Freon. A pump drawing off the vapour keeps the pressure on the liquid so low that it boils and robs the surroundings of heat. The vapour drawn off by the pump is pushed into small space (compressed) and prevented from getting hot at the same time, so that it turns into a liquid again, ready for re-evaporation. Some refrigerators (small domestic ones) are arranged to work without a pump, but they are too complicated to be explained here. A small gas flame or electric heating element is enough to keep them going. All big and efficient refrigerators, however, use a mechanically or electrically driven pump, and work on the principle described above.

CHAPTER EIGHT

WHAT IS HEAT?

UP to and even beyond the year 1800 men called heat "caloric" and believed it to be a kind of fluid that could be poured from one body into another. It seemed to flow from places of high temperature to places of low temperature, just as water will flow from a high level to a low level. Attempts were made to weigh heat, but it was found to be "imponderable" or weightless. Then it was noticed that heat could be "created" by friction. People cutting away the metal from great billets of bronze or iron in order to make guns noticed that the metal and the tool both became hot as the work proceeded. To-day everybody knows that friction causes heat to appear. The brakes on a car become hot when the car descends a long hill. If you slide down a rope too fast your hands become scorched by the heat generated when the rope slips through them.

How much heat is generated in this way? Careful experiments show that a man weighing 100 pounds sliding down a distance of $7\frac{3}{4}$ feet generates nearly enough heat to raise the temperature of a pound of water by 1 degree Fahrenheit. The product $100 \times 7\frac{3}{4}$ ($= 775$) of the man's weight in pounds by the distance of his fall in feet is the measure of the work he does in falling, and is referred to as 775 foot-pounds. The heat needed to raise the temperature of a pound of water 1° F. is called a

British Thermal Unit. It would appear from the most careful experiments that 772 ft.-lb. of work are equivalent to 1 B.Th.U. This is called the "Mechanical Equivalent of Heat," or Joule's Equivalent after the scientist who first measured it.

When a man slides down a rope the heat does not go into water but into the rope and into the skin of the man's hands, and although the amount generated is small it may produce a painful and destructive rise of temperature. This 1 B.Th.U. will not only serve to heat 1 pound of water through 1° F., it could alternatively heat a hundredth of a pound of water through 100° F., or a tiny part of your hand through several hundred degrees F.

Heat is always being created by things that rub against one another. The bearings of an engine become hot by friction, and if not well oiled they may become dangerously hot and melt. Electricity flowing along a wire makes the wire warm. If the electric current is big enough, the wire may become red hot (as in an electric fire) or white hot (as in an electric lamp).

If we have the necessary amount of energy to spend, we shall find heat is very easy to make; but a good deal of useful work or useful electricity does not make very much heat. You would be sorry if you had to heat up the water for your early morning cup of tea by pedalling a friction machine, because you would need to pedal hard and for a long time. A horse can do 33,000 foot-pounds of work in a minute when it is working steadily all day. You would have to work as hard as a horse for $4\frac{1}{2}$ minutes to heat a pint of water from 60° F. to boiling-point. From these considerations you can see that fuels such as coal, wood and so on are very valuable to us—they save us a lot of work!

WORK FROM HEAT

I have said a lot about obtaining heat from work, but nothing as yet about obtaining work from heat. If we can get 1 B.Th.U. from 772 ft.-lb. of work, could we not get 772 ft.-lb. of work from 1 B.Th.U.? This is a question that has engaged the attention of scientists and engineers for many centuries. To get heat from work is easy, but to reverse the process and get work from heat is not so easy. However, as heat causes things to expand and exert quite large forces in so doing, there seems a chance of getting heat to do work for us.

Before the year 1800 men like Newcomen and Watt were already applying the force of steam to useful tasks by means of crudely built engines. They did not receive 772 ft.-lb. of work in return for each B.Th.U. of heat given out by burning coal—what they got was more like 6 or 7 ft.-lb., the reason being that their engines wasted most of the heat and were thus very *inefficient*.

As the years went by, engineers were able to make their steam engines do better than this, and to-day we can get something like 270 ft.-lb. from each B.Th.U. of heat expended in the furnace. Using a Diesel engine and oil fuel, we can get even more from our B.Th.U.s—over 300 ft.-lb., but there are good reasons I cannot tell you about here for thinking that we shall never do much better than this with engines worked by burning fuel.

HEAT IS MOLECULAR MOTION

The discovery that heat could be created by an expenditure of work, or could be made to disappear in the production of work, taught men that it could not be a fluid. We are fairly confident to-day that heat is only an internal agitation or motion of the tiny particles of which all material things are composed. The hotter they are made the more vigorous the agitation. If a solid body be made hot enough the agitation of its particles loosens their hold on one another so that the body becomes liquid. Further heating causes the particles to fly completely asunder, so that the liquid turns into a gas. The separate particles of a gas are flying about in all directions at a great speed, and the bombardment of these tiny particles on anything that is put in their way gives rise to what we call pressure. If the gas is made hotter, the particles move faster; if the gas be compressed into a smaller space, more of them hit each square inch of the walls of the enclosing vessel in a given time, so, either way, there is an increase of pressure.

This motion of the particles or molecules comprising matter is not to be confused with motions inside the molecules themselves. These other motions have to do with atomic energy, and that is another story altogether.

CHAPTER ONE

THE AIR WE BREATHE

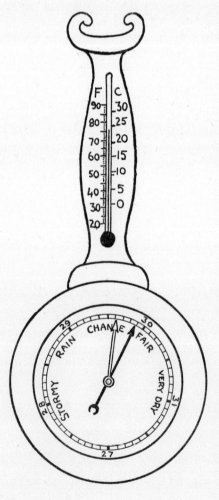

WHEN Mary reached her eleventh birthday Father gave her a barometer for her birthday present. It was a beautiful thing, something like a clock, with two hands, only it did not tell the time. Instead, it told what kind of weather was coming. When the big hand pointed to where twelve would be on the clock, it said "Change." To the right of this it said "Fair," and farther round still it said "Very Dry." If the big hand moved to the left instead of to the right it said "Rain," and then "Stormy." The little hand did not move itself. It was fastened to a knob on the outside of the glass, and Mary could turn it round by twisting this knob. Every evening she put the little hand so that it appeared to be on top of the big one, hiding it. Every morning she went to see if the big hand had moved from where it had been the night before. She could easily

286

By courtesy of the Royal Meteorological Society

Viewed from their own level, clouds are seen to be only large or small wisps of mist.

By courtesy of the Royal Meteorological Society

On a mountain above the clouds there is clear sunshine, while in the valley below the cloud blanket it is sunless and gloomy.

By courtesy of the Royal Meteorological Society

Festoon clouds are a more drooping and sorrowful kind than the ones
we call mackerel sky

By courtesy of the Royal Meteorological Society

These are man-made clouds arising from the exhaust gases of aeroplane
engines.

see whether it had moved, because the little hand stayed where she had put it, whereas the big hand generally went wandering round the dial.

On days when the big hand moved round to the left of the little hand Mary said, "Oh dear, it is going to rain, I think." On days when the big hand moved the other way she said, "Hooray, it is going to be fine." She was generally right too, but not always.

"How does it work, Daddy?" she asked Father one day. "It seems to be quite right about the weather most days, but not always. Can it smell the wetness coming, and does the wetness sometimes turn back and go the other way after all?"

"Oh no," laughed Father, "nothing like that. There is, however, a weather forecaster that works on a principle something like that."

MIST, DEW, CLOUDS AND RAIN

"A piece of seaweed hung up in the house will get hard and dry in fine weather, and it will go moist and limp when the air is nearly ready to let fall the water it carries. The air is always full of steam you cannot see, and when the air becomes cold, the steam becomes visible as clouds. Clouds are really huge crowds of tiny, tiny droplets of water. They are just patches of mist high up, and mist, as you know, is wet. The ground mists that form in the evening are caused by the air becoming colder and trying to get rid of moisture. At night the moisture often falls out as dew. The air is nearly cold enough for there to be a mist but not quite. Only when it touches really cold things, like trees and grass, does it reach what is called the dew-point and drop its load of water. If

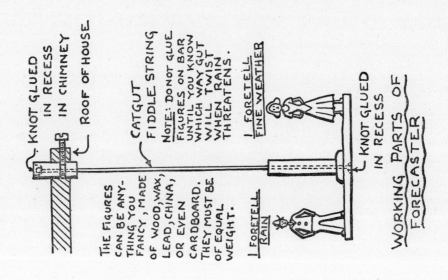

KNOT GLUED IN RECESS IN CHIMNEY

ROOF OF HOUSE

CATGUT FIDDLE STRING

NOTE: DO NOT GLUE FIGURES ON BAR UNTIL YOU KNOW WHICH WAY GUT WILL TWIST WHEN RAIN THREATENS.

I FORETELL FINE WEATHER

THE FIGURES CAN BE ANYTHING YOU FANCY, MADE OF WOOD, WAX, LEAD, CHINA, OR EVEN CARDBOARD. THEY MUST BE OF EQUAL WEIGHT.

I FORETELL RAIN

KNOT GLUED IN RECESS

WORKING PARTS OF FORECASTER

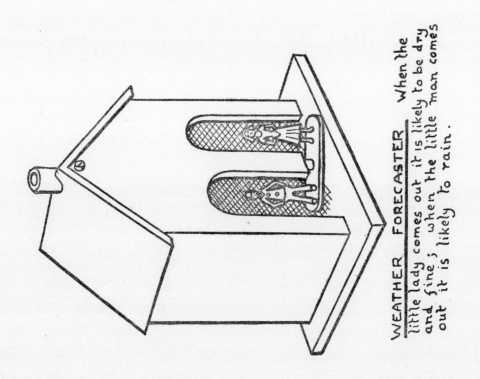

WEATHER FORECASTER When the little lady comes out it is likely to be dry and fine; when the little man comes out it is likely to rain.

large volumes of air reach the dew-point together you get mist or clouds. When the tiny droplets in a cloud come together and join up to form bigger drops you get rain. Once the drops start to fall, they catch up and collide with smaller drops and merge with them to form still bigger drops. Drizzle is the rain you get from low clouds: the drops have not fallen far enough to have collected together to any extent. Huge thunder drops come from great thick banks of cloud high up. The drops may have fallen several miles and picked up smaller drops all the way down.

"Well, as I said before, a piece of seaweed becomes limp when the air gets near the dew-point. Air begins to show its moisture either because it has absorbed all the water it can carry, becoming 'saturated,' or because it is getting colder."

A SIMPLE WEATHER FORECASTER

"A piece of catgut, such as fiddle strings are made of, is sensitive to moisture in the air in much the same way as seaweed. It twists and untwists, depending on whether it is dry or humid, which means moist. You can see little weather forecasters in the shape of a house. Indeed, you could make one yourself. The house has two doors; in one there stands a man and in the other a woman. The two little figures are mounted on a bar of wood that is hung up in the middle by a length of catgut. When the catgut twists or untwists the little figures move. The man comes out if rain is threatening. In dry weather the woman comes out. Usually the catgut is fixed to the chimney of the house, and by turning this you can adjust the positions of the figures so that they work properly. If you could not do this you might find that one of them was out all the time, the other being in. Changes of weather would cause the outside figure to move to and fro, but never far enough to go right in."

HOW A REAL BAROMETER WORKS

"Your barometer does not depend for its action on the humidity of the air, that is, on the moisture it contains, but on the pressure of the air. We live, you know, at the bottom of an enormously deep ocean of air that we cannot see, but only feel. The earth has to hold up all this air just as the sea-bed has to hold up millions and millions of tons of water. The air weighs quite a lot, and it is pressing down on the ground all the time. If you could weigh the air you would find that every little square of ground with its sides one inch long had to hold up air weighing nearly fifteen pounds. The weight varies from day to day, because the depth of the ocean of air varies. There are huge waves and currents in this ocean, just as there are in the sea; the currents you feel as winds, for the air is always rushing from places where the ocean is too deep in order to fill up places where it is too shallow. From time immemorial men have used the rush of the wind to drive ships and rotate wind-mills.

"Your barometer really measures the weight of the aerial ocean at the place where you happen to be.

"Inside your barometer is a bent tube full of mercury, which is a heavy silvery liquid. One end of the tube is swelled out to form a sort of jar, and this is open to the air; the other end is shut, and all the air has been taken out of it, so that on this side there is no weight of air to press on the mercury. The ocean of air presses on the mercury in the open end of the tube and tries to push it down. It succeeds in doing this, and so

By courtesy of Canadian Pacific Railway Co.

Freely available to all, the wind was the motive power of this great Atlantic trader, the *Lake Erie,* built in 1868.

By courtesy of The P. & O. Steam Navigation Co.

Early steamships had sails so that they could be helped by a favourable wind; modern steamships generally travel faster than the wind and could seldom benefit from sails.

"Jack and Jill," old disused windmills at Clayton, Sussex.

Once turned by the wind, this mill near Brighton, Sussex, used to grind wheat into flour.

the mercury climbs up on the other side. But the farther it climbs, the greater the force needed to keep it there. Eventually the force of the air is balanced by the force of the mercury trying to return and so become level in the two sides of the tube. The balance usually occurs when the mercury is about thirty inches higher on one side than the other. A thirty-inch difference is equivalent to a little less than fifteen pounds on the square inch. Whenever the atmospheric pressure varies, the column of mercury moves up or down, being thirty-one inches high some days and only twenty-nine inches high at others. The figures round the rim of your barometer show the height of the mercury column. A float on the mercury

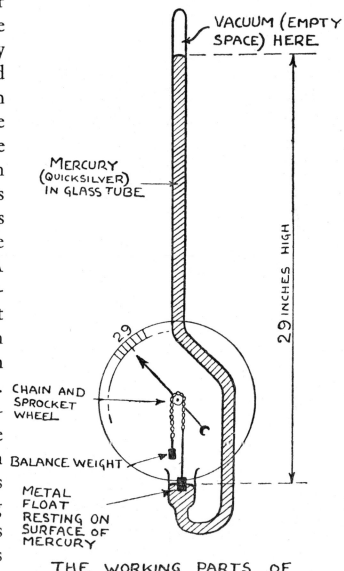

VACUUM (EMPTY SPACE) HERE

MERCURY (QUICKSILVER) IN GLASS TUBE

29 INCHES HIGH

29

CHAIN AND SPROCKET WHEEL

BALANCE WEIGHT

METAL FLOAT RESTING ON SURFACE OF MERCURY

THE WORKING PARTS OF MARY'S BAROMETER

in the open end of the tube works the pointer that tells you the barometric height.

"The height of the barometer is not a direct indication of what the weather is going to do, but it is a sort of guide. Thus, if the barometer falls, it means that you are at a place where the aerial ocean is getting too shallow. Soon you can expect a mighty wind to come and fill up the 'depression.' When your barometer (or glass, as it is sometimes called) moves to 'Stormy,' you can expect a gale, and if you live in England, gales usually come from the west across thousands of miles of Atlantic Ocean. They pick up a lot of water on the way, and so they are usually the cause of rain sooner or later. Winds from the other direction come across dry land—across Siberia. They are usually cold and dry. If, then, your glass falls because a strong easterly wind is on the way, it may say rain when actually no rain is coming, but only biting cold. This, however, is rather rare.

"The predictions of the barometer are made a little uncertain by the fact that winds usually travel in great circular sweeps, or cyclones, like the water on its way out of your bath when you pull the plug up. An east wind may be a current that has come from the west all round Iceland, over a bit of Europe and then across to England. Such a wind might bring you rain after all. So, you see, it doesn't do to believe or disbelieve your barometer too much when it says Rain, Stormy, Fair, Very Dry. All you can be absolutely sure about is the figure for the height of the mercury column. A cyclone on a very small scale with a whirl of only 50 to 100 feet across is called a tornado (see page 263). It is caused by the local uprush through cool air of hot air blanketing a sun-baked surface."

ANEROID BAROMETERS

"Daddy!" Peter butted in suddenly; "in the house of a friend of mine there is a natty little barometer like a small clock, with no room inside it for a long tube of mercury. How does that work? It has figures on the rim—twenty-eight, twenty-nine, thirty, and so on, just like Mary's; but if there isn't any mercury in it, how can it know what the height of the mercury column would be?"

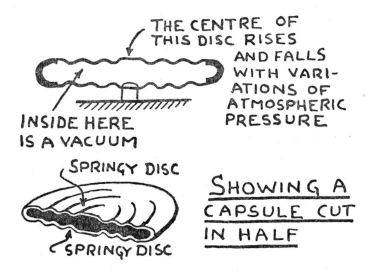

THE CENTRE OF THIS DISC RISES AND FALLS WITH VARIATIONS OF ATMOSPHERIC PRESSURE

INSIDE HERE IS A VACUUM

SPRINGY DISC

SPRINGY DISC

SHOWING A CAPSULE CUT IN HALF

"You can get barometers as small as pocket watches, and it is quite true that they have no mercury in them," replied Father; "they are called *aneroid* barometers, or simply 'aneroids.' Inside such a barometer there is a thing called a capsule. This consists of two discs of metal with a stiff rim round the outside to separate them. They are usually made wavy or corrugated instead of flat, so that they can 'breathe' in and out. The space between them is made quite empty. Air is pumped out of this space to make what is called a vacuum. The outside air presses on the outside of the corrugated discs, but there is nothing to push back again from the inside, so the discs are forced inwards. Because they are springy they go in so far and then stop. They stop when the pressure of the air balances their springiness. If the air pressure varies, then the

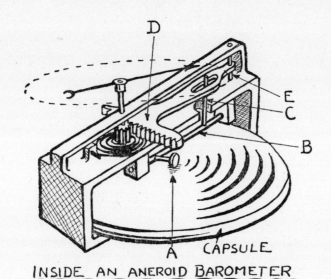

INSIDE AN ANEROID BAROMETER

KNOB "A" RESTS ON THE CAPSULE AND MOVES UP OR DOWN WHEN THIS EXPANDS OR CONTRACTS, THUS ROCKING SPINDLE "B". ARM "C", PROJECTING FROM "B", ENGAGES A SLOT IN TOOTHED SECTOR "D", THEREBY ROCKING IT ABOUT SPINDLE "E". THE SECTOR TURNS A PINION ON THE SPINDLE OF THE POINTER AGAINST THE FORCE OF A HAIR-SPRING.

discs move in or out a little. This movement is a measure of the change in the barometric height, so all you have to do is connect your capsule by means of levers to a pointer or hand working round a dial and, hey presto, you have a barometer. If you look inside an aneroid you will see that in some designs (not all) there is a strong spring to hold the two sides of the capsule apart and prevent them from being crushed together by the weight of the atmosphere. The movement of the connected end of this spring is transmitted through rods and cranks and a chain to a pointer on a spindle, this connection being of a kind to magnify the movement of the capsule which, after all, is very tiny. In another design (see illustration) a rocking bar operates the pointer through a toothed sector and pinion."

RARITY OF THE ATMOSPHERE AT GREAT HEIGHTS

"Aeroplanes are fitted with aneroids, aren't they, Daddy?" Peter asked.

"Yes," answered Father; "an aneroid is useful for telling you how high up you are. If you climb up a mountain carrying with you an aneroid, or any other barometer, you will see that the pointer falls steadily. The reason for this is that the earth high up on a mountain-side does not have to bear such a great weight of air as the earth near sea-level. You get nearer to the top of the ocean of air the higher you go. If you climb to the top of Mount Everest, which is twenty-nine thousand feet high, you have not very much more air on top of you, and so your barometer would show a small height of mercury column. In fact, the air up there is of such little pressure that it is hard work to get enough of it to breathe. It does not rush into your lungs like the air at sea-level. Nobody has yet climbed Everest to the very top, because the breathing is so hard that it tires men out before they have gone many steps. You can go higher than Everest in an aeroplane, because going high is easier when you can sit still. However, high-flying aeroplanes generally carry a supply of oxygen for the pilot to breathe."

IN THE "STRATOSPHERE" THE
AIR IS VERY RARIFIED: LOWER
DOWN IT IS MORE DENSE.

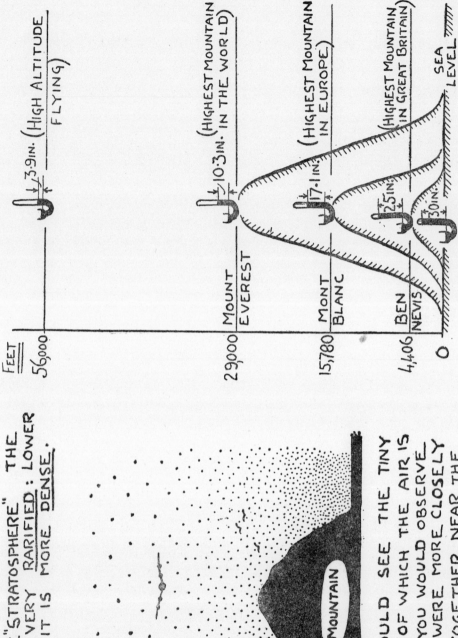

FEET
56,000 — 3·9 IN. (HIGH ALTITUDE FLYING)

29,000 MOUNT EVEREST — 10·3 IN. (HIGHEST MOUNTAIN IN THE WORLD)

15,780 MONT BLANC — 17·1 IN. (HIGHEST MOUNTAIN IN EUROPE)

4,406 BEN NEVIS — 25 IN. (HIGHEST MOUNTAIN IN GREAT BRITAIN)

0 — 30 IN. SEA LEVEL

BAROMETRIC HEIGHT AT DIFFERENT LEVELS

MOUNTAIN

IF YOU COULD SEE THE TINY
PARTICLES OF WHICH THE AIR IS
COMPOSED YOU WOULD OBSERVE
THAT THEY WERE MORE CLOSELY
CROWDED TOGETHER NEAR THE
GROUND THAN HIGH UP.

296

"How much does the barometer fall when you go up, say, a thousand feet?" Mary asked.

"Roughly one inch," Father replied. "That does not mean to say, however, that at thirty thousand feet the barometer would show no height of mercury at all. You lose one inch of mercury for the first thousand feet, and almost an inch for each thousand feet up to four or five thousand; then you lose less than an inch per thousand feet, possibly only three-quarters of an inch, then half an inch, then a quarter of an inch and so on. The reason for this is that air squeezes up under pressure into a small space and weighs quite a lot at sea-level—about eight hundredths of a pound (or more than an ounce and a quarter) for each bit you could put in a box one foot long by one foot wide by one foot high. If you took this squashed-up air in its box up a high mountain and then opened the box, most of it would rush out and leave you with much thinner air not weighing nearly so much. Your cubic foot of air might weigh only three or four hundredths of a pound at the height where you are. So you see, when you climb you push your way through layers of air that are less and less squashed up. To observe a difference of one pound per square inch in the pressure of air you need climb only about two thousand feet to begin with, but higher up you would have to climb four thousand or five thousand feet or even more to observe the same change.

"The aneroids used by airmen are not graduated in inches of mercury at all, but in thousands of feet. The dial has to be adjustable so that the instrument can be set to show nothing (or zero) when the aeroplane is on the ground, no matter what the barometric height may be. If the barometer is changing

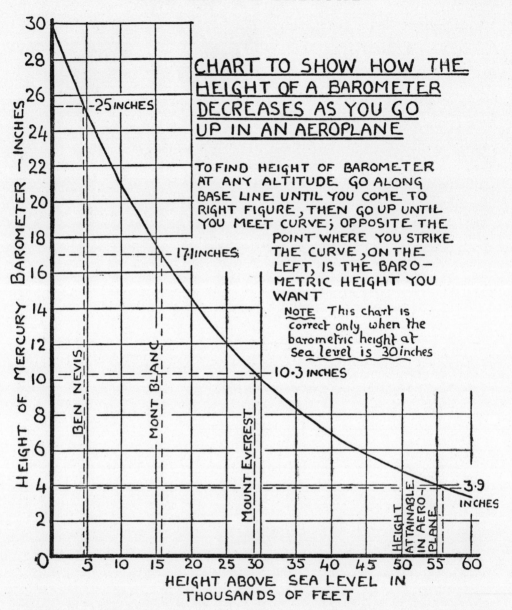

CHART TO SHOW HOW THE HEIGHT OF A BAROMETER DECREASES AS YOU GO UP IN AN AEROPLANE

TO FIND HEIGHT OF BAROMETER AT ANY ALTITUDE GO ALONG BASE LINE UNTIL YOU COME TO RIGHT FIGURE, THEN GO UP UNTIL YOU MEET CURVE; OPPOSITE THE POINT WHERE YOU STRIKE THE CURVE, ON THE LEFT, IS THE BARO-METRIC HEIGHT YOU WANT

NOTE This chart is correct only when the barometric height at sea level is 30 inches

rapidly, the altimeter (as the airman's aneroid is called) may become very inaccurate after a few hours' flight. It would not be safe to depend on its reading in a fog, or at night; you couldn't land your machine by saying to yourself, 'Now I am fifty feet up and I can begin to flatten out.' You might be still

By courtesy of Swiss Federal Railways

Photo by E. Gyger, Adelboden

The Jungfrau, a mountain in Switzerland more than 12,000 feet high, reaches up into considerably rarified air.

five hundred feet up, or you might actually have hit the ground. Airmen have to have other aids to enable them to gauge their height accurately when close to the ground. The altimeter is useful only as a rough guide."

MAKING AIR "HARD"

"Just now you said something about air being squashed up," Mary interposed. "Can you squash it up so tight that it is hard?"

"Yes," answered Father; "you can do that with a bicycle pump. Put your finger over the hole at the end and push, and

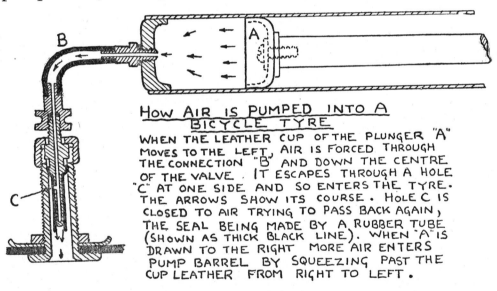

How Air is Pumped into a Bicycle Tyre

When the leather cup of the plunger "A" moves to the left, air is forced through the connection "B" and down the centre of the valve. It escapes through a hole "C" at one side and so enters the tyre. The arrows show its course. Hole C is closed to air trying to pass back again, the seal being made by a rubber tube (shown as thick black line). When "A" is drawn to the right more air enters pump barrel by squeezing past the cup leather from right to left.

you can feel the air inside behaving like a piece of rubber. You can squash it so hard in a tyre that the tyre hardly dents when you pinch it. If you pump the air in very quickly you make it hot. You can often feel the pump getting warm.

"Not everyone knows how a bicycle pump works, so I will sketch it for you, showing the tyre valve in the same picture.

The plunger of the pump is a leather cup. As you push it down the tube, air is forced through the connection to the valve. Here it squeezes through a small hole in a little pipe that is surrounded by a thin rubber tube. It squirms down between the metal and the rubber to find its way into the tyre. Directly it is inside, the air already there forces the rubber back against the tiny hole, so that no air can get back up the connection again. When you pull back the plunger of the pump, you make an empty space behind the leather cup. The only way air can get in to fill this space is by squeezing past the cup from the handle side to the connection side. This it can do because the rim of the cup can easily get smaller and leave a space round for the air to flow through. The air goes in very quickly, because there is a partial vacuum on one side of the cup and all the weight of the atmosphere (fifteen pounds to the square inch) on the other side. When you push down on the plunger the air in front of it tries to pass back the way it came, but in so doing it opens out the cup again, and when the cup fills the pump barrel it will not let the air go by. By pushing hard enough you force the air to go the way already described through the connection and the valve into the tyre."

SOME MEMBERS OF THE GAS FAMILY

"From all I have told you you will see that air is a very real thing, with weight and body, although you cannot see it. It is often referred to as a gas, but really it is a mixture of two gases called NITROGEN and OXYGEN. There is much more nitrogen than oxygen. There are many other gases that are invisible, like air. Some weigh more and some weigh less;

some smell and some are odourless; some will burn and others will not; some are harmless and some are deadly poison. An inflammable gas weighing very little is HYDROGEN. If you fill a balloon or airship with this it will float in the air just as a boat floats on water (see page 321). A fire often makes new gases out of air in combination with solid fuel. It makes CARBON DIOXIDE, which is odourless, invisible and relatively harmless, but it can also make CARBON MONOXIDE, which, while odourless and invisible, is a deadly poison.

" In the war of 1914–1918 poisonous gases were used to try to kill soldiers, and in the recent war it was expected that our enemies would try to use poison gases again. That is why we were all given gas-masks. The gases used in warfare are specially made, and I do not need to tell you anything about them. Most of them smell, some of them are visible as faint clouds in the air, and all of them are heavier than air, so that they will roll along close to the ground and not rise up like hydrogen, thus becoming lost. The gas we burn in the kitchen comes from coal. It is a mixture of several gases, all of them inflammable. I may tell you more about them some other time."

CHAPTER TWO

SYPHONS AND PUMPS

ONE very cold and frosty morning Mary wanted to get up early, as she had not been able to finish her school homework the night before. She went to the bathroom to have a wash, but when she pulled the plug out of the basin to let the dirty water run away nothing happened, because the waste pipe was stopped up with ice. She was still trying to empty it in cupfuls out of the open window when Father came in for his shave.

MARY TRIES TO BALE OUT DIRTY WATER FROM THE BASIN AS THE WASTE PIPE IS STOPPED UP WITH ICE

He guessed at once what had happened.

"The quickest way to get that water out of the window into the garden is to make a syphon," he said. "I will go and find a length of rubber tube."

While Father was gone, Mary wondered how the water could be made to go by tube out of the window, as the window-sill was two feet higher than the basin at least. "It will have to go uphill before it goes down," Mary said to herself; "I cannot imagine that it will be able to do that."

When Father returned with the tubing he put it in the basin so that it became full of water. Then, pinching both ends to close them, he took it out with the water still inside, holding it like a big **U** in both hands. He gave Mary one end, saying, "Pinch the end tight and hold it deep down under the water in the basin until I tell you to stop pinching."

Mary did as she was told, and then Father leaned out of the window, still pinching his end of the tube. With the hand that was holding the tube he reached as far down the wall of the house as he could, until his end of the tube outside the house was lower than Mary's end inside the basin.

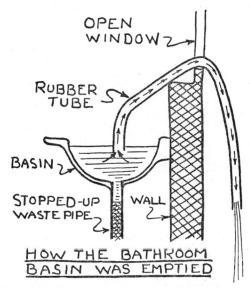

HOW THE BATHROOM BASIN WAS EMPTIED

"You can stop pinching now, Mary," he said; "but go on holding the end down at the bottom of the basin."

Mary let the pipe open under the water, and at the same time Father let his end open. Instantly the water in the tube poured out into the garden, and the odd thing was that, as it went, it seemed to suck in more water from the basin, so that instead of the flow ceasing in a second or two, it went on and on, until the basin was empty. At the finish, Mary's end of the tube gave a sucking noise as though it were eager to drink up the basin itself.

"Well!" exclaimed Mary, "I never saw anything like that before. The water actually ran *up* the pipe in its hurry to get out of the window, yet there was nobody sucking at the other end of the pipe. What is the explanation, Daddy?"

"Your barometer should give you the clue to the mystery," Father answered. "There you have a column of mercury, thirty inches high, held up in a tube because the top end is closed and no air can get in. It is held up by the force of the atmosphere trying to get up the tube and reach that little empty space at the top. If the liquid happened to be water instead of mercury, the pressure of the atmosphere would hold up a column of it more than thirty feet high, because water is not nearly so heavy as mercury.

"When I hung the rubber tube out of the window, there was about four feet of it dangling down. On your side of the wall, going up from the basin to the window-sill, there was less than three feet of tube. When I let go my end of the tube, the water in it tried to fall down, but it could not do this without making an empty space or vacuum at the top where the pipe rested on the window-sill. You must remember that your end of the pipe was filled with water too, so no air could come up that way. What the air did do, however, was push water in the basin up the tube to fill the emptiness, and it kept on doing this until the basin was empty.

"What decided the water to flow my way, that is, out into the garden, instead of your way, back into the basin, was the fact that on my side the pipe was longer, and consequently the water in it was heavier. If I had put only a few inches of pipe out of the window the water would have run back into the basin; to make a successful syphon you *must* have a pipe going *down* that is longer than the pipe going *up*.

"Syphons are very useful for emptying things you cannot

turn upside down. If you want to empty a tank with only a little hole in it at the top—a hole too small for your hand to pass through, you may have difficulty starting your syphon. However, all you have to do is poke the empty pipe into the tank, leaving a long piece dangling down outside which you can suck. By sucking you can get the water to rise up that part of the pipe which is in the tank. Once it comes over the bend at the top it will come rushing down, and it will keep on rushing. Often you can get your mouth away before the water reaches the outlet. This is just as well if the water happens to be dirty, or if the tank happens to hold some liquid other than water, with a nasty taste.

A SYPHON CAN BE STARTED BY SUCKING DOWN THE TUBE.

SUCTION PUMPS

" When you suck lemonade up a straw you do it by making something inside your mouth smaller. This leaves an empty space which the air tries to fill. In trying to do this it pushes lemonade out of your glass up the straw.

" A pump for getting water out of a well will work so long as the water is not more than thirty feet down. It has a plunger or piston, acting like the one of leather in a bicycle pump, only made differently. It is always a good fit in the pump barrel, but there is a little flap on the top which opens upwards. When the plunger is pulled up it leaves an empty space below. Air tries to get in, but as the little flap on the plunger opens

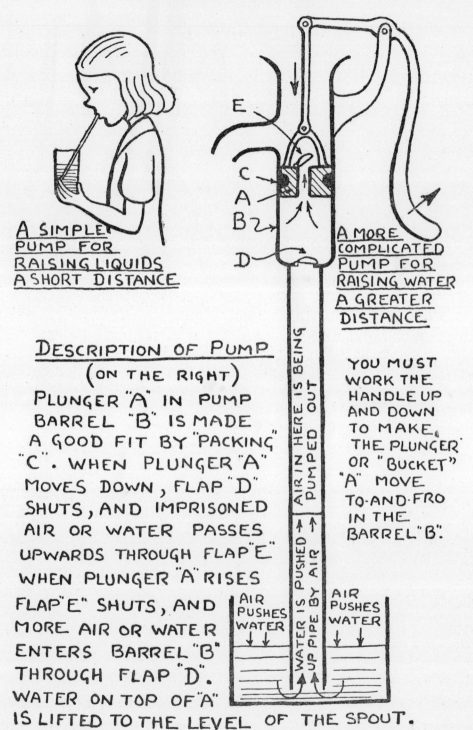

A SIMPLE PUMP FOR RAISING LIQUIDS A SHORT DISTANCE

A MORE COMPLICATED PUMP FOR RAISING WATER A GREATER DISTANCE

DESCRIPTION OF PUMP

(ON THE RIGHT)

PLUNGER "A" IN PUMP BARREL "B" IS MADE A GOOD FIT BY "PACKING" "C". WHEN PLUNGER "A" MOVES DOWN, FLAP "D" SHUTS, AND IMPRISONED AIR OR WATER PASSES UPWARDS THROUGH FLAP "E" WHEN PLUNGER "A" RISES FLAP "E" SHUTS, AND MORE AIR OR WATER ENTERS BARREL "B" THROUGH FLAP "D". WATER ON TOP OF "A" IS LIFTED TO THE LEVEL OF THE SPOUT.

YOU MUST WORK THE HANDLE UP AND DOWN TO MAKE THE PLUNGER OR "BUCKET" "A" MOVE TO-AND-FRO IN THE BARREL "B".

AIR IN HERE IS BEING PUMPED OUT

WATER IS PUSHED UP PIPE BY AIR

AIR PUSHES WATER

AIR PUSHES WATER

306

upwards, not downwards, air cannot get in that way. It has to come in from below, from the long pipe leading down to the water in the well. There is another upwardly opening flap covering the upper end of this pipe. This lifts to let the air in while the plunger is going up. It shuts again when the plunger starts to come down. The air imprisoned in the pump barrel cannot get back into the pipe again; its only way out as the plunger descends is through the flap in the plunger itself; this lifts to let it pass up and out. By working the plunger up and down you can empty the air out of the long pipe leading down into the well. But when you empty out the air in the pipe water will be forced up by the atmosphere to fill this emptiness. Eventually the water comes right up to the pump itself, and then the pump starts emptying water out of the long pipe. That is just what you want.

"If water does not start to flow after you have worked the pump for a few times it is because the plunger no longer fits the pump barrel very well. To make it a good fit there is a belt of soft stuff called 'packing' in a groove round its middle. If this gets hard and dry the plunger will cease to be an air-tight fit in the barrel and will let air leak past on the up stroke. To start your pump working you will then have to moisten the packing by pouring some water into the pump from the top. So, if you have to depend on a well for water, you should never let your buckets get quite empty lest the pump needs moistening—or 'priming' as it is called."

FIZZY DRINKS

Mary and Father were still talking about syphons and pumps at breakfast-time. Peter pricked up his ears.

" How does a soda-water syphon work? " he asked. " The air is outside the syphon, not inside; yet the soda water runs up the middle pipe and out of the spout against the force of the air. How is that? "

" Soda water is water that has had a gas called carbon dioxide

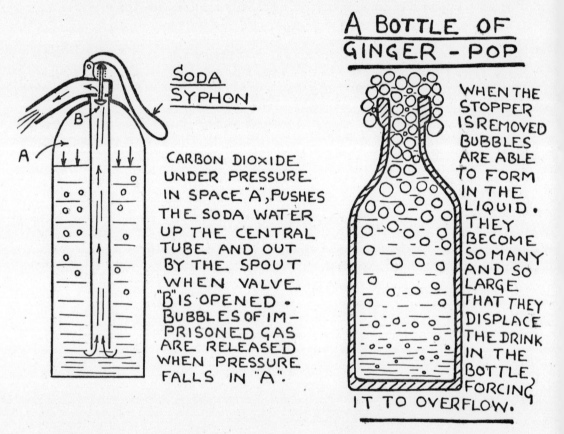

SODA
SYPHON

CARBON DIOXIDE
UNDER PRESSURE
IN SPACE "A", PUSHES
THE SODA WATER
UP THE CENTRAL
TUBE AND OUT
BY THE SPOUT
WHEN VALVE
"B" IS OPENED.
BUBBLES OF IM-
PRISONED GAS
ARE RELEASED
WHEN PRESSURE
FALLS IN "A".

A BOTTLE OF
GINGER - POP

WHEN THE
STOPPER
IS REMOVED
BUBBLES
ARE ABLE
TO FORM
IN THE
LIQUID.
THEY
BECOME
SO MANY
AND SO
LARGE
THAT THEY
DISPLACE
THE DRINK
IN THE
BOTTLE,
FORCING
IT TO OVERFLOW.

pressed into it," Father answered. " Water will dissolve this gas just as it will dissolve sugar, so that you cannot see it even as bubbles. To keep it there, though, needs the pressure of more carbon dioxide acting on the surface of the water. Inside the soda-water syphon, above the soda water, there is carbon dioxide under pressure. When you open the valve this gas is able to force the water up the tube and out. Its force diminishes, however, when the space above the water gets larger. Then some of the dissolved gas makes its appearance as bubbles in the soda water. It makes its escape and helps to keep the space above the soda water full of gas. So you can draw off your soda water to the last drop; the pressure of gas in the bottle always being more than that of the air outside."

" I had a bottle of fizzy drink yesterday," Mary said. " When I first unscrewed the stopper it was quite quiet in the bottle. After I had had half I put in the stopper and shook the bottle. Then, when I unscrewed the stopper, there was a tremendous fizz and the drink foamed up and started coming out. Why was that? "

" Shaking helps to release the gas," Father answered. " Some of it escapes into the neck of the bottle, and the rest only waits for the time when the pressure of gas in the bottle is released. Then bubbles form in the drink so fast that they do not leave room for the drink itself; this is forced up, foaming and bubbling, out of the mouth of the bottle."

CHAPTER THREE

IS WATER A SOLID?

WHEN you push your finger in a bowl of water it goes in very easily, as the water moves to one side and makes room for it. If, however, you fill a bottle with water to the very top, you will find it quite impossible to push in the cork. The water cannot make room for the cork because it already occupies the whole bottle. Nor will it "squash up" and make itself smaller

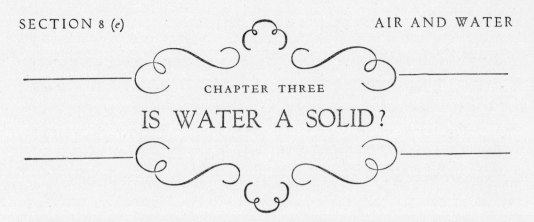

IRON SUPPORTS ITS OWN WEIGHT WITHOUT DEFORMING; SOFT RUBBER SAGS A LITTLE; AND WATER COLLAPSES ALTOGETHER, BECOMING A BROAD, SHALLOW PUDDLE

IRON   RUBBER   WATER

in the way that air would squash up. When water is confined on all sides it behaves exactly like a solid body, and it seems as hard as iron.

Water and most other liquids resemble solids in this peculiarity of theirs of entirely filling the space they occupy so that they cannot be made smaller. They are, to use the scientific term, almost *incompressible*. Rubber is incompressible too if it is firmly enclosed all round. If you want a piece of rubber, or a volume of liquid, to squash up in *one* direction, you must allow it space to expand or bulge in *another* direction.

Rubber offers some resistance to being squashed up, even if it is free to bulge sideways, but liquids offer no resistance at all if they are given a chance to go sideways. You cannot make water stand up on a table and support its own weight; it just spreads sideways until it makes a thin film over the whole of the available surface. A block of rubber may sag a little, but it

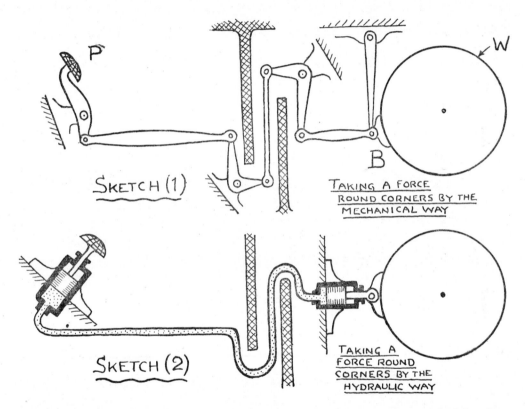

SKETCH (1)

TAKING A FORCE ROUND CORNERS BY THE MECHANICAL WAY

SKETCH (2)

TAKING A FORCE ROUND CORNERS BY THE HYDRAULIC WAY

will not spread sideways indefinitely. Iron or other solid bodies do not seem to sag at all. You could push down on them with a force of many tons before you could persuade them to squash out sideways.

The incompressibility of liquids in confined spaces makes them useful for transmitting forces round corners and to inaccessible places. Suppose, for instance, you wanted to make a pedal P apply a brake block B to a wheel W. To do it by means of levers and rods you would have to have all the complications shown in Sketch (1) here; but if you used a liquid for transmitting the force, you could have the simple arrangement shown in Sketch (2).

Many modern motor-cars have fluid-operated brakes working on what is called the Lockheed system, and, indeed, a lot of things are worked from a distance nowadays by oil or water

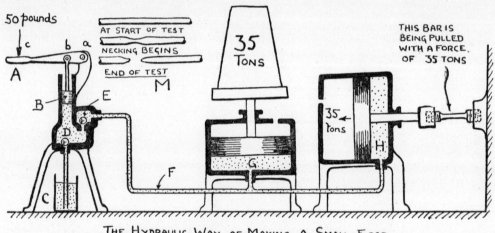

THE HYDRAULIC WAY OF MAKING A SMALL FORCE INTO A LARGE FORCE

being forced through long pipes. Oil and water are as strong as iron rods and bars, and will transmit any force you like to send, even forces amounting to hundreds and thousands of tons.

In a big factory you can often see what are called hydraulic presses: these are big pistons which are moved with enormous force by water. They can bend and cut a flat sheet of steel, forming it into the side of a motor-car body in a few seconds.

Using a small force-pump to drive water into a cylinder fitted with a big piston, you too could do the work of a giant. In the sketch you see here, A is the handle of a little pump with a

piston B of one inch diameter.   If you lift the handle, water
will rise from the tank C through the little ball valve D,
following the piston B.   When you push down on the handle
the ball valve D will shut and prevent the water from returning
to the tank C.   Ball valve E will open, however, and let the
water run along pipe F to the cylinders G and H, each of which
is fitted with a piston twenty inches in diameter.   When you
pump water into the spaces G and H, the big pistons will
slowly move along their cylinders, and you can make them
exert tremendous force, just by working the pump with your
own relatively weak arms.

If you can press down on the handle of the pump with your
whole weight of, say, fifty pounds, the piston B will press on
the water with a force of two hundred pounds, because the
handle is a lever with length *ab* only a quarter of length *ac*.
This force of two hundred pounds on a circle of only one inch
in diameter will be transmitted through the pipe E to the big
pistons which are each equal, not to twenty pistons of one inch
diameter, but to 20×20, or 400 pistons of one inch diameter.
The force on each big piston will therefore be four hundred
times the force on the little piston B; that works out to
$400 \times 200 = 80,000$ pounds, which is more than 35 tons!   So
you see, you could hold up a weight of thirty-five tons on the
piston in G, at the same time pulling in half a steel bar with
the piston in H.

Engineers use a simple machine like this, worked by hand,
for finding out whether iron and steel are of good quality.
They make samples into round bars about three-quarters of an
inch in diameter, and test them by pulling them till they break.
It is interesting to watch a steel bar break.   First of all it

"necks," or becomes thinner, at the weakest spot. Then it pulls out quite quickly, eventually snapping with a loud "bang" so that it looks like what I have drawn at M.

The incompressibility of water helps the plumber when he comes to un-stop your sink, which may have the waste pipe

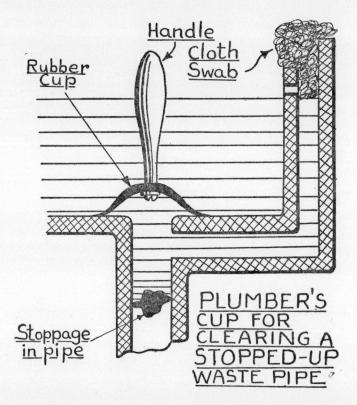

choked with fluff or tea leaves, so that the dirty water will not run away. The plumber brings with him a rubber bell, or cup, on a strong handle. To begin with, he fills the sink right up, and then he stuffs up the holes at the end with a cloth swab. Now he puts his cup over the waste outlet and forces the handle down with all his might. The water in the cup is driven down the waste pipe, where it pushes the obstruction with a force practically equal to the weight of the plumber. This usually shifts it and leaves the pipe clear. The reason why the holes at the end of the sink must be closed by a swab is clear to see. If these holes were not stopped up, the water from the plumber's cup would find an easy way round and up into the open air. In fact, as the plumber pushed on the handle of his cup, water might just squirt up from these holes and hit him in the eye! You see now how easy it is to have accidents if you are ignorant of science, or forgetful of its truths!

Well, the purpose of this short article was to tell you about the incompressibility of water and, indeed, of liquids generally. I hope that what I have said will enable you to appreciate this interesting and valuable peculiarity of liquids.

CHAPTER FOUR

PRESSURE AND VACUUM GAUGES

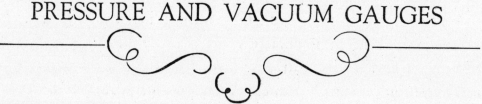

MARY had been to a party, and when she came home she was laden with little gifts. She had a funny paper hat and two toy balloons, but what pleased her most was the thing she called her "teaser." This was a flat tube of paper rolled up like a spring. When she blew into the mouthpiece the tube filled out and started to unroll. It went quite long and straight eventually. Mary kept blowing it at Peter, tickling him in the face with it, and then, when he wasn't looking, in the back of his neck.

MARY KEPT ON TEASING PETER

When Father came home from the office he stopped her.

"Don't tease," he said; "Peter will get mad in a minute and break your toy for you by snatching at it. That would be a pity, because it is an instructive thing and you can learn a lot from it."

"All right, Daddy," Mary answered; "I suppose this means another science lecture from you. What is it to be about this time?"

" You needn't hear it if you don't want to," Father answered crossly.

" Oh yes," Mary cried, " only I've just come from a party, you know, and you must expect me to be a little excited. It will take me some time to be myself again after all the fun I've had."

" I thought I would tell you how pressures are measured," Father went on. " The barometer measures atmospheric pressure very nicely, and you can use a bent tube full of liquid to measure other pressures. The tube is often called a ' U ' tube by reason of its shape, and a pressure gauge of this simple kind is called a ' manometer.'

" A manometer filled with water is often used to measure the pressure inside places where there is a partial vacuum, as for instance in the smoke box at the front of a railway engine. The blast of the exhaust steam rushing up the chimney takes air out along with it, leaving a partially empty space inside the smoke box. To fill up this emptiness air has to rush through the fire at the other end of the boiler, and this is how the fire gets the air it needs to make it burn well. The partial vacuum or ' depression ' in the smoke box is very important, and the manometer tells you what it is in ' inches water gauge.' A depression of 5 in W.G. is one causing water in a ' U ' tube to rise five inches higher on the smoke-box side of the ' U ' than it is on the side open to the atmosphere.

" You can use a manometer for measuring bigger differences of pressure; but if you use water, you will get a difference of level of about two feet for every pound on the square inch difference of pressure. This is too much for most purposes, and consequently a heavier liquid must be used instead. As you know already, mercury is the best liquid to use. With this liquid you will get a difference of level of only about two inches for a pressure difference of one pound per square inch. Even so, a difference of fifteen pounds per square inch requires a 'U' tube thirty inches higher one side than the other. Imagine

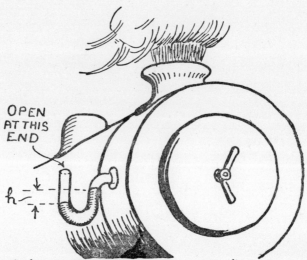

OPEN AT THIS END

h

A "MANOMETER OR "U" TUBE CONTAINING WATER, CONNECTED TO AN OPENING IN A LOCOMOTIVE SMOKE BOX WILL SHOW THAT WHEN THE ENGINE IS WORKING THE PRESSURE INSIDE THE SMOKE-BOX IS LESS THAN THAT OUT-SIDE. THE HEIGHT "h" MEASURES THE PRESSURE DIFFERENCE IN "INCHES OF WATER GAUGE".

what an awkward great thing a manometer would be for measuring pressures of a hundred or a thousand pounds to the square inch, pressures which are quite common in engineering!

" To measure these higher pressures you have a gauge working on the same principle as Mary's ' teaser.' A flattish metal tube is curled round to form three parts of a circle. When air or steam or any other fluid, liquid or gaseous, is pushed in

Photograph by W. A. Fortens, A.R.P.S.

Starting platform of the P. & O. liner *Stratheden*, showing Bourdon gauges for steam and other pressures.

under great pressure, the tube tries to straighten, because that way it makes more room for the fluid inside. In what is called a Bourdon gauge the moving end of the tube is connected by a sector and pinion mechanism to a pointer which records the pressure on a graduated dial. The Bourdon type of gauge is

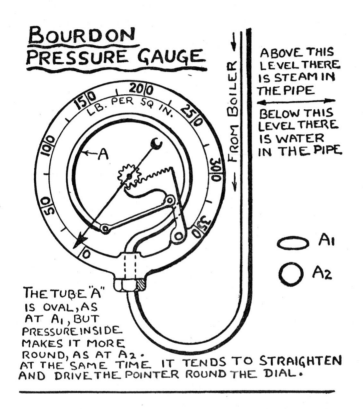

BOURDON PRESSURE GAUGE

LB. PER SQ IN.

150 200 250 300 350 100 50 0

FROM BOILER

ABOVE THIS LEVEL THERE IS STEAM IN THE PIPE

BELOW THIS LEVEL THERE IS WATER IN THE PIPE

A1
A2

THE TUBE "A" IS OVAL, AS AT A1, BUT PRESSURE INSIDE MAKES IT MORE ROUND, AS AT A2. AT THE SAME TIME IT TENDS TO STRAIGHTEN AND DRIVE THE POINTER ROUND THE DIAL.

very common, and you can see several of them in the cab of any railway engine or on the starting platform of a big steam-ship. They are set to read nothing at atmospheric pressure. What they record is the amount by which the pressure in a boiler exceeds the pressure of the air. Fifty or so years ago a gauge pressure of one hundred and eighty pounds per square inch was usual in railway engines, but nowadays engine boilers carry a pressure of two hundred and fifty pounds per square inch or even more. Remember that ' gauge pressure ' means pressure in excess of atmospheric. You must add atmospheric pressure (roughly fifteen pounds per square inch) to obtain the total or ' absolute ' pressure of the steam or whatever fluid is involved."

NOTE.—The springiness of the tube in a Bourdon gauge would be affected by heat, and therefore hot steam is not admitted directly to the gauge. The pipe connecting the gauge to the boiler is made with a dip in it, and this fills with water. The steam pushes relatively cold water into the gauge tube, but this water has the pressure of the steam behind it.

CHAPTER FIVE

WHAT MAKES THINGS FLOAT?

MARY and Peter were having a holiday at the seaside, and their
father had hired a rowing-boat for an hour. Already they were a
long way from the shore. Peter was peering over the side, trying
to see the bottom, but the water was too deep. All he could see
was the greeny-blue colour of the water. Mary gazed at the cork
in the bottom of the boat, and wondered what would happen if it
came out of its hole.

A HOLE IN THE BOTTOM
OF A BOAT (AS IMAGINED
BY A COMIC-PAPER ARTIST)

They were a glum pair.
Father saw that they
were rather nervous,
so he said, "What's
the matter, Mary?"

"Could you get that
cork back in its hole
again if it popped
out?" Mary asked,
pointing to the cork in
question.

"Of course I could," Father replied; "the pressure of the
water trying to come in is not very great. If I took it out you
would see a little fountain, but it would not come up any higher
than the water outside the boat. Look, I'll show you."

Mary cried out in terror, but she was too late. Father pulled out the cork, and water spurted into the air through the hole in the bottom of the boat. As Father had said, it did not rise very high, only about a foot.

" Put it back, Daddy, oh do! " cried Mary; " we shall sink! "

Father quietly pushed the cork back into its hole again and then mopped up the water in the bottom of the boat. He used an old rag, which he squeezed over the side.

" Anyone looking at the adventures of the folk in your comic

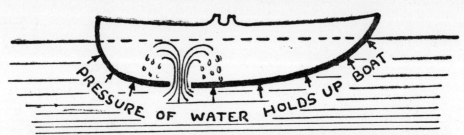

IN REALITY THE WATER FOUNTAIN COULD NOT RISE ANY HIGHER INSIDE THE BOAT THAN THE WATER OUTSIDE. THE FORCE ON THE CORK BUNG IS ONLY A TINY PART OF THE TOTAL PRESSURE ON THE UNDER-WATER SURFACE OF THE BOAT.

papers would think that water was waiting to rush into a boat with enormous pressure," he said; " for if anyone punctures a boat in one of the comic-paper pictures, a jet of water comes through with force enough to lift people right up in the air. Perhaps you get your own fear of a leak from seeing what comic artists imagine would happen if a boat developed a hole. The force of the water trying to come in, acting on the *whole* of the underneath of our boat is just equal to the weight of the boat with us inside it. That is what keeps us afloat. You can see that the cork has to withstand only a very *tiny* fraction of the total force, so tiny indeed that I can easily push it back again into its hole with one finger if it should come out."

"Yes, but don't do it again," Mary said, giving a little shiver.

THE MEANING OF DISPLACEMENT

"When you put stones into a jar of water you cause the water in the jar to rise. Æsop tells us in one of his fables of a clever bird that was unable to reach water at the bottom of a long-necked pitcher, but managed to do so at last by dropping in small stones to bring the level of the water well up the neck of the pitcher. If you drop heavy things into water, they are easily able to lift the water up, but things lighter than water do not overcome its weight. Instead of sinking down and displacing the water they float. They sink as far as they are able, displacing a weight of water

BY DISPLACING THE WATER WITH STONES THIS BIRD WILL SOON BRING IT WITHIN REACH OF ITS BEAK.

equal to their own weight, and then they stop sinking with part of themselves still showing above the surface. A boat floating on water is like two things balancing on a pair of scales. If the boat goes down deeper, the water it displaces must rise higher; if the boat bobs up again then the level of the water must fall."

THESE TWO JARS ARE OF THE SAME SIZE, AND THEY CONTAIN THE SAME AMOUNT OF WATER.

A BLOCK OF <u>IRON</u> MAKES ROOM FOR ITSELF IN THE JAR BY PUSHING (OR DISPLACING) WATER UPWARDS. A BLOCK OF <u>WOOD</u> OF THE SAME SIZE HAS NOT ENOUGH WEIGHT TO DISPLACE (OR LIFT) MORE THAN A FRACTION OF ITS OWN VOLUME OF WATER, SO IT CANNOT COMPLETELY SINK

<u>IN FLOATING THERE IS PERFECT BALANCE BETWEEN THE WEIGHT OF THE THING FLOATED AND THE WEIGHT OF THE WATER IT DISPLACES</u>

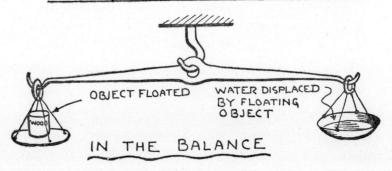

OBJECT FLOATED   WATER DISPLACED BY FLOATING OBJECT

IN THE BALANCE

"How can an iron ship float, Daddy?" Mary asked; "iron is heavier than water."

"You can make things of iron very light for their bulk by making them hollow," Father replied. "A ship made of iron displaces a lot of water, because the iron is beaten out into the form of thin plates which are riveted or welded together to make a thin hollow hull. You said iron, Mary, but actually ships are made of steel nowadays. Steel is a superior kind of iron containing carefully proportioned amounts of carbon and other substances in its composition. It weighs as much as iron, but it is stronger. A big modern ship of steel may displace 50,000 tons of water or more, and therefore it can be made to weigh at least this much itself, for the water will hold it up. The biggest ship afloat is the Cunard White Star steamship *Queen Elizabeth,* which has a displacement of about 80,000 tons. Knowing that the hull would push aside all this weight of water when it was afloat, the engineers were able to load it with heavy turbines, boilers and other things, confident that it would keep them all up off the bottom of the sea.

"It is really the volume of what is under the water that counts. For every cubic foot of water forced aside by a floating body you will get an up-thrust of about sixty-two and a half pounds, this being the weight of the displaced water. When you go into the sea to bathe, or when you get into your bath, you feel lighter because the water is trying to push back into the place you are filling, and it pushes with a force equal to sixty-two and a half pounds for every cubic foot of volume your body has.

"It was a celebrated Greek scientist called Archimedes who first realised that the loss of weight felt by a person in water was equal to the weight of displaced water. He lived about two hundred years before Jesus (well over two thousand years ago), and there is an amusing legend about him. It is said that he was in a public bath, thinking about the mysterious lightness of his body when in water. Suddenly he thought of the true explanation. He was so excited by his discovery that he cried,

'Eureka, I have it!' and leapt out of the water. Without waiting to put on any clothes he rushed through the streets to his house. He wanted to make some more experiments, and do some writing, and he could not waste his precious time

ARCHIMEDES SURPRISES SOME LITTLE GREEK CHILDREN

[ARCHIMEDES IS PRONOUNCED ARKY-MEED-EASE]

putting on clothes. The story may very well be true, for he was indeed an absent-minded man, and his absent-mindedness cost him his life. When his city was besieged and stormed by enemy soldiers, he went on working out scientific problems. He took no notice of all the noise of the fighting, and at last an enemy soldier came into the room where he was working and killed him."

THE PRINCIPLE OF ARCHIMEDES

" In school some day you may be told about ' Archimedes'
Principle,' which says what I have just been telling you,
namely, that the loss of weight of things in water is equal to
the weight of the water they displace. We could work out what
volume of water we displace in this little boat quite easily if
we knew our own weights and the weight of the boat. Suppose
our weights to be one hundred and fifty pounds for me, eighty
pounds for you, Mary, sixty pounds for you, Peter, and
three hundred pounds for the boat, then our total displacement would be 150 + 80 + 60 + 300, or 590 pounds. Since
we are afloat, there must be five hundred and ninety pounds of
water trying to get back into the place occupied by the under-
water part of our boat. The volume of this water, and hence of
the under-water part of our boat, must be 590 divided by 62·5.
I cannot do that in my head, so I will put down my oars and
work it out with pencil and paper."

Father put down the oars and did a division sum on the back
of a letter taken from his pocket. The result came to 9½ cubic
feet.

" Usually," Father went on, " boat builders know what
weights have to be carried, so they work out the volumetric
displacement, just as I have done, and then they plan their hull
to give them this displacement when it has submerged to the
right depth."

" I feel better now that I know what keeps our boat up,"
said Mary.

" So do I," Peter chipped in.

WHY BALLOONS AND AIRSHIPS FLY

" What makes a balloon or an airship float in the air? " Mary asked.

" Archimedes' Principle applies to that too," Father answered. " It is filled out with a very light gas, which may be HELIUM, but is more often HYDROGEN. The gas-bag displaces an immense amount of air, which tries to push back again into the space it fills. The balloon or airship loses weight equal to the weight of the air displaced. It loses more weight than it actually has, and so it feels a push upwards. It rises higher and higher, but the air it displaces becomes less and less dense (see page 295), and consequently the displacement measured in pounds becomes less and less. Eventually it displaces neither more nor less than its own weight of air, and then it ceases to rise any more. You would have to throw out ballast if you wanted to rise still farther. To come down you must reduce the volumetric displacement by letting out some of the hydrogen or helium.

" Helium is better than hydrogen, because it is not inflammable. It is, however, very expensive, and in the past hydrogen has generally been used for airships. There have been some horrible tragedies resulting from fires in airships. The British airship *R.101*, which I saw at the Hendon Air Pageant some years before the war, met with disaster when flying one windy night on its way to India. It only got as far as France, and there, due to leakage of hydrogen, it started to come down. It hit a hill and crashed. In a second it was ablaze, and everyone on board was burnt to death.

" Boats are much safer than airships. People have been

The great British airship R 101 which met with disaster on a flight to India.

The R 101 at Hendon. Following her destruction by fire, Britain decided not to build any more airships.

building them for thousands of years, and so long as they do not collide with rocks, icebergs or other boats, they keep afloat. All the time they enjoy the support of the displaced water, which gives them an up-thrust equal to this displaced water's weight——"

"Or so Archimedes said!" butted in Peter.

"Yes," agreed Father; "and Archimedes was right. Don't you forget that, my lad!"

"The hour is up," said Mary, looking at her watch. "We shall have to pay again for being late."

"Bother!" exclaimed Father, seizing up the oars and beginning to row for the shore.

CHAPTER ONE

MAGNETISM

WORKING with her scissors one day, the mother of Mary and Peter noticed that they had an attraction for needles and pins, which stuck to them as though they had been smeared with butter or treacle. Father was close at hand, and he explained that the scissors had become "magnetised." Magnetism is not any kind of stickiness, but an invisible force that reaches out from one thing to another. That is what Father said; and to prove it he laid a needle on the smooth shiny surface of the table and brought the scissors very gradually closer and closer to it until, quite suddenly, the needle gave a jump and stuck to them. "Treacle cannot draw things from a distance," said Father.

MAGNETISM IS "CATCHING"

"However did my scissors get like that?" Mother asked.

"Perhaps you let them fall with a smack on to a hard floor," answered Father; "the Earth we live on is a big magnet, and if a piece of steel is given a sharp knock or jolt while it is pointing North and South, it may become a magnet too. Magnetism is catching, like mumps, measles and whooping-cough, but only steel things can catch it. You cannot magnetise things made of brass or wood or aluminium, but only things made of steel.

"Many things that get hard usage become magnetised naturally. A file or other tool used in a workshop generally becomes magnetised sooner or later, because some day it gets a knock or a blow when pointing North and South. A steel poker, which is often dropped on the hearth, may become magnetised too, and then it will have this power to pick up needles and pins."

Mary was listening to her father while he was speaking, and an idea occurred to her. " If magnetism is catching," she

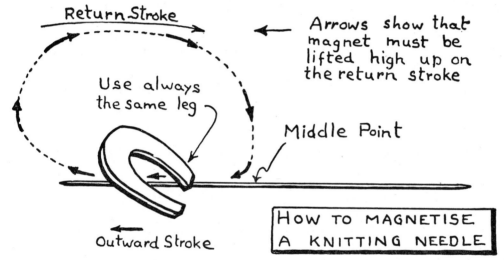

Return Stroke

Arrows show that magnet must be lifted high up on the return stroke

Use always the same leg

Middle Point

HOW TO MAGNETISE A KNITTING NEEDLE

Outward Stroke

said, " can a piece of steel catch it from another piece of steel as well as from the Earth? "

" Certainly," answered Father; " if you will bring me a really strong steel magnet, like the ones you can buy, I will turn a steel knitting needle into a magnet for you."

" Peter was given a little red magnet like a horseshoe last Christmas," Mary said; " will that do? "

" That will do very nicely," Father answered. So Mary ran to fetch it. She brought her steel knitting needles as well.

" Now I will show you that it is possible to make a knitting needle catch the complaint of magnetism from this magnet of Peter's," said Father. So saying, he took the knitting needle in his left hand, holding it near the middle, and stroked the projecting half with one leg of Peter's magnet. He used the *same* leg every time, moving it from the middle to the end of the needle, then lifting it high in the air and bringing it back to the middle again, ready for the next stroke. "If you move it back from end to middle without changing the leg, you will undo what you have done in going from middle to end," he said.

After Father had stroked the needle about ten times he showed that it was indeed a magnet, and quite a strong one, for it would pick up a lot of pins all together.

BALANCING A PIN ON ITS POINT

"Can you make a pin stand up on its point?" Father asked Peter.

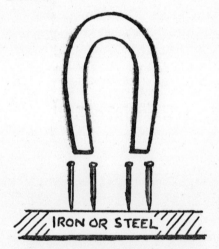

IRON OR STEEL

HOW TO MAKE PINS STAND UP ON THEIR POINTS

"Not without sticking it into something soft," answered Peter.

"I can make a pin stand up on a piece of hard steel," said Father; "in fact, I can make lots of pins stand up that way."

So saying, Father held a strong magnet about two inches above a flat slab of steel and then stood some pins, points downwards, on the piece of steel, directly under the magnet. The pins stayed standing upright, swaying from side to side. When he moved the magnet from side to side the pins leaned over first one way and then the other.

332

"These are steel pins," Father said. "I could not do this with brass pins, although, being silvered, they might look just the same."

A STRING OF PINS

"Can you join a lot of pins together head to point, head to point, head to point and so on to make one long string of them?" asked Father. "With the magnet it is easy. Look!" He held the magnet high up, and then let a pin hang from it, head downwards. He touched the head of this pin with the point of another pin, which he then let go so that it hung suspended by magnetism from the first pin. From the head of this second pin he hung a third pin, point upwards. He added a fourth pin to the third, a fifth pin to the fourth and so on. The string of pins grew longer and longer, but at last it became too heavy and then it broke.

A STRING OF PINS

HOW LONG CAN YOU MAKE IT?

"The first pin catches its magnetism direct from the magnet," said Father; "the second pin catches it from the first, the third catches it from the second, the fourth catches it from the third and so on."

MAGNETISM GOES THROUGH NEARLY EVERYTHING

"Things we let drop fall to the ground because the Earth attracts them," said Father; "but this force of gravity is different from magnetism, because it affects everything and not just steel things. The magnetism of the Earth is something quite separate from gravity, and it is so feeble that you would never notice it in the ordinary way. The force of gravity passes through everything. If you hold up a weight you can feel the Earth dragging it downwards, and this force still tugs at the weight even if you put screens between it and the Earth. Magnetism is another force that can pass through screens. Look at this."

Father rested some pins on top of a flat sheet of cardboard, and then he put the magnet underneath the cardboard. When he scraped the magnet along underneath the cardboard the pins on top followed it. They looked quite bewitched and full of life, as there was nothing visible to account for their movement.

" You can do this same experiment using a sheet of glass or of brass or of wood or of aluminium," said Father; " magnetism can pass through all these substances. The only thing you cannot use is a sheet of iron or of steel. That does stop the magnetism from getting through to the other side."

Mary and Peter used screens made of different materials to prove that Father was right, and some of these screens were thicker than others. They noticed that the pins were not so active when the screen was thick as when it was thin, and they thought that perhaps a thick screen did stop some of the magnetism.

" You are wrong in supposing that," said Father; " nothing can stop magnetism, but it spreads from the magnet like light spreads from a candle, filling all space, but becoming thinner or weaker the farther it is away from its source. The force of gravity becomes weaker too if you go a long way from the Earth, but because the Earth is so enormous in comparison with any distance you could go up in an aeroplane, you would never notice the weakening. With a magnet you notice this weakening because the magnet is tiny, and though its influence reaches out a long way, it soon becomes too feeble to be detected. It is the greater distance and not the greater amount of material in your screen that causes the magnetism to seem weaker when you use a thick screen instead of a thin one."

POLARITY

Mary was playing with Peter's strong horseshoe magnet and a darning needle she had magnetised with it when she noticed

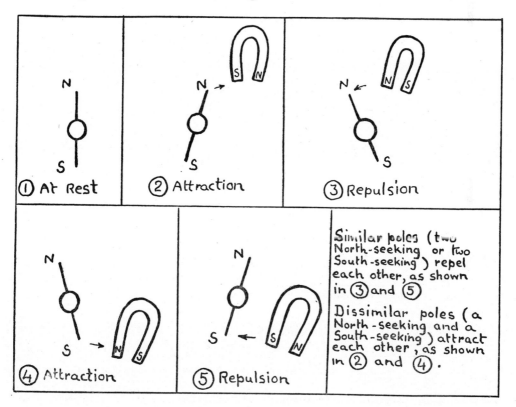

a very queer thing. The eye end of the needle would only go to one leg of the magnet, it shied away from the other one.

Similarly, the point of the needle had a liking for one leg of the magnet, but not the leg that attracted the eye end; it shied away from that one.

"You have discovered an important thing about magnetism," said Father, when Mary told him what had happened; "you

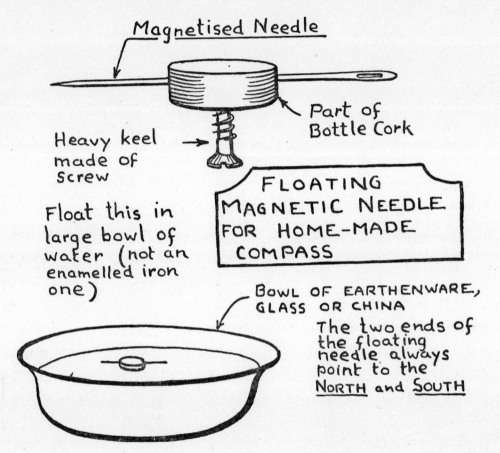

Magnetised Needle

Heavy keel made of screw

Part of Bottle Cork

Float this in large bowl of water (not an enamelled iron one)

FLOATING MAGNETIC NEEDLE FOR HOME-MADE COMPASS

BOWL OF EARTHENWARE, GLASS OR CHINA

The two ends of the floating needle always point to the NORTH and SOUTH

have discovered that a magnet has what is called polarity, being different at one end from what it is at the other. You can show this very well if you will stick your magnetised darning needle through a flat cork and float it on water. It can turn round very easily when it forms part of a little boat, and so you can easily see when one of its ends is being attracted or repelled.

336

You will find that one leg of Peter's magnet will attract the eye end, repelling the point end, while the other leg will attract the point end, repelling the eye end."

THE MAGNETIC COMPASS

" The Earth being a big magnet," Father went on, " you would expect to find one end of your darning needle drawn in one direction, and the other end drawn in the opposite direction. This is actually the case, and your freely floating needle, left to itself, will always go back to the same position in the water, as you may already have noticed. One end points South and the other end points North. This peculiarity of a magnetised needle is of great usefulness to travellers and especially to sailors, who must make voyages over the trackless ocean. A magnetised needle free to turn so that its ends always point North and South is called a compass, and every ship carries a compass to help the sailors steer a straight course at night or in a fog, or at any other time when they haven't the help of the sun or of stars to point out the way. You can get little pocket compasses in toyshops and in places that supply the needs of Boy Scouts and Girl Guides. Every boy and every girl should have a pocket compass. It is a help to them if they get lost when hiking through woods or over misty mountains. It

POCKET COMPASS

may even help them to find their whereabouts in a big town like London. And if you arrive at a strange hotel by night, you can find out which way your bedroom window looks before the sun gets up next morning. Without a compass you are always getting queer surprises, because it is natural to think of the way a strange house faces when you first find yourself in it, and you may easily imagine it to face North when it really faces South and *vice versa*. A glance at a compass will tell you at any time of day or night and in any weather which way you are looking. It would tell you this even if you were in a tightly shut box without any windows.

"Because of this inclination of every magnet to point with one of its ends to the North and the other end to the South we give the name of 'North-seeking Pole' or 'North Pole' to one end and 'South-seeking Pole' or 'South Pole' to the other end."

WHAT IS A MAGNET TRYING TO DO?

When Mary and Peter quarrelled and started pushing each other about, they generally pushed with some object in view. Perhaps Mary tried to push Peter out of the nursery, or Peter tried to push Mary into the gold-fish pond in the garden. They always had some idea of what they wanted to achieve when they started pushing. One day it occurred to Mary that a magnet might have some purpose in pushing one end of a needle and pulling the other end, so she asked her father about it.

"I am glad you asked me that," said Father; "a magnet does not just push away what it does not want and attract what it does. It really wants anything that helps its two poles to get into magnetic connection with one another, and it can use the poles of another magnet as we use messengers. If you put a little North pole near a big magnet, that big magnet will send it hurrying from its own North pole to its own South pole, and not out into empty space farther and ever farther away. In a similar way it will send a little South pole from its own South pole to its North pole. The two ends of the big magnet really want to get together, but if they cannot do so then they will send messenger poles to and fro instead. These messenger poles may have to follow paths that are straight or crooked, depending on how the little magnet they belong to is suspended, but if a messenger pole were quite free to do the bidding of the big magnet, it would generally go by way of a curved path. I will sketch

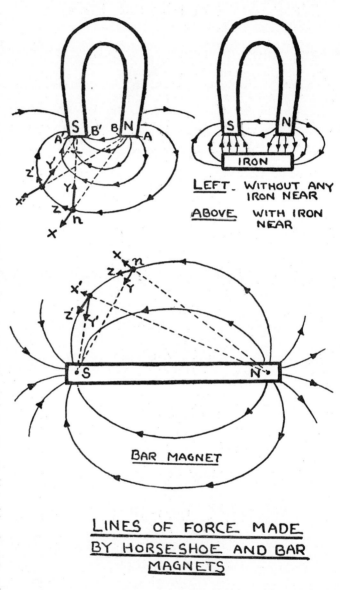

LEFT. WITHOUT ANY IRON NEAR

ABOVE WITH IRON NEAR

BAR MAGNET

LINES OF FORCE MADE BY HORSESHOE AND BAR MAGNETS

the sort of path it would take. Starting from A, it would follow the arrows to A'; starting from B, it would follow the arrows to B' and so on. I will draw lots of paths."

" Why do the messenger poles go such a roundabout way? "
Mary asked.

" They are urged by two forces," answered Father; " one
force is a push and the
other a pull. Look, I will
draw a messenger pole
here at n. The big pole
N is trying to send it
directly away from itself
in the direction of the
arrow X, but the big S
pole is trying to pull it
directly towards itself in
the direction of the arrow
Y. These two forces, the
push and the pull, are
affected by the distances
Nn and nS. The push
gets less and less as Nn
grows greater, while the
pull gets more and more
as the distance nS gets
less. The poor little pole
n cannot obey both forces
separately, any more than
you can obey Mother and
Father if they tell you to
do different things. What it can try to do, however, is please
both by doing something betwixt and between. The force
towards X, together with the force towards Y, really comes

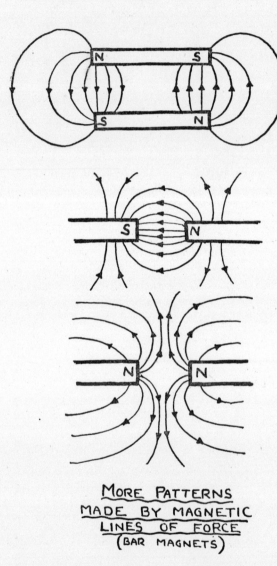

More Patterns
Made By Magnetic
Lines of Force
(Bar Magnets)

to the same thing as a force towards Z, and that is why the little pole *n* is going the way it *is* going. For the moment its path is in the direction Z. A little later the push and pull will be in the directions X' and Y', so that the little pole *n* will have altered the direction of its travel and will be going towards Z'. If you were a clever mathematician, you would be able to 'plot' the course of the little pole *n* with great accuracy, no matter where it started from. All these paths taken by the little pole *n* are what scientists call 'lines of force.' Round any magnet these lines of force make pretty patterns, and they become quite complicated patterns when two or more magnets are put near to one another. If there are two magnets for the little pole *n* to obey, then it will have four forces acting on it all at once—two pushes and two pulls.

"You can get an idea of how these lines of force run if you will put your magnet under a sheet of white paper and then lightly sprinkle the paper with iron filings."

THE ELECTRO-MAGNET

"When I tried knocking one of Mother's knitting needles about I only made it into a very weak magnet," said Peter; "how can you get a strong magnet like my shop-bought one?"

"You can do that by electricity," said Father. "Go round to the electricians' shop where they sell electric lamps and radios and other things and buy a reel of insulated wire—gauge thirty or thereabouts—and a flat torch battery. Insulated wire is wire covered with cotton or silk or enamel. Bare wire is wire without insulation, and it will not serve our purpose. Then see if you can buy a magnetic compass as well. We could use Mary's darning needle on its cork as our magnetic detector if we wanted to, but a proper compass will be more convenient."

When Peter returned with his purchases, Father wound a great many turns of wire round the knitting needle that Peter had tried to magnetise. Then he broke off the wire and joined the ends of what was wound round the needle to the two

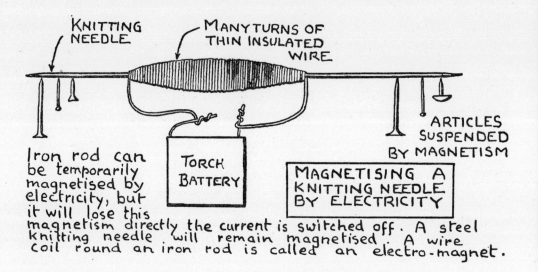

KNITTING NEEDLE — MANY TURNS OF THIN INSULATED WIRE

ARTICLES SUSPENDED BY MAGNETISM

Iron rod can be temporarily magnetised by electricity, but it will lose this magnetism directly the current is switched off. A steel knitting needle will remain magnetised. A wire coil round an iron rod is called an electro-magnet.

TORCH BATTERY

MAGNETISING A KNITTING NEEDLE BY ELECTRICITY

brass strips of the battery. The needle instantly became quite a strong magnet which picked up large nails and nearly picked up another knitting needle. (See also the chapter on "Electric Bells," Vol. II, page 318.)

"I will not keep the wires joined to the battery for long," said Father, "because I should soon run down my battery. But, in any case, to keep the current flowing is not necessary. If this needle is made of good steel it will remain magnetised even after I have switched off the current."

Father took the wires off the battery and then tried to pick up nails with the needle. It still picked up nails, but not quite so well as before.

" A magnet that is only a magnet while current is flowing round it is called an *electro-magnet*," said Father; " if it retains some of its magnetism afterwards it is then called a *permanent* magnet. The best electro-magnets are made with a soft-iron centre instead of a steel one. The soft iron magnetises easily and strongly, but almost all the magnetism goes when the current is turned off. Steel is not so strongly magnetised by a weak electric current, but it retains most of its magnetism when the current is switched off. Your shop-bought magnet is made of proper magnet steel, so that it has kept its magnetism well. It is probably an alloy steel, by which I mean steel with a trace of some other metal in it. The cheaper permanent magnets are made of tungsten steel, which is steel with a little tungsten in it. Better ones are made of steel with cobalt and chromium in it. They are very expensive, because cobalt is expensive. A more up-to-date material for magnets is nickel-aluminium steel. Unlike other magnet steels, this particular steel will go on being a magnet even though it be made very hot. Heat destroys the magnetism in cheap magnets."

CARE OF PERMANENT MAGNETS

" Why did I have to get a compass? " Peter asked his father; " we haven't done any *detecting* with it yet."

" To-morrow will do for that," answered Father; " it is getting late now and we must put our things away. Do you know how to put a magnet away? "

" I just put it in my box of lead soldiers," answered Peter.

" Do you put a keeper on it? " Father asked.

" What's a keeper? " countered Peter.

" A keeper is a little piece of iron or steel that you put across the poles or legs of your magnet to keep it from growing weaker as time goes by," answered Father.

" It had a little bit of iron on it when I was given it," said Peter; " but I thought it was no use, so I threw it away."

" That was wrong," said Father; " here is a nail for you to put across the two poles. Never put your magnet away without putting a keeper on it. If you ever take an electric machine to pieces and it has a permanent magnet in it, *always* put a keeper on the magnet when you pull out any part of the machine that

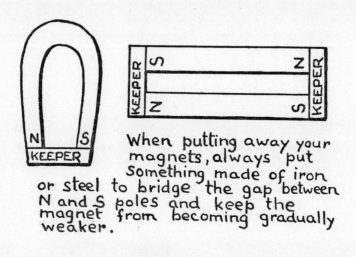

When putting away your magnets, always put something made of iron or steel to bridge the gap between N and S poles and keep the magnet from becoming gradually weaker.

normally runs from pole to pole. A magnet quickly demagnetises itself if it is left without a keeper on it. Hard knocks are bad for a magnet too. You can magnetise a thing weakly by pointing it North and South and then knocking it, but by careless knocking you can demagnetise anything that is already strongly magnetised. You can make its magnetism weaker That is why you should never drop a magnet or let it bump about in a box of old junk. Magnets, in the form of long bars, should be kept in pairs in a proper case, with two keepers to each pair."

CHAPTER TWO

ELECTRO-MAGNETISM

"I WANT to do some detecting with the compass I bought yesterday," said Peter to his father. "I've always wanted to be a detective."

"I want you to tell me how a piece of iron or steel can catch its magnetism from electricity," said Mary; "why should a coil of wire with a current in it make any difference to a piece of steel?"

"I think I can satisfy you both at the same time," said Father; "all I want is some wire, a com-

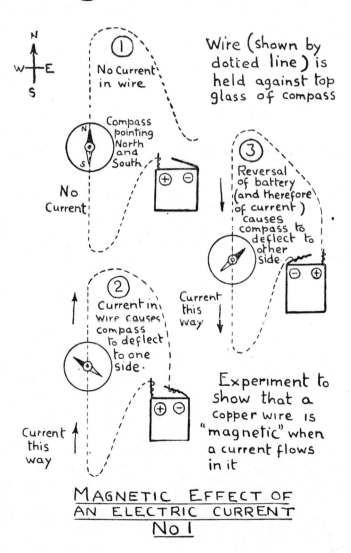

(1) No Current in wire

Wire (shown by dotted line) is held against top glass of compass

Compass pointing North and South

No Current

(3) Reversal of battery (and therefore of current) causes compass to deflect to other side.

Current this way

(2) Current in wire causes compass to deflect to one side.

Current this way

Experiment to show that a copper wire is "magnetic" when a current flows in it

MAGNETIC EFFECT OF AN ELECTRIC CURRENT No 1

345

pass and a battery. I put the compass on the table and then I join a fairly long piece of wire across the terminals of the battery.

Now I stretch a piece of the wire into a straight line and I make it point North and South, like the compass needle. Now I bring it over the top of the compass and lower it so as to try to make it hide the compass needle."

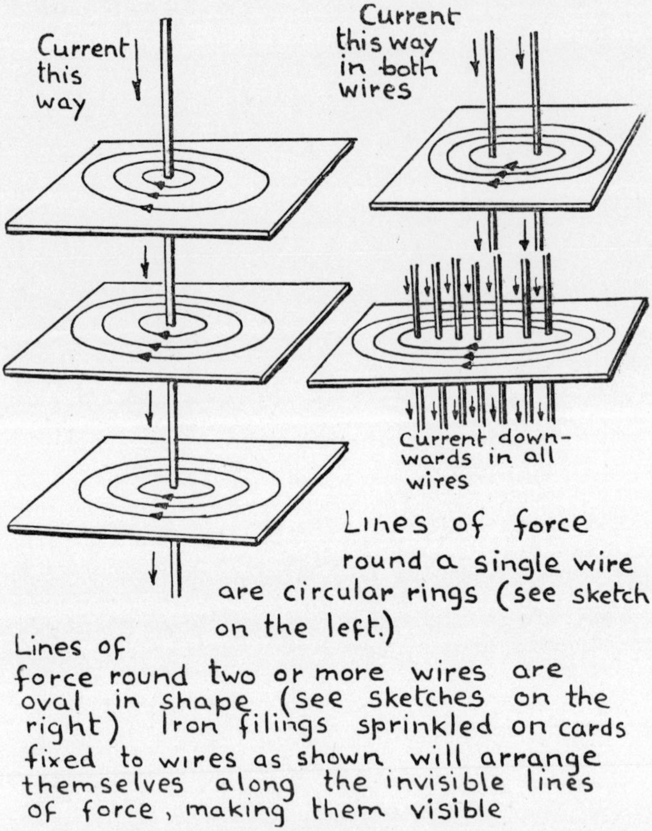

Current this way

Current this way in both wires

Current downwards in all wires

Lines of force round a single wire are circular rings (see sketch on the left.)

Lines of force round two or more wires are oval in shape (see sketches on the right) Iron filings sprinkled on cards fixed to wires as shown will arrange themselves along the invisible lines of force, making them visible

MAGNETIC EFFECT OF AN ELECTRIC CURRENT No 2

"Oh!" exclaimed Mary; "the compass needle won't let itself be hidden; it is turning round sideways with its ends pointing East and West."

"Yes," said Father, "the wire is surrounded by magnetism when it is carrying a current, and that is why the compass is disturbed by it. If you will disconnect one end of the wire from the battery while I still keep my part of the wire over the compass, you will see that when the current stops flowing the compass goes back to its original North and South position. Then, if you will connect the ends of the wire to the battery

346

the other way round, to make the current flow along my piece in the reverse direction, you will see that the needle of the compass deflects the other way. The North-seeking end does not point East this time but West instead."

"The compass detects a current in the wire," said Peter; "and it tells us which way the current is flowing."

"Quite right," answered Father; "it has also shown us that an electric current makes magnetism which a piece of iron or steel could catch from it, thus answering Mary's question. A little messenger pole put near a wire carrying a current would go round it in a complete circle. In fact, depending on where you put it to begin with, it would make many circles, just like I am drawing now. You could thread a piece of cardboard on to a straight piece of wire going up and down and then, when the wire was carrying a strong current, you could sprinkle iron filings on the cardboard. They would arrange themselves in circles like those I have drawn. If there were

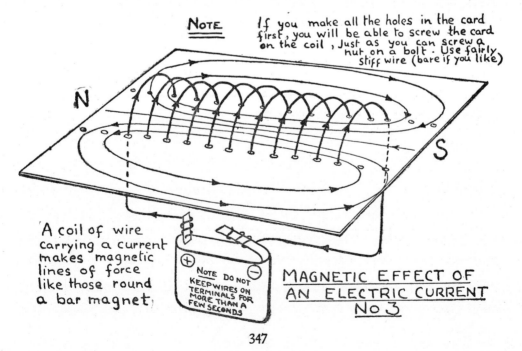

NOTE If you make all the holes in the card first, you will be able to screw the card on the coil, Just as you can screw a nut on a bolt. Use fairly stiff wire (bare if you like)

N

S

A coil of wire carrying a current makes magnetic lines of force like those round a bar magnet,

(+) NOTE DO NOT KEEP WIRES ON TERMINALS FOR MORE THAN A FEW SECONDS (−)

MAGNETIC EFFECT OF AN ELECTRIC CURRENT No 3

two wires passing through the cardboard fairly close together, they would not make two separate sets of circles: they would make oval shapes to go round both. More wires than two would make still longer oval shapes. The magnetism round two wires is stronger than that round one wire, and round three or four wires it is stronger still. You can use a lot of wires and get very powerful effects indeed. A coil of wire threaded through cardboard will give you lines of force just like those from a bar magnet. In fact, such a coil *is* a magnet, and you can easily show with your compass detector that it has North and South poles. If you put a bar of iron through the coil, it becomes magnetised at once. The two wire bobbins in an electric bell (see Vol. II, page 318) make magnets of the iron bars inside them."

POSITIVE AND NEGATIVE

"Electricity," said Father, "was once believed to be a kind of fluid which flowed along a wire from a place where there was plenty to a place where there was a shortage. The place where there was supposed to be plenty was said to be positive or + and the place where there was supposed to be a shortage was said to be negative or −. The terminals of all batteries are still marked + and −, and we still think of electricity as flowing from + to −, although, in reality, the flow now seems to be from − to +, as I shall explain when we speak of valves for the radio. In a flat torch battery the short brass strip is the + terminal and the long brass strip is the − terminal, and so, if we obey the old rule, we shall show one current flowing from the short strip to the long when we draw a wire joining these two strips together. I am now going to stretch my wire over the compass detector again, and I am going to make the south end of my wire + and the north end −, so that current flows (if the old rule can be believed) from South to North. The wire is over the needle, and I want you to notice which way the North end of the needle goes."

"It goes to the West," said Mary. (See diagram 2 on page 345.)

"Now I will make the North end of my wire + and the South end −, so that the current flows from North to South."

"The North end of the needle is going East now," said Mary. (See diagram 3 on page 345.)

"I could draw rings round the wire to show how a free messenger pole of North polarity would go round and round the wire, and this little experiment of ours shows which way round the messenger pole would make its journey. Looking along the wire from its + end to its − end (the way the current is supposed to go), we should see that the messenger pole was going round the wire in the same direction as the hands of a clock. I could put arrows on the lines of force (rings they are in this case) to indicate this direction. Another way to remember the direction of the lines of force is to imagine that you are tightening up a screw, making it go away from you in the same direction as your electric current. The lines of force go round in the same direction that you have to turn the screwdriver, assuming that the screw is an ordinary right-handed one. Knowing this rule for finding the direction of lines of force caused by an electric current, you can wind and connect up bobbins to give you magnets of the polarity you want. I am drawing a bobbin coil now; the current goes in at the left-hand end, over the top, round the back, underneath

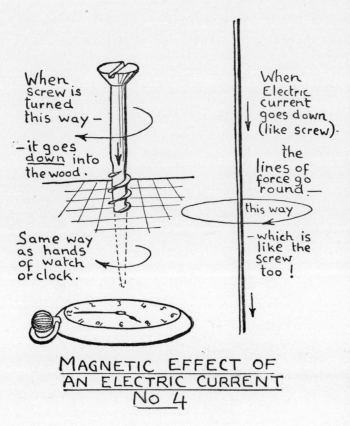

When screw is turned this way —

—it goes down into the wood.

Same way as hands of watch or clock.

When Electric current goes down (like screw)-

the lines of force go round —

this way

—which is like the screw too !

MAGNETIC EFFECT OF AN ELECTRIC CURRENT No 4

to the front again, up and over the top for the second time and so on. If you imagine yourself screwing a screw along this wire away from you, your hand turning clockwise, you will see that inside the coil a messenger pole would travel from right to left, so that a bar of iron in this coil would have North polarity on the left and South polarity on the right." (See diagram on page 347.)

THE ELECTRIC MOTOR

Father took three large books out of the bookcase and rested two of them on the table, one on top of the other. Then he laid two long steel knitting needles on the top book so that the ends overhung the table. He clamped them in position by putting the third book on top of them.

"Whatever are you doing?" asked Peter.

"You will see in a minute," Father said, and while he spoke he made a little wire swing to hang down between the knitting needles. The bottom part of the swing, where the imaginary rider would sit, he put between the poles of Peter's horseshoe magnet.

"We are ready now," he said; "if I join wires from my battery to the two knitting needles a current will pass through

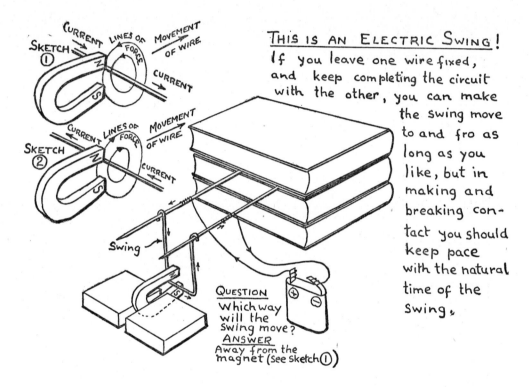

SKETCH ① CURRENT LINES OF FORCE MOVEMENT OF WIRE CURRENT

SKETCH ② CURRENT LINES OF FORCE MOVEMENT OF WIRE CURRENT

Swing →

THIS IS AN ELECTRIC SWING! If you leave one wire fixed, and keep completing the circuit with the other, you can make the swing move to and fro as long as you like, but in making and breaking contact you should keep pace with the natural time of the swing.

QUESTION
Which way will the Swing move?
ANSWER
Away from the magnet (see sketch ①)

the swing. The wire between the poles of Peter's magnet will have rings of magnetic force round it and the North pole of Peter's magnet will try to go round the wire in the way you could already discover for yourselves if I told you the direction of the current in the wire. The South pole of Peter's magnet will try to go round the wire the other way. Now the magnet is very heavy, so it cannot move, but the wire which is trying to move the magnet is itself lightly hung. So instead of the magnet moving, the wire moves. It is rather like you trying to push a heavy motor-car along a road when your two feet are standing on slippery ice. You do not budge the car an inch, but you slide yourself along the road away from it. The wire with the current tries to push the magnet away, but gets pushed away itself. Watch!"

Father touched the needles with the wires from the battery, and the swing moved out from between the poles of Peter's magnet towards the books. By reversing the direction of flow of the current Father made the swing move away from the books, so that it went farther than ever in between the poles of Peter's magnet.

"That is what happens when, instead of trying to push your car you try to pull it. You merely pull yourself closer to it."

Father started cutting two grooves in a large bottle cork. Then he pushed a darning needle through it and wound some wire round the grooved part. The two ends of the wire he stripped of insulation and then he threaded them through holes in two little cardboard discs which he made and pushed on to the needle.

"I am making an electric motor now," he said; "and this part of it is called the armature. It will buzz round at a great speed. We need a bigger magnet than Peter's: one from an old-fashioned motor-car magneto would suit us and, luckily, I have one. I bought it the other day.

"I put the magnet flat on a piece of cardboard. Midway between the poles I make a prick in the cardboard for the point of my armature spindle. The top of the spindle I can hold in position with a springy strip of card with a dimple made in it to receive its eye end. All we need now is someone to send current round the armature coil."

"I will hold the springy strip of card," said Mary, "and then you can show us how to do the rest."

Father made the end of each wire from the battery bare of insulation for about an inch and he straightened the bare parts.

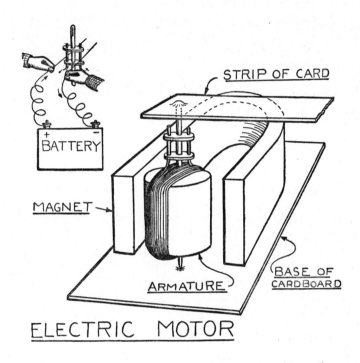

STRIP OF CARD

BATTERY

MAGNET →

ARMATURE

BASE OF CARDBOARD

ELECTRIC MOTOR

"These are my brushes," he said; "and with them I am going to touch the two ends of the armature coil. These two ends are supported between the cardboard discs on the spindle, and if I hold my two brushes against them in just the right way (see small sketch) the armature will start to buzz round at a great speed. Watch!"

It was just as Father said: the electric motor worked very well.

"Each wire in the grooves of my cork is behaving like the swing we were playing with just now," said Father. "On one

353

side of the cork the current in the wires is going one way, causing the wires to try to get out from between the poles of the magnet; on the other side of the cork the current is going the other way, causing the wires to try to get still farther in between the poles. The cork most obligingly turns to let them have their way, but when the wires are level with the poles of the magnet my brushes no longer make contact, so the current stops. The momentum of the armature keeps it turning, however, and soon my brushes make contact again. This time the current flows round the armature the other way: the wires that wanted to come in now want to get out and those that wanted to get out now want to come in. This helps the armature to go on turning, and, in fact, it goes on turning for as long as I like, and very fast. The little wires between the cardboard discs form what is called the commutator. With their help I can feed current into the armature winding, and what is more, I can feed it automatically first one way then the other through the wires.

"The motors of electric trains and trolley buses have armature windings and commutators like our toy motor, but instead of having only two slots for the winding, a real armature has many slots, and instead of having only two bars a real commutator has many bars. Our motor with two slots and two bars works rather jerkily, as it gives only two power impulses in each revolution. A real motor gives power impulses all the time, so it works very smoothly.

"A real motor uses an electro-magnet for the stationary part instead of a permanent magnet. This stationary part is called the field magnet, and a very strong magnet it is too. The body or core of a real armature is not made of cork, but of iron, and it fits the space between the poles of the field magnet as closely as possible, so that the lines of magnet force have hardly any distance at all to travel through air. They go most of the way through iron, which is much easier for them. It is very difficult to provide a strong magnetic field (many lines of force) in air, but easy to do so in iron. You could discover this for yourself; a bobbin without an iron rod inside it makes a much weaker magnet than one which has an iron rod inside it. An electric motor needs strong magnets to make it powerful, and so the path of the magnetic lines of force is 'paved' with iron wherever possible."

INDUCTION

"To get all our electricity from batteries would be very expensive," said Father; "batteries are really chemical laboratories inside, and they make electricity by using up valuable materials such as zinc, copper and so on. I am speaking now of the so-called 'Primary' batteries, which work directly they are made, but are useless when they have run down. The other sort of battery, called a 'Secondary' battery or accumulator, only works after it has been 'charged' or filled up with electricity from some other source. It can usually be charged again after it has run down. This sort of battery is a chemical laboratory too, but the substances used up when the battery gives out current are restored during the charging process.

"Batteries of all kinds have their uses, but they can only give us a very small part of the electricity we need. Fortunately, we know an easy way to get huge quantities of electricity quite cheaply, and now I will tell you about it. If I pushed my little swing quickly through the space between the poles of Peter's magnet, so as to cut all the lines of magnetic force therein, I should make a small electric current pass through any wire that happened to join the two knitting needles, and this current might be strong enough to be detected by the com-

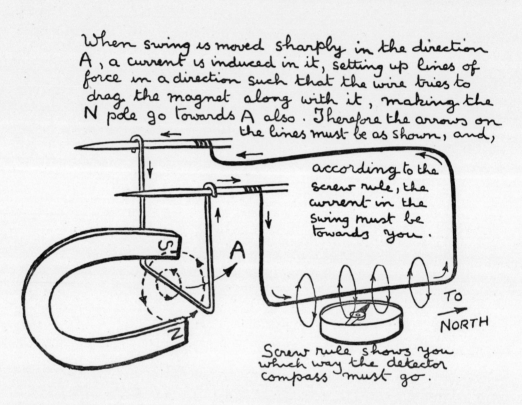

When swing is moved sharply in the direction A, a current is induced in it, setting up lines of force in a direction such that the wire tries to drag the magnet along with it, making the N pole go towards A also. Therefore the arrows on the lines must be as shown, and,

according to the screw rule, the current in the swing must be towards you.

TO NORTH

Screw rule shows you which way the detector compass must go.

pass detector. The current would be in the direction shown by the arrows I am making in this diagram I am drawing. Round the wire forming the swing this current will make lines of force in such a direction as to hinder the movement of the wire and make it more difficult for me to push it. Thus, if I am pushing the wire out from between the poles of Peter's magnet, the lines of force will be of the kind to make the wire want to pull itself farther in, and *vice versa*. By this rule you can always tell which way current will be induced in a wire when it is moved through a magnetic field in a direction to cut all the lines of force."

"Just a minute, Daddy," interrupted Mary; "shall we try the experiment you are speaking about?"

"No use," answered Father; "our detector is not sensitive enough for such a feeble current as I could make in the way I have described. To do this experiment we must first make a more sensitive detector, and then we must find a way to induce a rather bigger current. To make a more sensitive detector we will lay more than one wire over our compass needle and we will have wires underneath it as well. In fact, we will put our compass inside a coil wound with many yards of wire, making one hundred or more turns. Such an arrangement is almost worthy to be called a 'galvanometer,' and it will not take many minutes to make.

"We will replace the swing with a circular coil of wire also," went on Father; "the original swing had only one wire to cut the magnetic lines of force, but we will have about one hundred wires in our new one. It will not look like a swing any more, but it will serve the same purpose. We can wrap wire round a bottle to form our coils (using thin wire), and before slipping the wire off the bottle we can slip little short pieces under and round the turns to hold them together."

Father made the second coil so that it had as many turns as would slip easily between the poles of Peter's magnet. The free ends of this second coil he connected to the free ends of the coil belonging to the galvanometer. The children watched the galvanometer needle while Father took the movable coil and pushed one side of it between the poles of the magnet. They saw the needle swing over a little to one side.

When Father withdrew the coil the needle swung the other way.

Of course Father did his part of the experiment a long way from the galvanometer, so that the needle of the latter should not be disturbed by ordinary magnetism from the magnet.

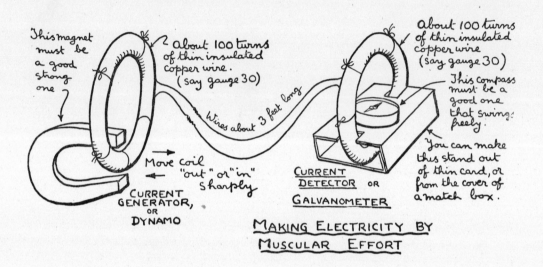

This magnet must be a good strong one

About 100 turns of thin insulated copper wire. (say gauge 30)

Wires about 3 feet long

Move coil "out" or "in" sharply

CURRENT GENERATOR, OR DYNAMO

About 100 turns of thin insulated copper wire (say gauge 30)

This compass must be a good one that swings freely.

You can make this stand out of thin card, or from the cover of a match box.

CURRENT DETECTOR OR GALVANOMETER

MAKING ELECTRICITY BY MUSCULAR EFFORT

This meant that fairly long wires had been used to connect the coil at Father's end to the galvanometer coil at the children's end.

"You will notice," said Father, "that the faster I move the magnet the stronger the current indicated by your detector. If I could measure the force I was exerting to make this current, I should find that double the current needed double the force to make it, treble the current treble the force and so on.

"To show you that the coil needs forcing to make it go through the lines of force between the magnet poles, I will join its two ends together to make it a closed circuit and then hang it up by a long thin thread. When the thread is quite untwisted and the coil is hanging quite still, I will pass the magnet poles

358

round one side of the coil. As the magnet approaches you will see the coil try to get away. When I pull the magnet back the coil tries to follow it. Thus there is a force between the

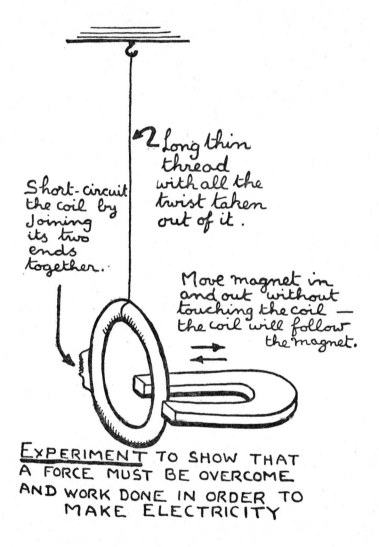

Short-circuit the coil by joining its two ends together.

2 Long thin thread with all the twist taken out of it.

Move magnet in and out without touching the coil — the coil will follow the magnet.

EXPERIMENT TO SHOW THAT A FORCE MUST BE OVERCOME AND WORK DONE IN ORDER TO MAKE ELECTRICITY

two of them. If I disconnect the two ends of the coil, leaving it open-circuited instead of short-circuited, nothing like this happens at all. The magnet only influences the coil when it can make a current flow round it."

THE DYNAMO

"What we have here is a simple dynamo," said Father; "and I am the engine that must do the work of moving the wires across the magnetic field. A real dynamo is made just like an electric motor, only instead of being fed with current it is forced to go round by an engine or turbine while its field magnet is energised, or excited, to create a strong magnetic field. The armature wires cut this field and send an electric current to the brushes, whence it can be led away to light lamps or drive electric trains. We cannot make electricity with our toy motor, because we have no way of spinning it round fast enough."

THE TELEPHONE

"You have seen me induce a current of electricity in a coil of wire by moving a magnet to and fro over one side of it," said Father; "I could do this in another way. I could wind wire round the poles of Peter's magnet to form bobbins on each, and then I could move a keeper to and fro in front of the two poles. When the keeper is on the poles, all the lines of force pass out of the magnet at the tip of the North pole round the keeper to the South pole. In this way they are bound to thread through both coils. When I take the keeper away, many of the lines of force jump across the gap between the poles before reaching the tips. These lines do not thread through all the turns of the coils. By moving the keeper to and fro I can make more or fewer lines of force thread the turns of my two coils, and while the number of lines is changing, the wires of the coils must be cutting through some of them. This is enough to induce a current in the coils. The earliest kind of telephone transmitter was just a permanent magnet with coils round its two legs and a keeper in the form of a thin metal diaphragm or disc spaced a hundredth of an inch or so from the pole tips. The telephone receiver was

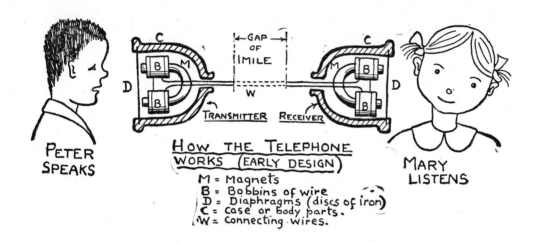

PETER SPEAKS

HOW THE TELEPHONE WORKS (EARLY DESIGN)

M = Magnets
B = Bobbins of wire
D = Diaphragms (discs of iron)
C = Case or body parts.
W = Connecting wires.

MARY LISTENS

made in exactly the same way, and the coils of transmitter and receiver were connected together by long wires. No battery was needed. When you spoke near to the diaphragm of the transmitter you caused it to vibrate with the sound of your voice (see articles on "Sound"), and as it moved to and fro it behaved like the moving keeper I was talking about just now. Tiny currents were induced in the coils round the limbs of the magnet. These currents flowed along the connecting wires over a distance of a mile or more to the coils of the receiver, the diaphragm of which was held near to the ear of the listener at the far end. As the current in the coils of the receiver waxed and waned, it strengthened or weakened the magnet of the receiver, causing it to attract the diaphragm of the receiver with more or less force. In this way the diaphragm of the receiver was caused to imitate exactly the movements of the diaphragm of the transmitter, and it made noises corresponding to those of the speaker, which the listener could understand perfectly as speech."

"How interesting," said Mary; "do modern telephones work in the same way?"

"The receiver does," Father answered; "but the transmitter has been simplified, and a battery is included in the circuit. The diaphragm of the transmitter presses on some grains of carbon, squeezing them up tighter or letting them go loose. Current from a battery passes through the carbon grains on its way to the receiver, and this current varies with the pressure on the carbon grains, becoming strong when they are squeezed together and weak when they are loose. This new kind of transmitter is called a microphone, and, as you know, the B.B.C. uses microphones to transmit speech and music to us."

A SHOCKING COIL

"Moving a bar magnet in and out of a coil of wire causes a current to flow to and fro in a wire joining the ends of the coil," said Father. "Instead of moving a magnet to and fro you could have a fixed magnet of variable strength. As the strength of the magnet increased, it would make more and more lines of force and all these would cut the surrounding coil, so inducing a current in it. As the strength of the magnet decreased, the lines of force would collapse and, in doing so, they would again cut the surrounding coil, thus inducing a current once more, but in the reverse way. A shocking coil works on this principle. The outer coil, which is cut alternately by increasing and decreasing lines of force, is called the 'secondary' winding. It consists of thousands of turns of very fine wire. The fixed magnet of variable strength is an electro-magnet. The core is a bundle of soft-iron wires, and surrounding these is a winding of fairly thick wire called the 'primary' winding. This is fed with current from a battery,

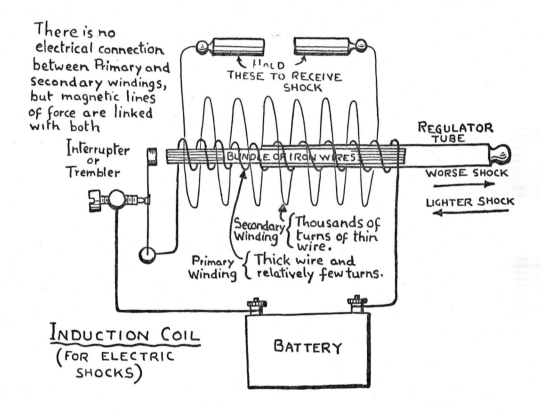

There is no electrical connection between Primary and Secondary windings, but magnetic lines of force are linked with both

THESE TO RECEIVE SHOCK

HOLD

Interrupter or Trembler

BUNDLE OF IRON WIRES

REGULATOR TUBE

WORSE SHOCK

LIGHTER SHOCK

Secondary Winding { Thousands of turns of thin wire.

Primary Winding { Thick wire and relatively few turns.

INDUCTION COIL
(FOR ELECTRIC SHOCKS)

BATTERY

and there is an interrupter in the circuit similar to that which you have in an electric bell. (See Vol. II, page 318.) The circuit is alternately made and broken so that the magnet is strengthened and weakened fifty or more times in a second. While this is happening, the secondary winding will be wanting to send a current first one way and then the other, so that if you catch hold of its two ends it will be able to have its wish, using you as the connecting wire, and you will experience a most peculiar sensation. Most shocking coils have some way of regulating the current from the secondary winding, so that you can vary it to suit your taste from one which causes a faint tingling to one which causes a painful muscular contraction. A mild electric shock is quite harmless, but a powerful shock can hurt you seriously and even kill you.

"The shock from a small shocking coil can be painful, but it is not dangerous. The way in which the secondary current is varied is ingenious. Round the bundle of iron wires there is a brass tube that you can pull out to uncover more and more of the iron. This tube acts as another secondary winding (a winding of only one turn) and as it is short-circuited on itself, it has a current flowing to and fro in it. The current is a strong one when the tube is pushed right in to cover all the iron, and it behaves in such a way as to prevent many lines of force from cutting the real secondary winding, the current in which is thus very weak. When the tube is pulled out to uncover some of the iron, the real secondary gets a chance to work, and it works more and more effectively the farther the brass tube is withdrawn from the iron core of the magnet. In other designs of shocking coil, the core itself can be pushed in or pulled out."

CHAPTER THREE

ELECTRICAL MEASUREMENTS

YOU may find the following article a little hard to understand at first, but you do not *have* to read it. The articles coming afterwards can be understood even if you miss out this one. In many books you will find the Ampere described as a current which performs a certain amount of electroplating in a given time, and the Ohm as the resistance of a special piece of metal, and the Volt as the pressure needed to send a current of 1 Ampere through a resistance of 1 Ohm. These definitions do not make you much wiser than you were before, but the definitions given in this chapter are the scientific ones, and learning them now will save you much confusion and mystification later on if you ever study electricity seriously.

Much of the pioneer experimental work in electricity was done by foreign scientists, namely Volta, Ampere, Galvani, Coulomb, Gauss, and so on; consequently, all the original measurements of distance and force and weight were made in foreign units. Instead of measuring lengths in inches, these scientists measured in centimetres, and there are 2·54 (roughly two and a half) centimetres to one inch. Weights were measured in grammes, and there are 454 grammes to 1 pound. The force needed to give anything an acceleration of 32 feet per second per second (32·2 to be precise) is its own weight (see page 15). Now 32·2 feet = 981 centimetres, so that the weight of the gramme mass will give to that mass an acceleration of 981 centimetres per second per second. The force needed to give it an acceleration of only 1 centimetre per second per second is the gramme weight divided by 981. This very tiny force is called the dyne.

In Great Britain we measure work in foot-pounds, this being the force overcome in pounds multiplied by the distance through which it is pushed back. The foreign unit of work is the dyne-centimetre or erg, a very small amount of work indeed. In a foot-pound there will be $12 \times 2.54 \times 454 \times 981 = 13,600,000$ ergs, because 1 foot is 12×2.54 cm., and 1 pound is 454×981 dynes.

British scientists have adopted the foreign units in all their electrical calculations, so I cannot explain to you what a " volt " is, or a " watt," or an " ampere " without first of all telling you all this about the centimetre, the gramme, the dyne and the erg.

MAGNETIC UNITS

The strength of a magnet is taken to be the force with which it repels or attracts a similar magnet to itself. You must imagine the two magnets to be rather long, so that if the North pole of one is put 1 centimetre away from the North pole of the other, the two South poles can be far enough away not to have any influence. If the magnets are exactly the same and their two North poles repel each other with a force of 1 dyne when 1 centimetre apart, then each North pole is said to have a strength of 1 magnetic unit; in fact, it is called a " unit pole."

A magnet will send messenger poles out in all directions along an infinite number of lines of force. If we draw a great many of these lines we shall find that they crowd closely together where the magnetism can be strongly felt, and spread far apart where the magnetism is weak. This gave our own scientist Faraday the idea that the strength or intensity of a magnetic field in two places could be compared by comparing the number of lines in those two places. He found it was true

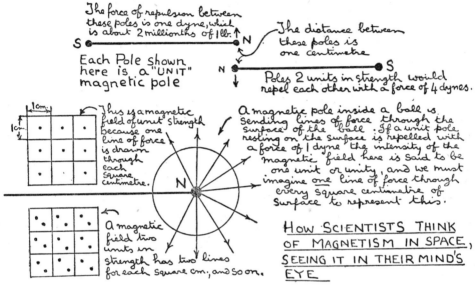

The force of repulsion between these poles is one dyne, which is about 2 millionths of 1 lb.

Each Pole shown here is a "UNIT" magnetic pole

The distance between these poles is one centimetre

Poles 2 units in strength would repel each other with a force of 4 dynes.

This is a magnetic field of unit strength because one line of force is drawn through each square centimetre.

A magnetic field two units in strength has two lines for each square cm., and so on.

A magnetic pole inside a ball is sending lines of force through the surface of the ball. If a unit pole resting on the surface is repelled with a force of 1 dyne the intensity of the magnetic field here is said to be one unit or unity, and we must imagine one line of force through every square centimetre of surface to represent this.

HOW SCIENTISTS THINK OF MAGNETISM IN SPACE, SEEING IT IN THEIR MIND'S EYE

to say that where there were twice or three times as many lines, there was also twice or three times the magnetic force. Of course, you could draw as many lines as you pleased; but Faraday said, " Let us draw only one line for a magnetic field that urges a unit messenger pole along with a force of 1 dyne and then, automatically, there will be two lines in places where the force on unit pole is 2 dynes, three lines in places where the force is 3 dynes, and so on." All scientists now observe this rule. If a magnetic pole at the centre of a hollow ball is exerting a force of 1 dyne on a unit pole resting on the surface of that ball, then we must consider one line of force to come out through the surface of the ball for every little square on that surface having its side 1 centimetre long. A square of this size is called a square centimetre, and the strength or intensity of a magnetic field is therefore stated as so many lines of force per square centimetre. A coil of wire of many turns carrying a good strong current of electricity may give you a field intensity inside of 400 to 700 lines per square centimetre. If a bar of iron is put inside the lines, threading through the coil will be enormously increased, so that you will get several thousand to a square centimetre. The field intensity without the iron might only be, say, 50 lines per sq. cm., but after the iron is put in, it could be as much as 10,000 lines per sq. cm.

UNIT OF ELECTRIC CURRENT: THE AMPERE

An electric current is measured by the magnetic field it can produce. If you have a wire bent to form a circle of 1 centimetre radius and send an ever-increasing current round it, you will produce an ever-increasing force on a messenger pole put at the centre of the coil. Suppose this messenger pole to be a unit pole, as described above, and suppose the force on it to be increased until there is 1 dyne for every centimetre of wire in the loop, then your current at this moment will be what scientists call "unit current." An Ampere is a tenth part of this scientific unit.

UNIT OF QUANTITY: THE COULOMB

When 1 ampere flows along a wire for 1 second, the amount of electricity passing in that time is called a Coulomb.

UNIT OF PRESSURE: THE VOLT

Thinking of electricity as a fluid flowing from a place of high pressure (denoted by +) to a place of low pressure (denoted by −), we shall see that there is another quantity

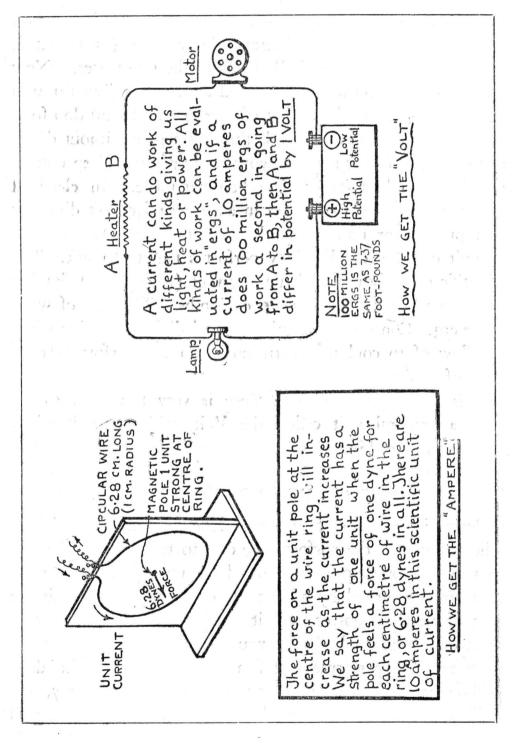

Motor

A Heater B

A current can do work of different kinds giving us light, heat or power. All kinds of work can be evaluated in "ergs", and if a current of 10 amperes does 100 million ergs of work a second in going from A to B, then A and B differ in potential by 1 VOLT

Lamp

High Potential (+) Low Potential (−)

NOTE
100 MILLION ERGS IS THE SAME AS 7·37 FOOT-POUNDS

HOW WE GET THE "VOLT"

CIRCULAR WIRE 6·28 CM. LONG (1 CM. RADIUS)

MAGNETIC POLE 1 UNIT STRONG AT CENTRE OF RING.

6·28 DYNES FORCE

UNIT CURRENT

The force on a unit pole at the centre of the wire ring will increase as the current increases. We say that the current has a strength of one unit when the pole feels a force of one dyne for each centimetre of wire in the ring, or 6·28 dynes in all. There are 10 amperes in this scientific unit of current.

HOW WE GET THE "AMPERE"

369

we must measure if we are to understand what is happening, and that quantity is the difference in pressure (or potential, as it is more usually called) between the two places. Now with water we know that a pound of it descending through a height of 1 foot in the bucket of a water wheel must do 1 foot-pound of work. If it descends through a pipe without doing any outside work, it may do work on itself instead, so that its speed of travel or its pressure becomes more. In electrical science we say that two places in an electrical circuit differ by unit pressure or unit potential if the passage between them of unit quantity of electricity performs 1 unit of work. The scientific unit of quantity is unit current (10 amperes) flowing for 1 second, and is therefore 10 coulombs. The unit of work is the erg. Consequently, unit potential difference exists when the flow of 10 coulombs corresponds to the performance of 1 erg of work.

This unit of potential difference is very tiny, and so we have a practical unit called the Volt, which is a hundred million times as big.

UNIT OF POWER: THE WATT

Power is the amount of work done in unit time. Thus, 1 horse-power is the performance of 550 foot-pounds of work in 1 second, or 33,000 foot-pounds in 1 minute. A current of 1 ampere, urged by a potential difference of 1 volt, is the unit of electrical power, and it is called the Watt. From what has been said above, you will see that 1 Watt must represent the performance of a tenth part of a hundred million ergs of work in every second—that is to say, ten million ergs of work a second. Shall we see what this means in intelligible units? Some pages back (page 366) I said that there were 13,600,000 ergs to every foot-pound. Therefore, 1 watt is not quite as much as a foot-pound a second—it is only 10/13.6 or 0.737 foot-pounds a second. How many watts are equivalent to 1 horse-power? As many times as 550 contains 0.737. The answer is 550/0.737 = 746. Every engineer remembers this important figure—746 watts=1 h.p.

THE POWER OF ELECTRICAL MACHINES

On every electrical dynamo you will find a brass plate telling you what it can do. It will tell you how fast it must be rotated (in revolutions per minute) and what voltage it develops across its terminals. It may tell you how many amperes of electrical load it will carry, and it is almost sure to tell you what the rated output is in "Kilowatts" (shortened to kW. or KW.). A kilowatt is 1,000 watts or 1000/746 = 1.34 horse-power, say, a horse-power and a third. A dynamo to give 500 kilowatts (and needing an engine of about 700 horse-power to drive it) was once considered quite large. Nowadays it is not unusual to see electrical generators for 50,000 kilowatts, and there are many that are even bigger, so that the steam turbine driving the armature against magnetic forces may have to exert more than 100,000 horse-power.

UNIT OF RESISTANCE: THE OHM

Much energy is wasted in sending electricity along wires that offer resistance to its passage. Thus, you might try to work a toy motor needing 4 volts from a battery giving you 4 volts and using long thin wires for your connections. If the wires are too long and too thin your motor may scarcely turn at all. Nearly all the battery's pressure of 4 volts may be used up merely in driving a current of 1 or 2 amperes through the long thin wire. When electrical energy is used up in a wire in this way it makes the wire warm, or even hot. A wire offering great resistance may become red-hot (an electric fire) or even white-hot (an electric lamp). When wiring up your toys or other things you must be careful to use thick enough wires, or else the results will be disappointing. Thinner wires will waste the energy in your battery without giving you the desired results.

A wire which requires the wastage of 1 whole volt to send a current of 1 ampere through it has unit resistance, and this unit of resistance is called the ohm. A 2-ohms resistance needs 2 volts to send 1 ampere through it, a 3-ohms resistance needs 3 volts, and so on.

FACTS ABOUT DOMESTIC APPLIANCES

A 60-watt lamp for a 240-volt supply consumes a current of $60/240 = \frac{1}{4}$ ampere. Its resistance would be 240 ohms if it passed 1 ampere, but since it passes only $\frac{1}{4}$ ampere, its resistance must be $4 \times 240 = 960$ ohms.

A bowl or bar fire taking a kilowatt (1,000 watts) consumes a current of $1000/240 = 4\frac{1}{6}$ amperes. Its resistance would be 240 ohms if it passed 1 ampere, but since it passes $4\frac{1}{6}$ amperes, its resistance must be 240 divided by $4\frac{1}{6}$, or $57\frac{3}{5}$ ohms.

Electricity is sold to us in kilowatt-hours at a price depending on the purpose for which we use it. A kilowatt-hour is the energy used by anything taking 1 kilowatt of power if it is left switched on for 1 hour. A 50-watt lamp could be on for twenty hours before it would use a kWh, because $1,000 = 50 \times 20$. The original charge for electricity was 4d. to 6d. per kWh, but to encourage people to use it for heating and cooking the power companies have all offered it at a much cheaper rate for these purposes. In many homes there are two electricity meters, one keeping count of the kWh used for lighting, and the other keeping count of the kWh used for heating, cooking and

Meter Reading on March 31st
2910·3

Meter Reading on June 31st
3150·2

power. Can you read an electricity meter? It is quite easy. The one in my house has 6 dials, as shown in the accompanying sketches. To read this you jot down the figures indicated, reading (and also writing) from left to right, putting a decimal point before the figure shown on the last dial on the right. If a pointer is between two figures, you must put down the lowest one. The reading shown in the top sketch is 2910·3, and this was taken on March 31. The reading shown in the bottom sketch is 3150·2, and this was taken three months later, on June 30. Thus the energy I have used is $3150 \cdot 2 - 2910 \cdot 3 =$ $239 \cdot 9$ kWh. If I am charged $5d$. a unit, which makes $5 \times 239 = 1,195d$. for the whole units and $4\frac{1}{2}d$. for the odd $0 \cdot 9$ unit, this comes to $1,200d$. less one half-penny, which is £4 19s. $11\frac{1}{2}d$.

THE DYNAMO AGAIN

In a dynamo you have wires on the armature cutting through a strong magnetic field at a great rate. To have a pressure of 1 volt induced in it a wire must cut a hundred million lines of force in every second. You can see now why there must be a strong magnetic field in a dynamo, and why the armature, besides turning fast, must carry many wires on its surface.

The dynamo for lighting on a motor-car gives us 6 volts or 12 volts, depending on the make of car. An ordinary accumulator gives us 2 volts per cell, so that a 6-volt accumulator has

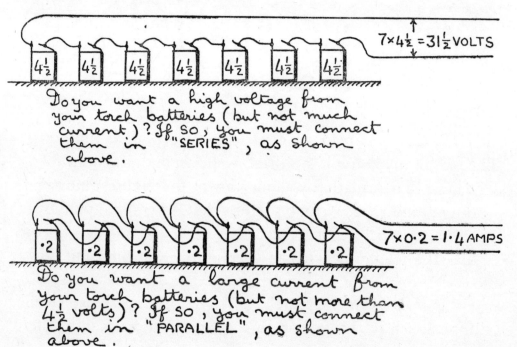

$7 \times 4\frac{1}{2} = 31\frac{1}{2}$ VOLTS

Do you want a high voltage from your torch batteries (but not much current)? If so, you must connect them in "SERIES", as shown above.

$7 \times 0 \cdot 2 = 1 \cdot 4$ AMPS

Do you want a large current from your torch batteries (but not more than $4\frac{1}{2}$ volts)? If so, you must connect them in "PARALLEL", as shown above.

3 cells, and a 12-volt accumulator has 6 cells. The dry battery gives us about 1½ volts per cell, so that a flat battery with 3 cells gives us 4½ volts and a round battery with 2 cells gives us 3 volts. A high-tension wireless battery is a dry battery with a great many cells connected together to give us 100 volts or more.

In a big electricity generating station the steam turbine will use about 8 pounds of high-pressure steam for every kilowatt-hour generated. The boilers making this steam will require to burn about 1 pound of good-quality coal to produce this 8 pounds of steam. Very roughly, then, 1 pound of coal gives us 1 kilowatt-hour. Is this a good result or a bad one? We can soon find out. 1 kW. is 1·34 h.p., and 1 h.p. is 33,000 × 60 foot-pounds an hour and 778 foot-pounds (772 was Joule's figure) are equal to the British Thermal Unit as defined on page 283. This means that a kilowatt-hour converted into heat would be:

$$\frac{1·34 \times 33,000 \times 60}{778} = 3,400 \text{ B.Th.U.}$$

In a pound of good-quality coal there would be about three times this number of B.Th.U.s, and so we see that our elaborate engine and dynamo give us only about a third of what we might expect. This result, however, is really very good, because we ought not to expect an efficiency of much more than a third from any heat engine. The dynamo can convert mechanical work into electricity with an efficiency of more than 90 parts in 100 (it gives you 9 electrical horse-power for every 10 mechanical horse-power you put into it), but a heat engine will not give you 778 foot-pounds for every B.Th.U. in the fuel. It will give you only about a third of this figure for reasons you may be inquisitive enough to ask about one day. Lack of space prevents me from telling you the reasons now.

CHAPTER FOUR

ALTERNATING CURRENT

IN the dynamo described by the father of Mary and Peter, the field magnet remained still and the armature revolved. It is quite possible to make a dynamo with the armature winding

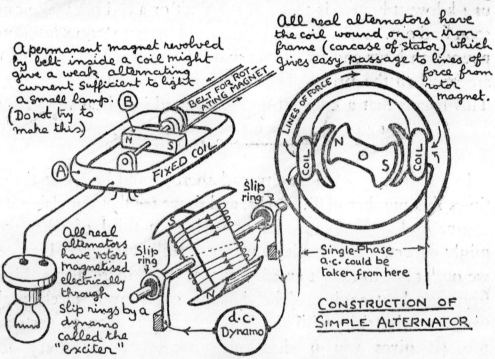

A permanent magnet revolved by belt inside a coil might give a weak alternating current sufficient to light a small lamp. (Do not try to make this.)

All real alternators have the coil wound on an iron frame (carcase of stator) which gives easy passage to lines of force from rotor magnet.

BELT FOR ROTATING MAGNET

FIXED COIL

LINES OF FORCE

COIL   N   S   COIL

Slip ring

All real alternators have rotors magnetised electrically through slip rings by a dynamo called the "exciter"

Slip ring

← Single-Phase a.c. could be taken from here

d.c. Dynamo

CONSTRUCTION OF SIMPLE ALTERNATOR

stationary and the magnet revolving. It is also possible to do without any commutator. The accompanying sketch shows an electrical generator with a fixed winding A and a revolving magnet B. If the ends of the winding are connected to a lamp, as shown, and the magnet be then revolved, current will flow through the lamp, but it will not be unidirectional or direct current. A little thought will show you that the current must flow through the lamp first one way and then the reverse way, afterwards the first way again, and so on, back and forth for ever or at least for as long as the magnet is turned. The current flows once in each direction for every revolution of the magnet, and our biggest dynamos or generators actually make current of this to-and-fro kind. It is called "alternating" current, and so the generators making it are called "alternators." The current from an alternator is said to be cyclical, because it varies in a way that keeps repeating itself. Each to and fro repetition is called a cycle, and the

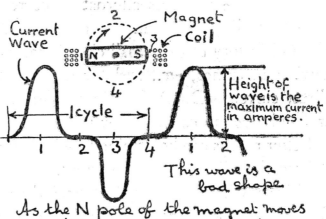

Current Wave

Magnet
Coil

Height of wave is the maximum current in amperes.

←—1 cycle —→

This wave is a bad shape

As the N pole of the magnet moves to positions 1, 2, 3, 4, 1, 2 etc. the current in the coil grows big in one direction, then stops, then grows big in the reverse direction then stops again, then grows in the first direction once more, and so on.
Each revolution gives one cycle. Main Supply Frequency is usually 50 cycles a second so that the power-station alternators must revolve at 50 revolutions a second, or 3000 r.p.m.

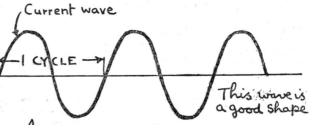

Current wave

|←—1 CYCLE —→|

This wave is a good shape

A well-made alternator gives a wave of this shape. You have seen that sound waves are of this shape too. It is called the "SINE" wave, and in the section "Sound" you have been shown how to draw it.

377

number of cycles in a second is called the frequency or periodicity of the supply. An alternator with a two-pole magnet, turning at 3,000 revolutions a minute or 50 a second, gives us a supply with a frequency of 50 cycles a second (written 50 ~). This alternat.ng current is perfectly satisfactory for lighting lamps or for fires and cookers, it is also satisfactory for the small electric motors in vacuum cleaners, sewing machines, etc., and for radio, but it is not so good as direct current (D.C.) for big motors, and neither trains nor trolley buses can conveniently use it.

Better results can be obtained with motors using what is called "three-phase" alternating current. A three-phase alternator has three windings spaced at 120 degrees as shown in the diagram on page 379. It is possible to connect three of the coil ends together and "earth" them, using the remaining three to transmit power to the consumer. Lamps or fires can be connected across any two of the wires, but all three wires are taken to motors which, like the alternator, are made with three stator windings. The advantage of a three-phase motor as compared with a single-phase one is that it will start itself and give quite a good turning effort in so doing. Also, a three-phase motor has a very simple rotor—merely an assemblage of copper bars called a squirrel cage. No brushes are needed, and there is no commutator.

THE ADVANTAGES OF A.C. AS COMPARED WITH D.C.

All things considered, most engineers would prefer to have a D.C. supply in a factory, but A.C. is nearly as good, and it is infinitely easier to generate and distribute. The alternator

By courtesy of The Brush Electrical Engineering Co Ltd.

Brush-Ljungström turbo-alternator giving an output of 50,000 kilowatts (about 70,000 horsepower).

By courtesy of Brighton Corporation

Inside a substation, showing oil-cooled transformers in the background, high-tension switchgear on the left, and low-tension switchgear on the right.

By courtesy of The Hackbridge and Hewittic Electric Company Ltd.

A Hewittic mercury-arc rectifier for converting alternating current to direct current as needed by trolley-buses or electric trains.

being simple, and without brushes or commutator, it can be wound to generate at a very high voltage—10,000 or more. Then the pulsating current can be sent to a thing called a transformer, which is like a shocking coil, but without an interrupter, and here the voltage can be stepped up to 30,000,

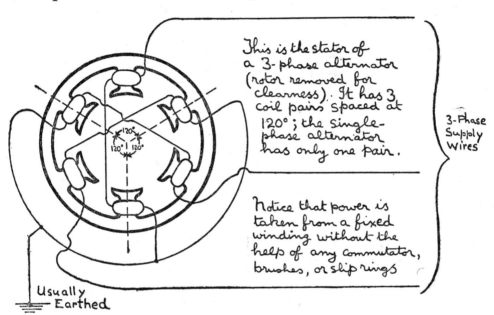

This is the stator of a 3-phase alternator (rotor removed for clearness). It has 3 coil pairs spaced at 120°; the single-phase alternator has only one pair.

3-Phase Supply Wires

Notice that power is taken from a fixed winding without the help of any commutator, brushes, or slip rings

Usually Earthed

60,000, 100,000 or even more volts. The current from the secondary winding of a transformer is much smaller than that put into the primary, but it represents the same amount of electrical power as before, because the pressure or voltage behind it is so enormous. And this comparatively tiny current can be taken over many miles of country through very thin and cheap wires. These wires are carried on pylons, and you see them everywhere. Any three of these slim-looking wires may be transmitting the whole output from a huge generating station, equivalent to 500,000 horse-power or more! To do this at a low voltage would involve the transmission of a very heavy current (thousands of amperes) and the cable needed would be very fat and costly, and very wasteful as well because of its resistance.

When the small high-voltage current has travelled over the countryside to the place where it is needed, there are more transformers to step down the voltage to a safe figure of about

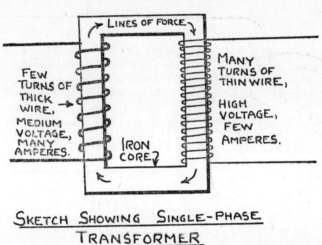

LINES OF FORCE

FEW TURNS OF THICK WIRE, → MEDIUM VOLTAGE, MANY AMPERES.

IRON CORE?

MANY TURNS OF THIN WIRE, HIGH VOLTAGE, FEW AMPERES.

SKETCH SHOWING SINGLE-PHASE TRANSFORMER

Transformers are very efficient, but they become hot in service and are therefore kept in tanks full of oil. The oil is cooled by convection in tubes outside the tank.

460. From the low-voltage secondary windings of these huge transformers come very heavy currents which divide up to serve all the hundreds of factories and homes needing current. If D.C. is needed anywhere, part of the A.C. current is fed to a rectifier which cleverly converts A.C. to D.C. in queer-looking glass bulbs filled with dazzling violet light. This D.C. is useful for electric trains or trolley buses, which must have the best kind of motors, capable of starting "in harness."

No important power-station generates D.C. to-day, though a few small factory power-stations do so. All large ones generate A.C. The reason why A.C. first came into favour was that it made the utilisation of water power possible. Away in remote mountains, hundreds of miles from any big town, there are great waterfalls which can be made to operate water turbines developing tens of thousands of horse-power. To make use of all this power, it must be transmitted to distant towns. Trans-

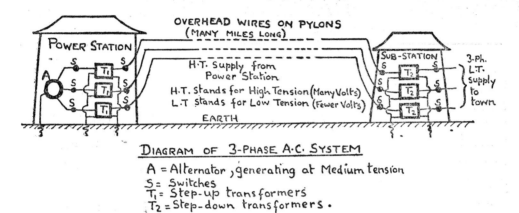

DIAGRAM OF 3-PHASE A·C· SYSTEM
A = Alternator, generating at Medium tension
S = Switches
T_1 = Step-up transformers
T_2 = Step-down transformers.

mission of low-voltage D.C. would be impracticable, and high-voltage D.C. cannot be got (or be converted back to low-voltage D.C.) without untold expense and complication; consequentiy, the inevitable method of generation and transmission was by A.C.

CHAPTER FIVE

BEWARE!! ELECTRICITY CAN BE DANGEROUS!!!

MANY young folk are killed every year because they meddle with household electrical fittings, or because something goes wrong with these fittings. Others burn themselves or cause fires by being careless with electrical apparatus.

Nowadays the electric wires in a house are put inside iron tubes (conduits), so that if the insulation frays, or becomes perished, and bare wire touches its surroundings, it merely blows a fuse (see Vol. II, page 326). This is because the circuit can be completed through the iron tube, one end of which, together with one wire of the main supply, is "earthed," meaning to say, connected to the ground by way of a water-pipe, drainpipe or in some other convenient way. Amateur electricians may install extra lights or power-plug points and use cheap wire tacked to walls or wainscoting. This is dangerous, because if anything goes wrong with this wire it may cause things in contact with it to become "alive." Some innocent person—the baby, for instance—may touch an electrified fender and be instantly electrocuted. Or there may be a stray current strong enough to cause sparks and heat, thus setting fire to the house. My advice to you therefore is never try to improve on the wiring in your home unless you have a competent electrician at your side to help you do it.

Playing with safe little batteries may have given you the idea that you have to touch *two* wires in order to get a shock. This is not true in a house, where one of the wires is earthed. All you have to do to kill yourself is put your hand on a water tap, or stand in a bath of water and touch *one* wire. Lots of people meddle with electrical gadgets while in their bath, and the result is nearly always fatal. If the bathroom light switch is faulty, or the bulb needs renewing, do not attend to it while you are wet or standing in water. If you do you are liable to become part of the main circuit, and your little spark of life will be extinguished before the fuse has time to blow. This is not meant to be funny, it is true.

A Mr. Know-All once explained to his family that it was safe to touch the wires going overhead on pylons so long as only one wire was touched at a time. He climbed up the steel pylon to demonstrate, touched one wire and was killed instantly. He forgot that one of the other wires of the system was earthed and therefore in direct connection with the steelwork of the pylon.

An old lady once asked if she would get a shock by putting one foot on the tram-lines. " Not unless you put your other foot on the overhead wire," answered the jovial tramway official. This the old lady obviously could not do, but children straying on to an electrified stretch of railway—trespassing to pick flowers, maybe—are often killed because they step on to the live rail. There is no need to step on two rails to get a fatal shock, because the earth itself counts as the second rail. The safe rule here is not to trespass, but if you do, then for good-ness' sake know something about electricity before you go near the live rail, and step *over* it not *on* it. Duty may one day compel you to venture on a railway (to rescue a strayed baby, for instance); if you do this, then watch your step.

I saw a man drop half a crown on to a live rail once and then dare a friend to get it off—never play stupid games of this sort.

Fires can be caused in all innocence by leaving electric irons standing with the current on. If the telegram boy brings an important message while you are ironing (this is a word to girls), you can easily forget all about the iron. This will get slowly hotter and hotter if it has not any work to do, and presently it will be red-hot. It can easily set fire to things when it is in this condition. You must never leave an electric iron without first of all standing it up on its proper metal stand. If you are likely to be away for more than a minute, you should switch off the current.

Electric bulbs become quite hot, and if they are decorated with crêpe paper at Christmas time they will become hotter still—hot enough to cause a fire. So never wrap up a bulb in paper or cloth or anything that could prevent the natural escape of heat. A 60-watt bulb *must* get rid of 204 B.Th.U.s in every hour. If it cannot do this it will just accumulate heat in itself until it can burn a way free of all coverings. A lady once discovered this when she used a 60-watt bulb as a bed warmer on a cold night. She set fire to her bed!

In an electric kettle there is a spiral of high-resistance wire that becomes very hot, when current passes, so warming the water in the kettle. This hot-wire element is carefully insulated from the kettle and from the water so that the water does not actually touch it. The kettle would become alive and electrocute you if water reached the element, because water is quite a good conductor of electricity. A clever boy once sat in his bath until the water became rather tepid and uncomfortable. Thinking he would warm the water up again, and thus prolong his period of comfort in the bath, he took the bowl electric fire, which was glowing merrily beside the bath, and plunged it under the water. He thought it would be the same as the arrangement inside an electric kettle, but he never lived to tell anybody so. He received a terrific shock that killed him instantly.

Inspection lamps used by people in garages are a common cause of fatal accidents. They are held in the hand, and often have a wire cage to shield the bulb from knocks that would break it. If the flexible wire that trails over the rough garage floor becomes frayed or perished, it may make contact with this wire cage or with the motor-car on which work is being done. Either way, the user is likely to receive a fatal shock. Modern hand-lamps are made of plastic and so also are modern switches, lamp-holders, etc., etc., inside the house. Metal things like vacuum cleaners and irons have an extra wire to connect their outside metal parts to " earth," so that if any live wire touches them they themselves do not become alive. They merely pass the current to earth, causing a short-circuit and blowing a fuse. Lots of modern appliances with two main wires and an earth wire are used in conjunction with old-fashioned two-hole plug sockets, with no third hole for the earthing wire. Used in this way a modern appliance is dangerous unless it is kept in very good order. A point to watch is the place where the flex goes into the appliance. Constant bending and chafing here may wear the insulation away and cause a live wire to make the whole appliance alive. Heat may accelerate the process of deterioration in appliances like irons and bowl fires. A good rule is never to touch these electrical things unless you are standing on dry ground—wood, carpet, linoleum or brick. Never hang on to a gas cooker or a water tap while you are carrying electrical appliances. If they do happen to be alive, this would be the worst possible way of finding it out.

The tiny fingers of a baby can easily find their way inside the holes of wall plugs. Such plugs should always have sockets in them, even if the sockets are not connected to anything, and they should be made stiff enough not to come out without a good hard grown-up tug. The pins on the plug are split down the centre, and if opened a little with the blade of a knife, they will fit tightly enough for safety.

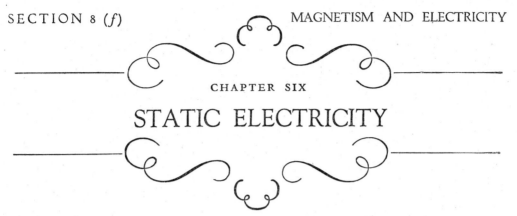

CHAPTER SIX

STATIC ELECTRICITY

THE existence of electricity was, for countless centuries, a well-kept secret of Nature, for unlike heat, light or sound, electricity does not play any very obvious part in the daily round. It becomes manifest in a large way only when something goes wrong with our weather—then we get a thunderstorm. If Old Man Electricity has to keep quiet on most days, he certainly lets himself go when this chance presents itself. A good storm is a perfect riot of light and noise compared with which even the biggest and best of firework displays seems feeble.

Very observant people have had glimpses of electricity at other times than when lightning crackles and thunder peals. A girl combing her long hair is troubled by the way the hair clings to the comb, even following it from a distance; and she may hear the crackling of tiny sparks. Electricity is the cause of both phenomena. A boy peeling off his vest on a frosty night, just before getting into bed, hears cracklings, and may see tiny lights if the room is quite dark. This is electricity again. The schoolboy rubs

MY HAIR HAS BECOME VERY SCIENTIFIC!

his vulcanite fountain-pen on his sleeve, and thereafter it behaves like a magnet, showing the power of attraction for small things, especially tiny pieces of paper. Once more electricity has been produced in a small way. Pussy's fur crackles and makes sparks when it is stroked on a cold dry night, minute quantities of electricity being generated by the stroking.

I have told you already (see page 282) that friction generates heat; now I must tell you that in favourable conditions it generates electricity too. Rubbing anything of metal may make electricity, but we shall never be conscious of the fact, because metal is a good conductor of electricity besides being a good conductor of heat, and any electricity generated will instantly escape into the surroundings and become lost. To make electricity that we can detect, we must rub things made of materials that are non-conductors or insulators. A pen of vulcanite, a glass tube, a stick of sealing-wax, a piece of amber or a sheet of brown paper can be electrified by friction if previously warmed until perfectly dry; it only needs to be rubbed in a suitable way. The paper can be brushed with a stiff brush (also made warm and dry); the glass can be pulled through the hand several times while being clasped with a silk handkerchief, and so on.

By experimenting with electrified bodies you will soon find out that there seem to be two kinds of electrification. Things rubbed together are electrified in the two different ways, and they will attract one another, as for instance the comb attracts the girl's hair. Things electrified in the same way, however, exert forces of repulsion on each other. Thus the separate hairs on a girl's head spread out as far from one another as they can in their endeavour to get away from one another. If they were electrified strongly enough they would stand up like the bristles of a porcupine.

Things oppositely electrified will cause sparks if they are brought very close together. You can hear sparks when a girl is combing her hair because comb and hair are oppositely electrified, and when the friction between them ceases, electricity tries to pass back from one to the other and make things normal again. If you fold a piece of dry and warm brown paper (the rough dark kind) into a strong spill a foot or more

THE ELECTRICIAN'S DAUGHTER
(BEWARE OF HER —SHE IS FULL OF SPARKS)

long, and rub this by pulling it two or three times between your arm and your side, you will electrify it strongly enough to get tiny sparks from it. If you hold the electrified paper close to your nose you will feel a slight pricking sensation and hear a tiny crackling sound. This is the pent-up electricity in the paper making its way back from the paper to your body through which it passes to that part of your jacket between your arm and your side which was oppositely electrified by the rubbing.

It would almost seem that friction causes one substance to be robbed of something by the other, and that the sparking is a giving back of the thing stolen. We get our idea of positive, or +, electricity and negative, or −, electricity from these simple experiments. The substance which we believe to be the gainer we say is positively electrified, while the substance we believe to be the loser we say is negatively electrified. This idea of gain and loss helps us to understand the attraction which oppositely electrified things have for one another; the one is able to supply a want of the other. Things electrified in the same way cannot do any good to each other, so they tend to separate. We see, then, that electrified things are almost human in their treatment of one another.

The attraction and repulsion between electrified bodies is yet another of these mysterious natural forces that can exist, like magnetism and gravity, in "empty" space. All three are distinct from one another, and all are operative even in spaces that have been exhausted of air. In the ordinary way a wire or a rod is needed for the transmission of force from one place to another, but Nature can send a pull or a push across a gap with no visible means of propagation in between.

Electricity residing in a comb or a piece of glass or a fountain-pen after rubbing is called "static" electricity. When oppositely electrified things are brought within sparking distance of each other, the electricity ceases to be static and becomes a current. Static electricity is in no way different from the electricity we get from batteries or dynamos, but things electrified by friction are given a very high potential (or voltage) compared with what is usual in a battery. At the same time the quantity of electricity involved is very tiny. When electrified bodies are brought near enough together for a spark to pass, there is a very tiny current for a very tiny fraction of a second, and then all is over. The voltage of several hundred between the two bodies is reduced to nothing in the twinkling of an eye. A battery is able to make much more electricity, so that it can maintain a small voltage difference between its terminals, even though quite considerable quantities of electricity continually pass from one to the other.

Various machines have been invented and made for generating electricity by frictional means. A very simple one consists of a disc of glass or ebonite (a gramophone record would do) which is revolved between pads anointed with an amalgam of zinc and mercury. A comb within sparking distance of the disc collects the electricity from the disc, which can then be made to pass across a spark gap and along a wire to the earth, whence it travels back sooner or later to the oppositely electrified pads.

This machine makes a continuous stream of very thin

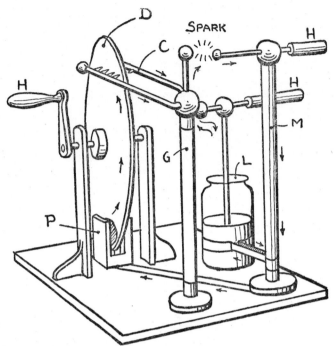

FRICTION MACHINE FOR MAKING "STATIC" ELECTRICITY
D = Disc of glass or ebonite
P = Pad holder (soft pads for making friction)
C = Collecting comb (Points near, but not touching disc)
G = Insulating pillar of glass. Brass knobs on top.
M = Metal pillar with brass knob on top.
L = Leyden Jar condenser.
H = Ebonite handles
Arrows show path of electric charges.

sparks. A spark passes when the comb has received enough electricity from the disc to raise its potential to a value sufficient to overcome the resistance of the air gap. At this critical moment the insulation of the air gives way, and a current flows. The comb loses its high potential when it loses its electric charge, and so the current ceases to flow. Then the potential builds up again and soon another spark passes.

CONDENSERS

Sparks can be made much more vigorous if the storage capacity of the comb be increased. A good storage for static electricity can be made from a jam-jar by covering the inside and outside with tin-foil. Such a contraption is called a condenser, and this particular form of it is called a Leyden jar,

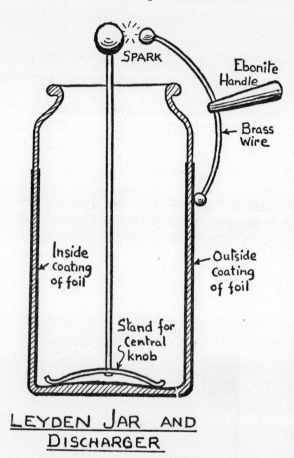

SPARK

Ebonite Handle

Brass Wire

Inside coating of foil

Outside coating of foil

Stand for Central knob

LEYDEN JAR AND DISCHARGER

after the name of the place where it was invented. Electric charges passing to the outside covering of foil attract charges of the opposite kind to the inside covering, and as they hold each other there by mutual attraction it is possible to put an indefinite amount of electricty into this mystic store. Eventually the potential difference, or voltage, between the two coverings may be enormous—enough to give you a terrific shock should you be unwise enough to grab hold of the jar. A charged Leyden jar should have its coverings short-circuited by a " discharger " before it is touched by hand.

When connected to an electric machine, the Leyden jar delays the rise in potential of the comb, for now it needs more electricity from the disc to charge it to the extent needed to produce a spark. You may have to wind the handle of the machine through several turns before anything occurs, and then at last a spark jumps the gap. There being so much more electricity wanting to escape than before, the spark is much fatter and brighter, and it makes a loud "crack," almost like a pistol shot. You may have to go on turning for a second or two before another such spark occurs, but eventually there is a second "crack."

When your machine is without a condenser, and is passing a continuous stream of thin sparks, you can safely touch any part

CONDENSER SANDWICH

of it, and even draw off sparks by your own knuckles; but I would not advise you to try any such tricks after you have fitted a Leyden jar to it. The electricity now stored up to make sparks is enough to give you a nasty shock.

Condensers are used a great deal in radio and other branches of electrical engineering. Very often they are made by putting together sheets of tin-foil with waxed paper in between, and then rolling the sandwich up into a small space so that it can be squeezed into a little container. You can charge such a condenser by connecting it for a moment across a battery. If the battery voltage is high enough (say 200 volts), you can then get a shock from your condenser by touching its terminals. The charged condenser will show a voltage of 200 at first, but this voltage quickly falls if the condenser be left standing, because the charge leaks away, and every tiny loss of charge is reflected as a drop in voltage. Unlike a battery, then, a condenser has no definite voltage of its own. It acquires whatever

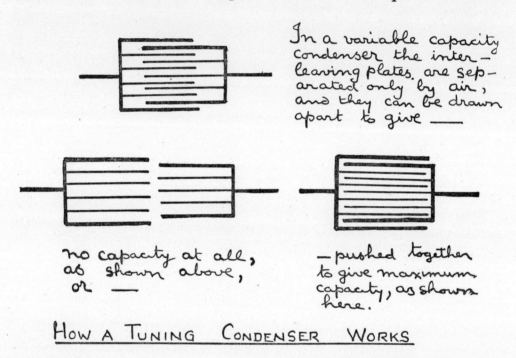

In a variable capacity condenser the inter-leaving plates are separated only by air, and they can be drawn apart to give ___

no capacity at all, as shown above, or ___

___ pushed together to give maximum capacity, as shown here.

HOW A TUNING CONDENSER WORKS

voltage you like to give it, and the more electricity you put in it the higher its voltage becomes.

If a condenser is so large that a Coulomb of electricity raises the potential difference between its plates by only 1 volt, then it is said to have a storage capacity of 1 Farad. Condensers in common use would have their voltage raised to a high figure by a tiny fraction of a Coulomb, because their storage capacity is only a few millionths of a Farad. A millionth of a Farad is called a micro-Farad (written mF), and a condenser with a capacity of 1 micro-Farad would have its voltage raised to 1 by a charge of one-millionth of a Coulomb. The Coulomb, you will remember, is the amount of electricity represented by 1 Ampere flowing for 1 second.

Electric sparks up to an inch in length can be made with comparatively small static electricity generators, or by inexpensive induction coils, but longer sparks than this need more ambitious equipment to produce them. However, scientists and engineers can make electric sparks several yards long, and there is not now any doubt at all that these are of the same nature as the lightning flashes we get in a thunderstorm.

THUNDER AND LIGHTNING

The loud bang made by a big spark is due to the effect of the heat expanding the air suddenly. The rapid burning of gunpowder, or T.N.T., produces a bang in just the same way. A close-by flash of lightning is followed without delay by a terrific bang. It is only when the flash is some way off that the sound is drawn out into a long rumble. Going at only 1,100 feet a second, the sound from a flash of lightning takes nearly 5 seconds to traverse 1 mile. On their way east, west, north and south, the sound waves impinge on hills, trees and buildings and become reflected. What we hear are the waves that reach us direct, mingled with others that arrive by reflection. The reflected waves generally arrive later than the direct ones, so prolonging the sound. Sound waves do not need to strike solid objects in order to be reflected. Passing from hot air to cold air, or into a bank of cloud, they are to some extent reflected, and that is why distant thunder is heard as a rumble rather than as a sharp "bang" even at sea. The bang of a gun is transformed into a rumble in just the same way.

Nobody is quite sure how thunderstorms are first started, but changes of temperature caused by the ascent of warm moist air seem to be mainly responsible. Perhaps the violent chafing of contrary winds sets up friction. Anyhow, great bodies of our atmosphere, generally moisture-laden bodies, acquire huge electrical potentials in favourable circumstances, and then they seek to unburden themselves of mighty electric charges. Lightning is seen flashing from cloud to cloud, or from cloud to earth, and we either enjoy the fun or we run to hide under the stairs, depending on our temperament.

Thunderstorms seem to follow always the same tracks across the country—up particular river valleys, round particular hills or towns and so on. The lightning seems, moreover, to pick out the same places to strike again and again. You hear of unlucky cottages that are struck repeatedly, and of trees that share a like misfortune. I once knew an old man who was struck twice by lightning in less than three years, while sitting at his own fireside. Nearby, in a field, was the skeleton of a tree that had also received the attentions of lightning. I do not think I should have cared to live in that old man's cottage!

Lightning does not always kill. It may pass over the moist outside of your body instead of through your vital organs, and then the only harm it will do is rip through the soles of your shoes, or tear the clothes from your back. You will be left rather dazed, and the absence of garments may cause you to feel rather shy, but otherwise you will be all right.

Knowing the truth about thunderstorms, and how slight is

Lightning is the sudden discharge of atmospheric electricity. Thunder is the sound which results, often muffled and delayed by distance, but sometimes shatteringly loud and almost coincident with the flash.

your chance of being struck, you should be able to enjoy them instead of feeling scared. You will not need to run about putting away the knives and turning mirrors to the wall as many ignorant people do. Instead, you will be able to sit near a window and watch the black clouds approaching. Only when the flashes are becoming very near do I advise retiring from the window, and that is not because the lightning is likely to strike you, but because an exceptionally brilliant flash might injure your sight. You ought to enjoy a thunderstorm as a freely given firework display, but I do not recommend you to go so far as the American scientist Benjamin Franklin, who actually flew a kite in a storm in order to attract some atmospheric electricity for his experiments. That was a brave thing even for a scientist to do! In many foreign places thunderstorms are of regular and very frequent occurrence, but in England they are rather rare, and one or two a year are all you are likely to witness. There may be two or three days of really lovely summer weather, hot and still; then these conditions are brought to an end by a thunderstorm. The thunder clouds come up in a contrary direction to what you would expect by looking at a weather-cock. Thus, if there is a gentle summer breeze from the north, the thunderstorm will come towards you from the south. Just before the storm breaks, the northerly breeze will die down and there will be an ominous calm. Truly dreadful-looking rolls of soot-black cloud sweep over your head, and then the distant trees begin to rock and sway in a mighty wind that the storm brings with it from the south. In a second the wind breaks where you are standing, and the air becomes thick with flying leaves and dust. The rain may begin to fall at this moment, but often the wind dies down again before rain comes. In tropical parts the sudden tempest of wind may be violent enough to do great damage to trees and houses. At sea it may cause a sort of tidal wave and upset small boats. When you see a bad storm coming it is a wise precaution to shut all windows and doors, and if you are at sea, you should take down the sails of your boat.

When the storm is over, the period of summer weather is usually over as well. Weeks of dull, cold, rainy weather may follow. In time summer conditions may return, only to be ended inside a week by yet another thunderstorm. The English summer is not a thing to be depended upon. Occasionally we get some months of genial weather, but often we look forward to settled conditions from May till September and then realise that there isn't going to be a summer at all.

CHAPTER SEVEN

RADIO AND TELEVISION

ALTHOUGH I have told you that gravitation, magnetism and electrical attraction are forces that can be felt across empty space, scientists will not quite agree with this. According to their view there is no such thing as empty space. The absence of air or of other material substances does not make space empty. All space is filled with a " something " we do not know much about, but which we call the ether or aether. The forces of gravity, magnetism and electrical attraction we believe to be caused by stretching or straining this ether. If the amount of stretch or strain is altered very suddenly, a wave action is set up, just as waves can be set up in a long spring (see page 66) by jerking one end of it. Something is happening all the time inside hot bodies to cause waves in the ether. These are the waves of light and radiant heat that come to us from fires or lamps. Heat and light waves come to us from the sun across an ether-filled space of about 90 million miles. They come to us at the rate of 186,000 miles a second. The wave length, or distance from crest to crest, is very tiny, so that in a distance of 1 metre (about 3 feet 3 inches) there are 1·32 million waves of red light and 2·33 million waves of violet light.

ULTRA-VIOLET RAYS AND X-RAYS

Just how rapid must be the vibrations which cause these waves you can judge for yourself if you consider how many metres there are in 186,000 miles and remember that this number, multiplied by the waves in each metre, is the frequency with which the waves are generated. And yet there are even shorter, and more frequent, ether waves than this. They are the ultra-violet waves (which, though invisible, have a great effect on photographic films) and the X-rays, which are so tiny that they can find their way through solid substances. A shadow caused by ordinary light shows your whole person in outline, but a shadow by X-rays shows only your bones, as your flesh does not stop them. Doctors and others make X-ray shadows of things to help them in their work. If you swallow a marble, the X-ray lamp will show the doctor or nurse exactly where it is inside you, because it stops more of the rays than your flesh, and casts a shadow on a screen or on a photographic plate.

INFRA-RED RAYS

Waves of radiant heat are longer than light waves. In between light waves and heat waves are the infra-red waves which cannot be seen, but which will affect special photographic plates. By infra-red wave photography you can take pictures of things through fog or clouds, and you may have seen panoramic views taken from aeroplanes by infra-red photography that show details of the view from distances much greater than that at which normal vision ceases. On a hazy day you could go up over London in an aeroplane and take quite a good infra-red picture showing the south coast, although places at half that distance away would be blotted out by the haze.

"WIRELESS" WAVES

Heat waves are still very short, and we do not know much about ether waves longer than heat waves until we get to waves in a different class altogether—waves running from several centimetres to 1,000 or more metres in length. These much longer waves can be created by electric sparks or other electrical disturbances, and we make use of them in radio communication, or "wireless telegraphy" as it used to be called. The so-called short-wave system of communication uses waves of only a few metres in length. These resemble light waves to some extent in being directional. They can be focused into a beam and be sent in one particular direction. They are easily stopped by obstacles in their path, but in the absence of obstacles they go much farther than the longer unfocused waves used in ordinary broadcasting, which have a length of 200 to 2,000 metres. They compare with the light of a lamp, which goes farther when concentrated into a beam by a searchlight reflector.

The long waves used in ordinary broadcasting spread in all directions and bend readily round obstacles in their path. Light waves bend round obstacles by only an infinitesimally small amount, but waves of many metres in length will bend much farther, and it is fortunate for our broadcast listening that they do so, because were it otherwise, we should feel the screening effect of hills and houses and trees much more than we do.

Sometimes a wave is described as being of so many kilocycles a second instead of so many metres in length. This is a measure of the number of waves passing by in a second, and is the same thing as the frequency of vibration of the wave generator. A kilocycle is 1,000 waves per second, and a wave 186 miles long would have a frequency of 1 kilocycle per second. To find the frequency in kilocycles of waves of any other length, you must divide 186 miles (converted to metres) by the wave length in metres. A mile is equal to 1,600 metres, so that the formula for conversion is 186 × 1600 ÷ L, where L is the length of wave. A wave of 200 metres in length is equivalent to 1,488 kilocycles, whereas one of 2,000 metres in length is equivalent to only 148·8 kilocycles.

MAKING WIRELESS WAVES

The easiest way to make wireless waves is to use a very powerful shocking coil (see page 363) in conjunction with a spark gap and an aerial. To make the coil more effective a condenser is connected between the contacts of the interrupter. This makes the primary circuit of the coil into what is known as an oscillatory circuit. I must explain this in more detail. In an ordinary shocking coil, when the interrupter opens the circuit to stop the primary current, the magnetic lines of force linked with the primary winding begin to collapse, and besides inducing a voltage in the secondary winding, they cut the primary winding and induce a voltage in this too. The voltage is in a direction to make the interrupted current try to go on flowing, and it may succeed in doing this by jumping across the interrupter contacts as a spark. This delays the collapse of the magnetic lines of force and minimises the voltage or pressure induced in the secondary winding. The purpose of the condenser is to side-track this induced primary current; instead of sparking across the interrupter it flows into the condenser and charges it to quite a high voltage. Once the charging of the condenser is completed, there is nothing to prevent it from discharging by sending a reverse current round through the primary. It does this, and at once re-creates magnetic lines of force linking the primary. The current flows until the condenser is discharged, and then, for a second time, the collapsing magnetism causes the current to go on flowing. It actually charges up the condenser the reverse way, and when

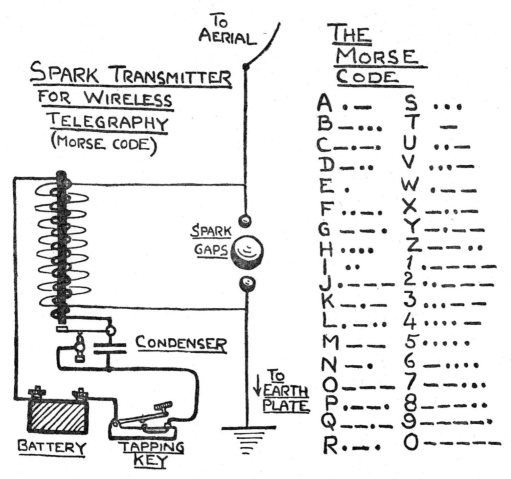

it stops flowing in one direction the condenser sets it going in the first direction again. The effect of the condenser, then, is to send current surging or oscillating to and fro through the primary winding. These oscillations of current die away after a certain number of repetitions, but while they last they are very rapid, and the related changes in the magnetic lines linking the primary and secondary windings are very rapid too, so that a very big oscillating voltage is generated in the secondary. This causes the sparking to be much more energetic in a coil with a condenser fitted than in one without. Each

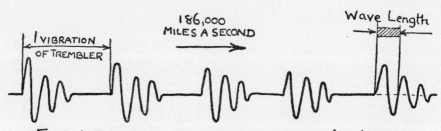

Each interruption of primary current by trembler sends out one bunch of waves (5 bunches shown)

Only three whole waves are shown in each bunch, but in reality there may be 200 waves in each bunch. Five trembler vibrations make the waves shown.

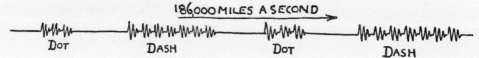

Waves drawn to a smaller scale. Here the trembler is made to work for short and long intervals by use of the tapping key. Three trembler vibrations make a "DOT" in the above picture and seven vibrations make a dash. In reality there might be about 30 and 70

WAVES MADE BY SPARK TRANSMITTER

spark, moreover, is really a series of sparks, possibly 200, for every interruption by the trembler of the primary current.

If these energetic oscillatory spark discharges are caused to take place between knobs connected to the ground on one hand and an overhead aerial on the other, ether waves will be sent out, one wave to each individual spark or 200 for each vibration of the interrupter. The precise frequency of the wave, or the wave length, can be adjusted by altering the capacity of the condenser already mentioned. A small-capacity condenser will reverse the primary current flow more quickly than a large-capacity one, so causing shorter or more frequent waves to be transmitted.

Early wireless transmitters consisted of modified shocking coils as described here. They sent out little bunches of waves which followed close on each other's heels, for as long as the transmitting key was depressed to keep the interrupter trembling. A long chain of wave bunches corresponded to a dash in Morse telegraphy, and a short chain to a dot.

RECEIVING WIRELESS WAVES

I will not describe the earliest wireless-wave receivers, because the later ones are just as easy to understand and much more satisfactory in action. The first essential of a wireless receiver is a tuned aerial circuit. You have an overhead aerial connected through a coil of wire and a variable-capacity condenser to an earth plate. The coil of wire and the condenser form an oscillatory circuit like the primary of the spark transmitter in conjunction with its condenser. The very tiny effect of the passing ether waves on the aerial is enough to start an oscillating current in the aerial circuit, provided that this be " tuned " to have a natural frequency of oscillation the same as the frequency of these passing waves. The condenser is made variable in capacity, so that it can be adjusted to give the right result.

You might think that a telephone receiver connected across the coil in the aerial circuit would vibrate in response to the oscillations of potential in this coil. However, it is not so. The oscillations are far too rapid to be followed by any diaphragm. To make the telephone responsive it is necessary to " rectify " the current passing through it. Included in the telephone circuit is a device which lets current flow one way but not the other. When a wave bunch is received, each of the 200 or so waves may try to make the diaphragm go first one way and then the other, but this device, called a rectifier, only allows

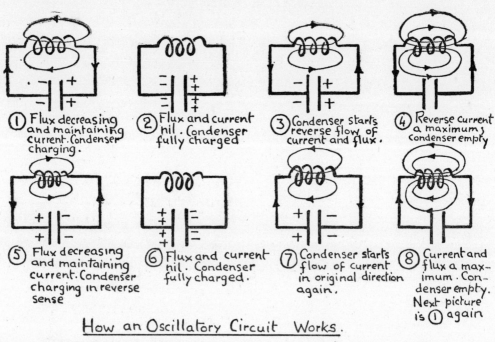

① Flux decreasing and maintaining current. Condenser charging.

② Flux and current nil. Condenser fully charged

③ Condenser starts reverse flow of current and flux.

④ Reverse current a maximum; condenser empty

⑤ Flux decreasing and maintaining current. Condenser charging in reverse sense

⑥ Flux and current nil. Condenser fully charged.

⑦ Condenser starts flow of current in original direction again.

⑧ Current and flux a maximum. Condenser empty. Next picture is ① again

How an Oscillatory Circuit Works.

Note Flux is another name for magnetic lines of force

the waves to exert a force one way. Instead of getting 200 impulses on one side, alternating with 200 on the other, the diaphragm gets 200 impulses all acting the same way. These are effective in moving it. Each bunch of 200 waves moves the diaphragm out and back again once, and the consequence is that the diaphragm starts buzzing at exactly the same rate as the interrupter of the transmitting coil. It buzzes for the same length of time as this interrupter, and if the interrupter is caused to buzz intermittently (long buzzes for dashes and short buzzes for dots), the telephone will do exactly the same. And this is really the whole story of wireless, for it tells you how messages can be sent across "empty" space by ships at sea, by aeroplanes and so on.

RECTIFIERS

The simplest sort of rectifier is a lump of crystalline substance —called a crystal—in contact with a little metal wire made in the form of a spring. This wire is called the "cat's whisker." Current will flow in one direction through this, but not in the opposite direction.

Another kind of rectifier is the thermionic valve. Everyone in these days knows what a valve is, but not everybody knows how it works. The British scientist Fleming discovered that if an ordinary lamp bulb had a plate fitted into it at one end he could pass a current through the "empty" space between the filament and the plate directly the filament was made white-hot. This current, in fact, started on its own if plate and filament were connected by an external wire. The current would go only one way, and it made the plate positive in relation to the filament, which was thus negative.

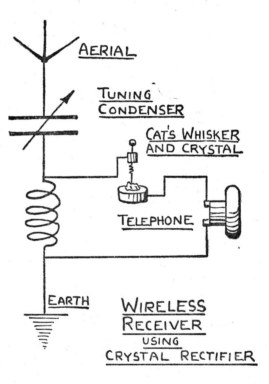

AERIAL

TUNING CONDENSER

CAT'S WHISKER AND CRYSTAL

TELEPHONE

EARTH

WIRELESS RECEIVER USING CRYSTAL RECTIFIER

You might think from this that the current flowed from plate to filament, but it would seem that our old ideas about + and − are wrong, because actually, in a valve, the flow is from filament to plate or − to +. The filament throws off minute charges of electricity, called electrons, and these pass to the plate in an endless stream. An electric current is now thought of as a stream of electrons flowing from − to +, but

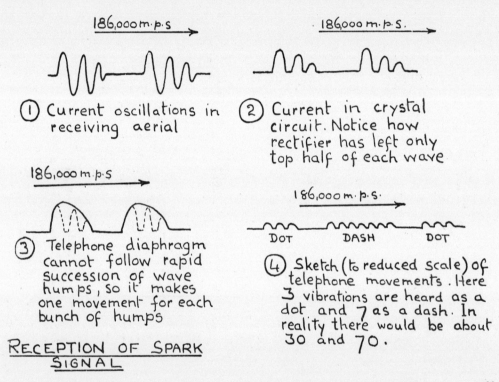

1. Current oscillations in receiving aerial

2. Current in crystal circuit. Notice how rectifier has left only top half of each wave

3. Telephone diaphragm cannot follow rapid succession of wave humps, so it makes one movement for each bunch of humps

4. Sketch (to reduced scale) of telephone movements. Here 3 vibrations are heard as a dot and 7 as a dash. In reality there would be about 30 and 70.

RECEPTION OF SPARK SIGNAL

in every branch of electrical engineering, except radio, we still draw arrows on our wires to show the current flowing from + to −. This is confusing until you are used to it.

Now, in a valve, the current flow from filament to plate can be made very energetic by connecting a big high-tension battery (100 volts or more) in the plate circuit. This current can also be stopped very easily by fitting a wire-mesh plate, called a grid, between the filament and the plate and making its potential negative in relation to the filament. The negative grid repels the negative electrons from the filament and prevents them from reaching the plate.

THE VALVE RECEIVER

You can see now that by connecting the filament and grid of a valve across the coil in a receiving aerial you can make the plate current respond to wireless waves. When the oscillations

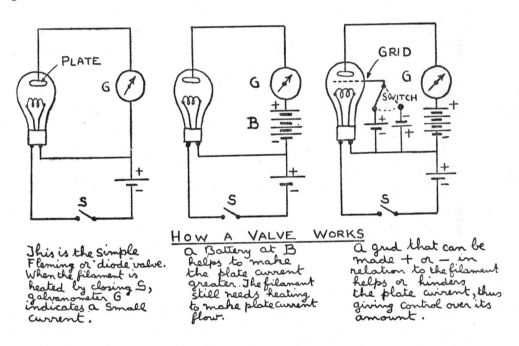

HOW A VALVE WORKS

This is the simple Fleming or 'diode' valve. When the filament is heated by closing S, galvanometer G indicates a small current.

A Battery at B helps to make the plate current greater. The filament still needs heating to make plate current flow.

A grid that can be made + or − in relation to the filament helps or hinders the plate current, thus giving control over its amount.

in the aerial circuit make the grid potential +, a plate current flows, but this current ceases to flow when the grid becomes −. A bunch of 200 waves will make the grid + 200 times, and there will be 200 pulses of plate current, all the same way. If therefore a telephone receiver be put in the plate circuit, you will hear its diaphragm move once for each bunch of waves,

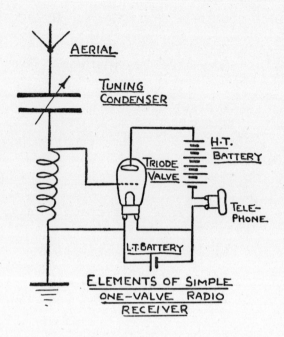

the net result being a buzz that faithfully echoes the buzz of the interrupter at the transmitting end.

The beauty of this arrangement is that it does not depend on the feeble current from the aerial to work the telephone (as happens with a crystal receiver), but uses this current to control the much larger one obtainable from the high-tension battery. You get much more noise from your telephone this way and, in fact, the receiver will respond to much weaker signals so that you can hear transmitters from a much greater distance.

VALVE TRANSMITTERS

By a sort of transformer arrangement linking the plate and aerial circuits of a valve, the valve can be made to vary the potential of its own grid, and if this be arranged properly, violent electrical oscillations will be set up in the aerial circuit. The aerial will then act as a transmitter, sending out continuous waves of any length you like to make them by altering the tuning of your aerial circuit. A wireless broadcasting station uses valves in this way, to send out waves, but these waves would not be detected by any receiver unless they were chopped up into bunches at the transmitting end and then rectified at the receiving end. Better than arranging for them to be chopped up, however, we can "modulate" them. To do this a microphone (see page 362) must be put in the grid circuit of the transmitting valve. This varies the resistance to the oscillations, and makes them stronger or weaker in a way that faithfully follows the movement of the diaphragm against which the broadcast artist is speaking or singing. When the resulting waves are rectified at the receiving end, the telephone

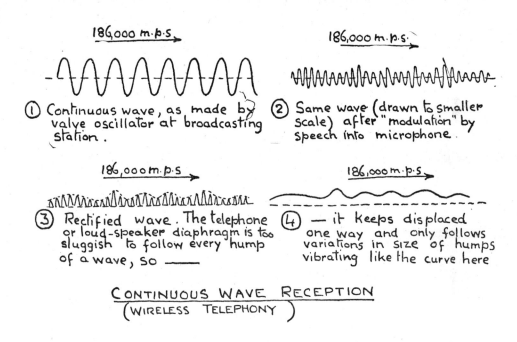

① Continuous wave, as made by valve oscillator at broadcasting station.

② Same wave (drawn to smaller scale) after "modulation" by speech into microphone.

③ Rectified wave. The telephone or loud-speaker diaphragm is too sluggish to follow every hump of a wave, so ——

④ — it keeps displaced one way and only follows variations in size of humps vibrating like the curve here

CONTINUOUS WAVE RECEPTION
(WIRELESS TELEPHONY)

or loud-speaker diaphragm imitates the movements of the microphone diaphragm, and so gives us the same sounds as are being made in the broadcast studio.

If you have experimented with valves and made up simple wireless sets yourself you will know that things are not quite so simple as I have made them appear here. Valves have to be coaxed to do the right thing, and this coaxing may involve fitting them with grid-bias batteries, grid leaks, etc., etc. Modern valves may have two extra grids to serve one purpose or another, so we have our "screened-grid" valve and our "pentode." The simple valve made by Fleming, with only a plate and a filament, would be called a "diode" nowadays, and the valve with a plate, a filament and a single grid would be called a "triode."

RADAR

If ether waves are only a few centimetres in length they become more like light waves, and they can not only be directed as a beam, but they can be reflected back again. This made them very useful in the last war. By sending out short waves into space it was possible to locate enemy aeroplanes in the dark. The beam would be reflected by the aeroplane when it was directed in the right way, and it would be received back again as a reflection in an interval of time that depended on the distance between plane and beam transmitter. A plane 93 miles away would give a reflection or echo that returned in a thousandth of a second.

This location of things by wireless waves is called "Radar," and it has war-time applications in naval as well as aerial campaigning. It can also be used in many ways in peace-time. Thus radar-fitted ships can go at full speed through the thickest fog, because their radar equipment tells them all the time how far away they are from other ships, rocks, icebergs, etc.

The curious thing is that bats (see Vol. I) find their way about in the dark in much the same way as radar-equipped ships, but they employ ordinary sound waves. They squeak continually with a very high note—so high that few people can hear it—thus making very short sound waves. These come back to them from the surrounding objects, so giving the bat an idea of where these objects are and how far they are away. The method of the bat is so effective that it can thread its way safely through a dark room that has strings and wires stretched across it.

You might wonder how anyone could be conscious of a time interval of a thousandth of a second, but there is no mystery here. When waves interfere with one another they may be in step or out of step. If they are in step they make a loud noise or give a big effect; if they are out of step they cancel each other out completely. The difference between one condition and the other is caused by the waves being only half a wave length apart, and half a wave length with short wireless waves corresponds with a time interval of not thousandths but millionths of a second. What the radar apparatus does (and the bat must do the same) is mix the outgoing and the reflected waves to find out what the result is. The distance away of the reflecting body can be instantly gauged from this result.

TELEVISION

In television use is made of a device called a photo-cell, which is an electrical resistance affected by the brightness of light falling on it. The thing to be televised is "scanned" by a swiftly moving light, which darts a ray over its whole surface line by line, many times in a second. The reflected light varies in intensity with the brightness of the thing illuminated, and this variation is caused by a photo-cell to vary the strength of radiated wireless waves. At the receiving end is a cathode-ray tube, which is a device for directing a stream of electrons against a screen of special material which glows with a greeny-white light at the spot where the electrons strike it. The stream of electrons is caused to " scan " the screen in step with the light ray scanning the televised object at the transmitting end, and the strength of the electron stream (which governs the brightness of the spot on the screen) is varied by the variable-strength wireless waves. Thus when the distant light ray falls at some point X on the televised object and is brightly reflected, the electron stream strikes the cathode-tube screen at the corresponding point X' and it makes a bright spot. A moment later the ray may be dimly reflected by some point Y of the televised object; the electron stream will make a dim spot at the corresponding place Y' on the cathode-tube screen. The secret of clear definition is to have the scanning done so fast and over so many lines that you do not see any flicker or any " stripiness " in the picture on the cathode-tube screen. The received picture at any one instant of time is really only a single dot, but the dot travels and varies in brightness at such a rate that your eye cannot follow it, and it seems therefore to be filling the whole screen, just as a thin propeller blade seems to fill a whole round space when it is whirling fast enough.

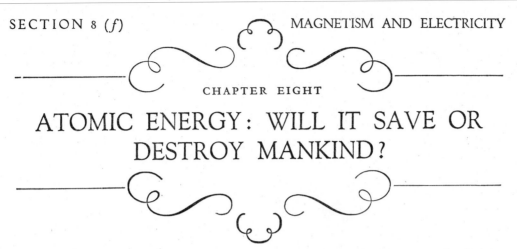

CHAPTER EIGHT

ATOMIC ENERGY: WILL IT SAVE OR DESTROY MANKIND?

ELECTRICITY has taught scientists that the material things we know so well and think of as so solid are not really solid at all. They are made up of minute particles called molecules or atoms, but each atom is in reality little more than so much space.

STRUCTURE OF THE ATOM

At the centre of the atom is a tiny something charged with positive electricity, and round it there spin in endless circles the even tinier electrons. The atom may be an atom of some solid, liquid or gas, but the only differences between different atoms lie in the number of electrons or negative electric charges encircling the positive nucleus, and in the size of that nucleus. It is thought that if an atom could be magnified to appear as a ball $2\frac{1}{2}$ miles across, the electron would look as large as a golf ball, and the nucleus as large as a fair-sized house. You will see from this that there is really plenty of room inside solid bodies, and this explains why certain kinds of ether waves manage to pass through them so successfully.

The number of positive charges in the nucleus of an atom is equal to the number of electrons circling round, and if an electron is removed to change the nature of the atom, a proton or positive particle must be removed too.

RADIO-ACTIVITY

In radium, and other radio-active substances, there is a continual loss of electrons and protons, causing the substance to change into other substances. At the end of the process the radium converts itself into lead.

This degradation of radium is very slow but, even so, much energy is released in the process, and for many years scientists have believed that if only they could split up atoms more quickly than Nature does it they could get limitless amounts of power for their trouble. Rutherford and other British scientists have managed with great difficulty to split single atoms, but until recently nobody could split unlimited numbers.

SPLITTING THE ATOM

The method of splitting an atom is to take shots at its nucleus with tiny particles and knock this to bits. The nucleus is very hard to hit because it is so tiny, and also because it is protected by a screen of whirling electrons. To try bombarding it with electrons (from radium, for instance) would be useless, because electrons are too small. Protons are better, but being positively charged they attract electrons and are repelled by the nucleus itself, so they either miss their mark or only strike it feebly. The success attending later experiments was due to the fact that scientists discovered a new kind of particle, called the neutron, which is not electrically charged at all. This can be aimed at its target and be depended on to go straight there.

THE ATOMIC BOMB

A special kind of uranium, very hard to make, gives off neutrons all the time. Most of these escape into space if the piece of uranium is small, but a few knock against the uranium atoms and release more neutrons. If the piece of uranium is big enough, there are enough collisions to start the whole lump disintegrating, and it does this with fearsome violence, about 4 pounds of it giving an explosion the equal of 20,000 tons of T.N.T.

The atom bomb is simply a container with two small pieces of the special uranium kept apart inside it. These pieces are brought close together in order to make one big piece, and that is sufficient to explode the bomb.

CAN ATOMIC ENERGY BE USED IN PEACE-TIME?

By embedding small pieces of uranium in a lump of carbon, like plums in a cake, the process of atomic disintegration can be made to take place slowly, and then heat is generated at a rate that can be controlled. The heat generator is called a "pile," and it will work for many years. To regulate its output metal screens in the pile are pulled out or pushed in.

The uranium pile has its uses, but so far it has not given the high-temperature heat wanted for power generation. Even so, it is a dangerous thing to approach because, like radium, it gives off rays that can destroy human flesh and blood. To be safe it must be kept in a case of thick lead or concrete, and this makes it rather clumsy for most practical purposes.

PROGRESS OR SELF-DESTRUCTION?

The discovery of a way to liberate atomic energy is the most important ever made, but it puts fearful powers into human hands. If men are wise enough to use these powers kindly and for the good of all, untold benefits may result; but if men are going to continue fighting and quarrelling among themselves, using atomic bombs for their weapons, it will not be long before everything in civilisation is wiped out. Then towns, ships, farms and people will all be destroyed.

Science is full of promise, but whether for good or evil depends entirely on the success or failure of teachers to make growing children more good-tempered and tolerant of one another than their forefathers have been. We badly need a new science to show us how to get an improved kind of human nature.